PELICAN BOOKS

A310

THE ETRUSCANS

M. PALLOTTINO

THE ETRUSCANS

BY M. PALLOTTINO

*Professor of Etruscology
and Italic Archaeology in the
University of Rome*

TRANSLATED FROM THE ITALIAN BY
J. CREMONA

PENGUIN BOOKS

Penguin Books Ltd, Harmondsworth, Middlesex
U.S.A.: Penguin Books Inc., 3300 Clipper Mill Road, Baltimore 11, Md
CANADA: Penguin Books (Canada) Ltd, 47 Green Street,
Saint Lambert, Montreal, P.Q.
AUSTRALIA: Penguin Books Pty Ltd, 762 Whitehorse Road,
Mitcham, Victoria
SOUTH AFRICA: Penguin Books (S.A.) Pty Ltd, Gibraltar House,
Regents Road, Sea Point, Cape Town

—

First Italian edition, 1942
Second Italian edition, 1947
Third Italian edition, 1954
Published by Penguin Books 1955

Made and printed in Great Britain
by Hunt, Barnard & Co, Ltd, Aylesbury
Collogravure plates by Harrison & Sons

CONTENTS

LIST OF TEXT FIGURES

LIST OF PLATES

Photographs originating from commercial sources and from the British Museum are duly acknowledged in the list below. The remaining plates have been obtained from the photographic archives of the Institute of Archaeology in the University of Rome, the Museo Nazionale di Villa Giulia in Rome, the Musei di Roma (Sezione Antica), the Sopraintendenza alle Antichità di Bologna and from the author. Though the majority of the photographs in the Italian third edition have been incorporated here, it has not been possible to include them all; on the other hand, a substantial number of photographs of objects kept in the British Museum have been added as it was felt that they may be of especial interest to British readers. I should like to take this opportunity to express my warmest thanks to Mr D. E. L. Haynes of the Department of Greek and Roman Antiquities, British Museum, for his help and advice in choosing a representative selection.

THE TRANSLATOR

Carthaginians for the supremacy of the Western seas (*Paris, Louvre*). See E. POTTIER, *Vases antiques du Louvre*, 1897, D 150, p. 40, plate 34.

4 (A) Lid of a small terracotta urn representing the dead man and a female figure, possibly his wife. This group is a good illustration of the original tendencies towards expressivity in Etruscan art (*Volterra, Museo Guarnacci*).

 (B) Lid of urn from Volterra, with the figure of the deceased man. The man may be seen wearing a plaited wreath and holding a *phiale omphalos* in his left hand and in his right, a drinking horn ending in the fore-part of a caparisoned horse. (*Phot. British Museum.*)

5 A master-piece of Ionic Etruscan art: detail from the Apollo of Veii (*c.* 500 B.C.), now in the Museum of Villa Giulia in Rome. See M. PALLOTTINO, *La scuola di Vulca*, 1945, and in *Archeologia Classica*, II, 1950, pp. 163 ff.

6 (A) Lid of sarcophagus from Tarquinia (Tomb of the Triclinium), belonging to the early fifth century B.C. (*Phot. British Museum*).

 (B) Alabaster statue of woman holding a bronze gilded dove in her left hand; Vulci (Polledrara Tomb), first quarter of the sixth century B.C. (*Phot. British Museum*).

7 Two yoked winged horses in painted terracotta from the pediment of the 'Ara della Regina' at Tarquinia (fourth-third century B.C.), a sample of Etrusco-Italic art under classical influence (*Tarquinia, Museo Nazionale*). See P. ROMANELLI in *Le Arti* I, 1938–9, p. 436, plates CXXXI ff. and in *Notizie degli Scavi*, 1948, pp. 254 ff. (*Phot. Anderson*).

8 (A) Terracotta statuette of a woman seated on a block, found at Cerveteri (*Phot. British Museum*).

 (B) Archaic female mask, taken from an antefix, Cerveteri (*Phot. British Museum*).

9 (A) Young woman's head in terracotta, showing Hellenistic influence (*Vatican, Museo Etrusco Gregoriano*).

 (B) Daemon's mask in terracotta (*Orvieto, Faina Collection*).

10 Sepulchral urn in the form of a standing man of life-size. The body is hollowed to receive the ashes, the head and neck serve as stopper; from Chianciano, near Chiusi (*Phot. British Museum*).

11 (A) Two antefixes mounted on the cornice of a roof (restored from fragments); from Lanuvio (Civita Lavinia) (*Phot. British Museum*).

altar with snake. This painted plaque, found at Cerveteri and now at the Louvre in Paris, has been much restored.

21 Mythological scene: painted plaque with frieze belonging to the end of the sixth century B.C. found at Cerveteri and now at the Louvre in Paris. The influence of archaic Greek art may be seen in this painting.

22 Circus scenes: pugilists, pyrrhicists and dwarfs. Detail of mural painting in the Tomb of the Monkey at Chiusi (*Phot. Alinari*).

23 Jugglers and musicians: detail of mural painting in the Tomb of the Monkey at Chiusi (*Phot. Alinari*). See R. BIANCHI-BANDINELLI, *Clusium. Le Pitture delle Tombe Arcaiche (Monumenti della Pittura Antica in Italia)*. 1939, pp. 130 ff. plate IV.

24 (A) Tuchulcha, daemon of the Etruscan Hades, among the shades of ancient heroes: detail of a mural painting in the Tomba dell' Orco at Tarquinia. See M. PALLOTTINO, *La peinture étrusque*, pp. 112 ff.

   (B) A piper playing the double-pipes: detail of a mural painting in the Tomb of the Triclinium at Tarquinia and now in the Museo Nazionale, Tarquinia. See M. PALLOTTINO, *La peinture étrusque*, pp. 74 ff.

25 (A) The goddess Uni (Juno) giving suck to Hercle (Hercules), according to an Etruscan myth: graffito on the back of a mirror found at Volterra and now at the Museo Archeologico, Florence (*Phot. Alinari*). See G. MONACO, in *Rendic. della Pont. Accad. di Archeologia*, VIII, 1932, pp. 163 ff.

   (B) Pava Tarchies (Tages ?) teaching the hero Tarchunus (Tarchon) the art of divination: from a mirror found at Tuscania and now in the Museo Archeologico, Florence. See M. PALLOTTINO, in *Rendic. della Accad. dei Lincei*, 1930, pp. 49 ff.

26 (A) Gold votive fibula with serpentine bow and richly decorated with granulation; from Vulci (seventh century B.C.) (*Phot. British Museum*).

   (B) A gold votive braceleto from Tarquinia (eighth-seventh century B.C.): the braceleto is covered with fine patterns and designs in granulation (*Phot. British Museum*).

   (C) Ornamental gold disc (*Phot. British Museum*). The use of these discs is not certain, but they were probably ear decorations worn by Etruscan women, though they may also have served as fibulae.

FOREWORD

In spite of the wealth of means of study at our disposal, the sharp weapon of scientific method and the intelligent toil of research workers, far too many problems still remain unsolved concerning the history and culture of ancient peoples.

What in fact do we know of the ethnic origins of those builders of pyramids, the ancient Egyptians, and what is the true chronology of the oldest landmarks in their history? How and whence was the Phoenician alphabet born, mother of all modern writing? Up to what point are the poems of Homer the work of a single artist and the mirror of true historical figures and events? When and why did the ancient inhabitants of Malta raise the prodigious piles of their many megalithic 'temples'?

Great questions, chosen at random from among a great number – some of them going back many a long year. There is no need to conceal the fact that modern science has not yet been able to provide final answers to these questions, answers that would be accepted unanimously by all scholars.

Why is it then that so much interest, both expert and lay, focuses with ever-renewed vigour upon the problems of the origins and the language of the ancient Etruscans, almost as if they were the most fascinating 'mystery', the 'sphinx' *par excellence* of all ancient history?

One of the reasons is the following: the Etruscan 'mystery' is not merely one of science's curiosities, or the appeal of a world that is far from our own, both in time and spirit. It is the mystery of the budding of a civilization that was the first to flourish on Italian soil, at the very roots of the history of Rome and, hence, of western civilization. At the very time when love for research on the primitive life of peoples appears to be so profoundly active, we see in the Etruscan 'mystery' a key to the question of Italic origins and the foundation stone on which to base the difficult reconstruction of Italy's most distant past.

This lively and deep-felt interest of the public for the history and civilization of the Etruscans deserves the scholar's attention. Naturally, neither analytical research nor the slow and painstaking reconstructions found in scientific essays can satisfy the widespread and impatient desire to know and understand. But, at the same time, most works of vulgarization, by generalizing and simplifying the complex structures built by science, fail to satisfy the demands of those – by far the most numerous – who do not care to be left at the temple's door but wish to be led inside to the very centre of the problem, to the heated and troubled terrain of scientific controversy.

It is for them especially that this book is meant: for its author has striven to keep close both to matter and method and has even, in a few cases, put forward what he hopes may be new contributions to the problems under discussion. It attempts to be neither a work of analysis nor a rigid and impartial exposition; differing in this respect from such well-known monographs as K. O. Müller and W. Deecke's *Die Etrusker* (1877), P. Ducati's *Etruria antica* (1927), or B. Nogara's *Gli Etruschi e la loro civiltà* (1934), it seeks to give an up-to-date interpretation of the people and of the chief problems concerning them, an interpretation striving towards serenity and sound documentation but none the less personal and vivid. A number of obscure aspects of the civilization of Etruria and firm convictions which, till now, have only cautiously been put forward by the author in other works will here be brought into the full light of day and weighed and defended with tenacity and wealth of argument.

Amongst these, first and foremost comes the thesis of the autochtony of the Etruscans: a nation which, as a historical entity, became formed and defined in Italy, between the banks of the Tiber and Arno, even though many ethnic and cultural contributions may have reached it from near or far off regions, especially during the earliest stages of its development. This thesis is now set upon a scientific footing and its acceptance no longer requires an act of faith, though the whole problem has too often been obscured by that anxious search for relationships and provenances that contributes little to the study of the dawn of Italian history. It is a thesis that stands out particularly against the over-simplified myth of a migration from the east, bag and baggage, of the first

Etruscans: a myth born out of the comparison of ancient literary testimonies with archaeological clues made before more recent researches and excavations had taken place, but, unfortunately, a myth still widely spread – as undisputed and acquired fact – beyond the confines of etruscology, even to the pages of school books.

The bibliographical references will be found in notes gathered at the end of each chapter and are limited to the scope of this volume. They are not systematic in character if we except works of a general nature embracing the whole of our discipline or its major sections. For the remainder, references try to furnish material for discussion and the checking of more controversial data, concentrating especially upon little known or very recent works not included in the etruscological manuals of Ducati or Nogara. This policy, of proved utility not only to the more serious reader and the student, but also to workers in allied fields, has been further stressed in this third edition of the work, a considerably expanded version of its two predecessors.

MASSIMO PALLOTTINO

Note to the English Translation

A CERTAIN difficulty was experienced in rendering into English many of the place-names of Etruria. We have generally referred to Etruscan towns by their Latin name, usually the best known in this country (e.g. Caere, Vulci, Veii, etc.); the modern Italian name of the site is often added in brackets for reference if necessary. At the risk of being taxed with inconsistency, we have used modern Italian names for those Etruscan centres whose light never dwindled in the past two millennia and whose Italian names are therefore more familiar to the English reader (e.g. Perugia, Fiesole, Volterra, etc.). Reference to the map on p. 107 (where both names are given in every case) should settle any difficulty that may arise.

J. CREMONA

PART ONE

The Etruscans and their place in the history of Italy and of the Mediterranean

CHAPTER ONE

ITALY AT THE DAWN OF HISTORY

The Myth of the Northern Invasions

WHEN dealing with the legends of antiquity on the foundation of Rome, Theodore Mommsen, the father of historical philology, wrote: 'History must first make a clean sweep of these fables which, though purporting to be history, are nothing more than somewhat simple improvisations.'[1] Little did he dream that the cumbersome archaeological and linguistic elaborations of modern science were soon to build up, in attempting to explain the origin of the Italic peoples, a whole series of reconstructions and hypotheses no less fabulous or fantastic than those originating in ancient pious traditions or in the fertile imaginations of mythographers, even though they were buttressed by the would-be excellence of method and authority of undisputed scholars.

Much blame has been laid upon antiquity for inventing such founder-heroes as Romulus and Remus, for creating out of sheer fancy such peoples as the Aborigines or the Pelasgians. What ought we to say then of a modern science that created the Villanovans on the mere basis that certain primitive peoples in Italy had in common a certain type of cinerary urn, discovered for the first time at Villanova in Aemilia? or of a science that believed for a long time in the existence of an original Italic language because of certain features Latin had in common with Umbrian and Oscan, whereas the unity of Italic peoples was in point of fact only realized as the result of the cohabitation of Indo-Europeans in Italy and of the spread of Latin? or, again, of a science that literally invented an Indo-European civilization in

Italy, whereas the concept of Indo-Europeanism is a purely linguistic one, in no way reflected (as far as we can say at the present moment) by manifestations or changes of culture? All these theories, however sketchy or absurd they may appear in the light of the latest advances of Etruscan studies, have nevertheless been current for many decades and exhibited a dogmatism verging at times on intolerance. They have left so deep a mark on research that even to-day, when bringing forward new concepts to replace the old, we unconsciously tend to use the terms and expressions which they created.

Is the fact that nineteenth-century science substituted its own 'myths' for the myths of antiquity a sufficient reason for too severe a judgement on our part? The youthful ardour of research-workers in a completely new field, where the last mists of eighteenth-century baroque learning were fast melting away; the possession of a new weapon – method – believed to be infallible; their faith in progress and their contempt for the intellectual activities of the past; all these causes explain, if they do not justify, the complacent attachment felt for the first results obtained and a certain intolerance in their attitude. Nor must we forget that, from many points of view, everything had still to be sorted, to be classified. It would be ungracious to complain of the makeshift plank that first enabled us to cross the river, though now we can, and must, build a far stronger and better bridge.

When a clean sweep had been made of the complicated ethnographic legends about primitive Italy inherited from classical times, historians and archaeologists of the end of the last century were faced with the following problems: when, and how, did the Indo-European peoples come to Italy? by what ethnic changes can the successive cultures revealed by Italian prehistory be explained?

As was only natural, the answers to these questions soon

led to an attempt to reconcile linguistic and archaeological facts within a single, all-embracing synthesis. It is worth recalling that, in linguistics, the concept of Indo-European unity, heroically fought for and consolidated during the nineteenth century, implied an original close relationship of peoples dispersed in historical times, such as the Celtic, Germanic, Italic, Greek, Slav, Armenian, Iranian, and Indian peoples. This in its turn implied an original point of departure and a particular moment of arrival in the various regions they are known to have inhabited in historic times. The arrival of a language could only signify the arrival of a people. Hence the idea of vast prehistoric migrations on the lines of the barbarian migrations at the time of the decline of the Roman Empire (with this important difference, that the Germanic peoples that spread over Europe and the Mediterranean world did in fact impose their language only in the British Isles and in a few marginal territories of the Empire). Hence again the concept of an 'Italic' invasion of prehistoric Italy.

On the other hand, prehistoric archaeology had at the same time made sufficient progress to recognize the existence of successive phases of culture. These came to be known as the palaeolithic (or chipped stone) age, the neolithic (or polished stone) age, the bronze age, and the iron age, the latter immediately preceding historical times. The then current method of chronological classification was of a typological and evolutionary nature, according to which the internal development of types of objects such as instruments, vases, weapons, and metal *fibulae* reflects a regular succession of periods common to the whole cultural area under consideration. A Swedish scholar, Oscar Montelius, after studying prehistoric remains of all kinds and particularly material found in tombs, succeeded in classifying the most recent phase of Italian prehistory into a 'bronze age' comprising four periods and an 'iron age' comprising six![2]

The first appearance of a bronze culture in Italy (occurring at the end of the neolithic stage when copper weapons and instruments were already in use, and hence labelled 'aeneolithic', 'cuprolithic', or 'chalcolithic') was assigned to the beginning of the second millennium B.C. and took the form of the Po valley *terremare* – prehistoric settlements built on palisades and surrounded by an embankment and a ditch to protect them from flood-waters. A connexion was seen between the *terremare* and a few rather meagre tombs that showed evidence of cremation as a funeral rite. The fact that the *terremare* were an isolated phenomenon, limited to northern Italy, and related structurally to the pile-dwelling system adopted by the prehistoric inhabitants of the Alpine lakes, the appearance of the cremation rite in neolithic tombs across the Alps (in France and Germany), the affinities between the *terramara* and the bronze cultures of Central Europe, all favoured the hypothesis that the bronze culture was introduced into Italy from over the Alps. This hypothesis appeared to be an historical and cultural reality of fundamental importance in the development of Italian prehistory, and it seemed obviously to indicate to scholars such as Gaetano Chierici, Wolfgang Helbig, and Luigi Pigorini, that the Indo-Europeans, i.e. the invading 'Italic' tribes, arrived in the peninsula as an already constituted people.[3]

This thesis, labelled 'Pigorinian', after its keenest and most famous exponent, acted as a keystone for the interpretation of the linguistic and archaeological facts of prehistoric Italy. It assumed in effect that the beginnings of Italy's cultural development were the result of a decisive ethnical impulse of transalpine origin. Whether this change was held to be solely due to the *terramara* wave, or whether it was thought that other invasions from the Danube basin followed it (thus giving rise to the iron civilizations of Italy, as others have believed), the civilizing wave always seemed to proceed from north to south. Rome itself was said to be linked in its earliest days to the northern *terremare;* and the square city, the Roman system of building its streets in chessboard pattern pointing towards the four directions of the compass, the very name of Palatine, all seemed to favour the theory according to which descendants of the inhabitants of the *terremare* founded the Eternal City. Thus the myth of the *terramaricoli* was substituted, in the name of science, for the myth of Romulus and Remus![4]

Position of Contemporary Criticism

Voices were already being raised however in opposition to the Pigorinian theory; they belonged to Edoardo Brizio, to Giuseppe Sergi the anthropologist, and to the archaeologist Giovanni Patroni, and warned against over-estimating the importance of the *terramara* civilization. The discoveries of Paolo Orsi in Sicily and Calabria, those of Giuseppe Angelo Colini and Ugo Rellini in central Italy, have revealed during the last fifty years the existence of a very flourishing bronze civilization that blossomed out without any break in continuity on the oldest aeneolithic sites. This civilization was entirely independent of transalpine influences: the funeral rite, for example, was the primitive rite of burial. If anything, it received the cultural waves that spread with greater and greater frequency from the Mediterranean islands and the East, where for centuries already civilizations of a superior type had been thriving: the Egyptian, the Mesopotamian, the Anatolian, the Minoan-Mycenaean. It was particularly as a result of Rellini's intense research and of his conclusions that this bronze civilization (known at first by the still controversial name of 'extraterramara', and now more appropriately renamed Apenninic) was shown to have played a preponderant role in the material and intellectual development of primitive Italy and was taken as a likely external pointer to the formation of the Italic *ethnos*. Upon it in fact were grafted the later iron cultures which already existed by the first millennium B.C. and are proper to the Italic peoples at the threshold of their history. It was observed that the Italic peoples in their most ancient and secluded settlements still preserved burial, proper to the Apenninic culture, as their funerary rite. The Pigorinian equation: Italic peoples = cremation peoples, was thus seriously invalidated.[5]

Owing to the presence as far as northern Italy of the Apenninic bronze culture and of inhumation rites, the *terramara* culture – limited to parts of Aemilia and lower Lombardy – appeared to be, and in fact was, no more than an episode of purely local importance, and essentially due to the peculiar geographical conditions of an alluvial region covered by a network of large rivers. Doubt was even cast on whether the cinerary urns should be attributed to the inhabitants of the *terremare*: for scholars tend to date the latter even earlier than the beginning of the actual bronze age. The original formulation of the problem was thus reversed, and Pigorini's theory was overthrown by the facts.

Once more, therefore, the need to answer the following questions arises: When did the Indo-Europeans come to Italy? How can the cultures of prehistoric Italy be explained? What was the origin of the Italic peoples?

As we proceed along the path of science we cannot help noticing the extreme complexity of phenomena which at one time appeared to be simple and clear-cut. The very simplicity, relatively speaking, of Pigorini's explanation is a clear indication of its insufficiency. Any attempt to marshal the facts of such a remote and obscure past into a straightforward and coherent pattern, with clear and precise statements, leads inevitably to the dangers of oversimplification, to the premature statement of general conclusions without sufficient knowledge of factual data.

In attempting to reach not a reconstructive synthesis (this is not possible for the moment, and perhaps never will be) but a guiding principle that would conform as far as possible to factual reality, we must begin by separating and analysing singly, without bias or haste, the data provided by linguistics and archaeology.[6]

Linguistic Outline of Primitive Italy

The present state of our knowledge provides us with the following linguistic outline of pre- and proto-historic Italy.[7] At the time of the spreading of the art of writing, i.e. between the sixth and fifth centuries B.C. the north of Italy and the greater part of the Alpine region seem to have been inhabited by peoples whose dialects are not yet properly classified but are usually referred to as 'Ligurian', for they roughly coincide with the area occupied by the Ligurians of history. In these dialects Indo-European elements seem to be superimposed on a pre-Indo-European substratum.[8] Along the whole of the valley of the Adige, in north-east Italy, there are traces of a 'Raetic' language belonging to a pre-Indo-European stock and possessing certain affinities with Etruscan.[9] Over the middle and lower Po plain, the slow spreading of Etruscan was taking place. In Venetia, Istria, and Carniola, a dialect was spoken that was certainly Indo-European: Venetic. Tyrrhenian (western) central Italy constituted the original area of diffusion of Etruscan, an essentially non-Indo-European language with Aegean and Asian affinities. In Latium, there was Latin, to which were probably related the primitive dialects of Tyrrhenian southern Italy, from Campania to Calabria. Along the backbone of the Apennines, stretching from Umbria to Lucania and spreading unevenly towards either shore, were scattered those linguistically related, pre-eminently 'Italic' peoples that spoke Umbrian and the Sabellic dialects, from which there derived, after the conquest of Campania at the hands of the Samnites, the Oscan language.[10] Along the Adriatic shore, in the region of Picenum, there are traces of

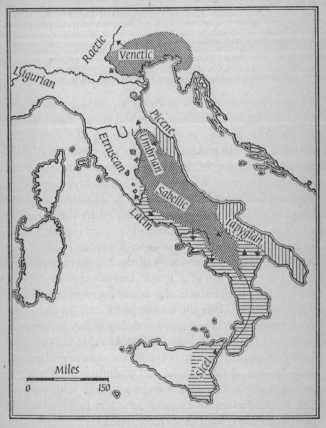

Figure I – THE LANGUAGES OF ANCIENT ITALY

Areas speaking a non-Indo-European language are left in white. Horizontal hatching indicates western dialects (Latin and Sicel); oblique hatching, falling to the left, dialects of the Umbro-Sabellic group; oblique hatching, falling to the right, Venetic; vertical hatching, other Adriatic dialects.

at least two very little known dialects, probably with Indo-European elements, but of uncertain origin. In Apulia, Iapygian (or Messapic) was also of Indo-European stock and possessed certain affinities with Illyrian. In eastern Sicily, an Indo-European dialect was spoken that possessed certain similarities with Umbro-Sabellic, but also significant affinities with Latin.[11] In the western half of the island, in Sardinia and in Corsica, languages were spoken which (though we have no direct supporting evidence) may be considered as non-Indo-European; they were probably related, even though indirectly, to African, Iberian, and Ligurian idioms.[12] We should finally mention the languages of colonization: Doric and Ionic Greek dialects in southern Italy and Sicily, Punic in the Carthaginian settlements of western Sicily and Sardinia, and finally Etruscan itself on the coasts of Campania and Corsica.

Thus, the linguistic picture is one of extreme complexity. We are a long way from the over-simple 'Italic' unity of certain scholars of the past; and we are a long way too from the conditions reigning in other countries, such as contemporary Greece, with its linguistic evenness broken only by dialect variations, quite negligible in most cases and soon destined to be smoothed by the literary κοινή of Attic culture.

In attempting to bring a little order into this intricate state of affairs, we must first distinguish those dialects that certainly belonged to the Indo-European stock from those foreign to it or that appear to have been influenced by it only in a limited way. The latter ('Ligurian', 'Raetic', Etruscan, and in all probability the island idioms) belong to the west, whereas the Indo-European dialects occupy the eastern areas of continental and peninsular Italy. The boundary dividing the two groups follows an imaginary line that roughly corresponds to the twelfth meridian, from the Trentine Alps to the mouths of the Tiber; the line is then carried over to Sicily, dividing the island into two. The linguistic, geographic, and historical importance of this fact cannot escape anyone: for if we suppose, as everything leads us to suppose, that the non-Indo-European linguistic area is older than the Indo-European area, the latter's position shows very clearly that Indo-Europeanism must have advanced from east to west rather than from north to south.

Within the sphere of the Indo-European dialects themselves a classification is both possible and useful.[13] The independence of Latin and of the Osco-Umbrian group has been definitely demonstrated. All the known Indo-European idioms of Italy can be thus divided into three fundamental groups:

(1) Latin, probably the dialects of the Tyrrhenian zone of southern Italy, and, perhaps, Sicel;

(2) Umbrian, the Sabellic dialects, Oscan;

(3) Venetic, partly (perhaps) the Picene dialects, Iapygian.

The geographic position of these three groups is significant: the first occupies the extreme western or Tyrrhenian regions and is in contact with the non-Indo-European area; the second is spread along the centre of the peninsula following the crest of the Apennines; the third, or eastern group, borders on the Adriatic. The affinities which have been found to exist between Venetic and Latin could be explained by the peculiar position of the former: for although it belongs to the Eastern or Adriatic group, it is, like Latin, in direct contact along its western border with the non-Indo-European linguistic area.[14] The Adriatic dialect-areas are not contiguous, and, as far as we are able to tell, do not constitute a single linguistic whole. Toponymic data, and tradition, refer us to the coasts of Illyria and to the Illyrians, though there is as yet no full agreement amongst scholars on the exact meaning to be attached to the word

'Illyrian', especially since present-day Albanian dialects, believed to be its surviving descendants, do not possess any affinities with ancient Venetic or Iapygian. It is probable that ethnic and linguistic influences from the opposite Adriatic shore also exerted themselves on Picenum, where we encounter little-known dialects and where there lived a people which the Umbrian text of the Iguvine Tablets designates by the name of *Iapuzci*, cognate with the *Iapodi* of Istria and the *Iapygi* of Apulia.

The area covered by the three Indo-European linguistic groups in Italy makes, in our opinion, the history of their original diffusion sufficiently clear. They are spread on three bands of territory that divide the Italian peninsula longitudinally, thus giving the impression of three successive waves. Since the eastern band is contiguous with the Indo-European zones of the Balkan peninsula and the western band borders on the non-Indo-European zone, it is self-evident that the linguistic waves must have spread from east to west and that the oldest must have been the one to which Latin belongs ('proto-Latin' according to Devoto's terminology). This in fact concurs with what is known of some of the marginal (and therefore archaic) characteristics of Latin when compared with other Indo-European languages. The Umbro-Sabellic wave that followed afterwards must have pushed these peoples back to the extreme margins of the peninsula and of Sicily, placing them in close contact with the surviving non-Indo-European areas and influencing their original languages, as is perhaps the case with Sicel. The oldest Umbro-Sabellic occupation zone was in the southern central Apennines and it is from this area that, in proto-historic and historical times only, speakers of these dialects spread northwards towards Romagna, westwards in the direction of Latium and Campania, and southwards to the extremity of the peninsula. Contrary to common opinion (established on the strength of the Pigorinian theory and still held to-day by some scholars) there is no certain trace of the presence of Umbro-Sabellic peoples in northern Italy before the Umbrian invasions of historical times. We have therefore no concrete proof of their having immigrated over the Alps. The hypothesis that makes them cross the Adriatic from the Balkan peninsula is far more likely to be true. That this was possible is proved by the third linguistic wave which our linguistic outline has caught, so to speak, in the act of crossing the Adriatic, having already established bridgeheads on the Italian shores (Apulia, Venetia and, perhaps, Picenum) while its bases are still on the Illyrian shore opposite.

The problem of the classification and the diffusion of the Indo-European languages of Italy may be further complicated by the recently examined likelihood of yet other Indo-European linguistic currents finding their way (in presumably very ancient times) to the peninsula.[15] This eventuality should be considered in connexion with the concept of 'Proto-Italics' put forward by Devoto, though it is a cultural rather than a linguistic concept. At any rate it is important to bear in mind that the structure of these languages and dialectal variations of historical times (Latin, Oscan, Umbrian, etc.) cannot without great difficulties be referred back to prehistoric times, i.e. to times when the Indo-European linguistic prototypes were introduced into Italy. It is likely that the historical idioms attested through inscriptions are only the culmination of a long and complicated process of concentration and specialization on the part of linguistic currents only approximately identifiable, of which, for various reasons, some may have developed in vigorous fashion, others may have been considerably mingled and altered, while yet others may have completely disappeared. This supposition is strengthened by analogy with events occurring in historical times, when we see the Oscan idioms impose themselves over southern Italy only to be submerged, together with their neighbours, by their sister Latin.

The arrival in Italy of the various Indo-European linguistic waves obviously presupposes an earlier non-Indo-European phase. But since the latter is a good deal older than the adoption of writing, we can only form an idea of it from the languages (i.e. Etruscan) of the western zone (though these are hardly better known), and from toponymy, i.e. the study of place names, which often stubbornly resist linguistic change and evolution. This type of research is of course extremely difficult; it is impossible to be too cautious, and results are always uncertain and subject to revision. The latest researches however seem to arrive at the recognition in the Mediterranean linguistic substrata of the Italian region of three sufficiently well-defined types: a Libyco-Iberian group in the islands, a 'Ligurian' group in northern Italy, and a third, 'Tyrrhenian' or 'Raeto-Tyrrhenian' in the eastern Alps, in the lower Po valley and over the rest of the peninsula.[16] The latter type is thought to be mainly related to the non-Indo-European languages of the Aegean basin and of Asia Minor, whereas the first two groups ought probably to be connected with the primitive idioms of Europe and western Africa. The arrival on the scene of the Indo-European languages from the East would then have pushed the older languages (Ligurian in the north-west and 'Tyrrhenian' in Tuscany) towards the western edge of the Italian peninsula. It is also possible however that the east-to-west movement of the 'Tyrrhenian' linguistic wave might be due to causes analogous to those that brought about the great speed of the Indo-European languages in Italy.[17]

Bronze and Iron Cultures in Italy

Such is the broad outline of the linguistic prehistory of Italy sketched on the basis of reliable factual data. It gives us no

indication however as to when or how the Indo-Europeanization of Italy took place; the process, that is, by which the
peoples of historic Italy were first formed. It only provides
us with a relative chronology of events, and not with the
absolute chronology we need in order to localize them in
history; nor does it explain the actual mechanism of linguistic transformation: whether it was due to large migrations, to a slow infiltration, or to cultural or political
influences.[18]

We should therefore also examine the question of the
Italian prehistoric cultures, freed from the preconceptions
of the Pigorinian reconstruction. But let us first of all note
the birth of a new method in ethnological and palethno-
logical research in opposition to the old evolutionary and
typological method: we refer to the historico-cultural
method first introduced by F. Gräbner and by Father W.
Schmidt. Cultural facts are no longer studied on the basis
of an *a priori* supposition that a general and continuous
evolution took place from simple to complex forms. The
new basis assumes that every centre of culture created its
own peculiar conditions of life, and that the genius of single
individuals may have achieved in certain places conquests
and inventions that later became general, while in other
places very ancient or even primitive forms of life may have
survived for a long time. Once this is assumed, it is certainly not a given type of object that will furnish any precise idea of the age to which it belonged. An ordered classi-
ficatory system such as the one elaborated by Montelius
must of necessity be invalidated by the possibility that cultures of a more archaic type may survive other more progressive types. Instead of a general and continuous development, a new concept has been evolved, based on present-
day observations, especially amongst primitive peoples:
that of centres of development spreading their innovations
and civilizing influence in surrounding areas to a greater or

lesser degree. Instead of the idea of transitional cultures linking one phase to the next, we now have that of cultures uniting elements that originated in several different centres, or successive irradiations from the same centres.[19]

It is obvious that once the problem is set in this way we can no longer speak of a regular succession: stone age, bronze age, iron age, except on the broadest lines of time and space. Whereas the East (Egypt and Mesopotamia) rapidly developed an early civilization that from the beginning of the third millennium B.C. transformed its ancient stone and aeneolithic cultures into an advanced bronze culture that included cities, religious monuments, complex political organizations, writing, scientific, and artistic documents, etc., the majority of the inhabitants of Europe were to live for a long time yet at the stone age level, with rare influxes from the East and only a very limited use of copper weapons and instruments. In Italy the actual bronze culture spreads slowly, perhaps only as a result of the effulgence of the Aegean civilization which had as its first and most resplendent centre the island of Crete. One can only speak of a true bronze age in Italy during the second half of the second millennium B.C., and it is possible that aeneolithic cultural traditions thrived on in secluded areas up to the end of the bronze age. Similarly, in an isolated territory such as the island of Sardinia, the iron age was not even able to establish itself, so that the Sardinians lived at the bronze culture level till they were conquered by the Romans, during the third century B.C.

Aeneolithic culture itself varied greatly from region to region, whereas the 'Apenninic' bronze culture possesses a relatively uniform character in central and southern Italy: it appears to have been especially vigorous in the Adriatic regions. Its ramifications are found in the direction of northern Italy, Umbria, Tuscany, and Campania, whereas on the Apulian coast, in Sicily and in the Lipari islands the direct

influence of Mycenaean culture can be detected. The latest
phase of the bronze culture, following its Apenninic
flowering, appears to be represented in southern Italy (and
in the Lipari islands) by a cultural phase that has received
the name of 'Ausonian'.[20] The Po valley displays the
phenomenon of the *terremare* which, as stated before, appears to have been geographically rather circumscribed: it
is probably also late in character and is related on the one
hand to forms of life belonging to the Alpine lake-village
system (Polada culture) and on the other with the late
Apenninic and 'Ausonian' cultures.

But the different regions of Italy present notable variants
only with the appearance of iron culture, characterized by
the spread of the use of the new metal alongside bronze, in
the fashioning of arms and tools and by the use of geometrical decorative patterns with a preference for the
straight line. It corresponds to a phase of history that followed the end of the Mycenaean civilization of Greece (the
so-called geometric period), and represents the beginning
of the cultures of the Italian peoples of historical times.[21]
In Italy, as also in central and western Europe, its establishment took time in becoming effective; its progressive penetration amongst the late bronze cultures varied from place
to place.[22] The principal regional varieties of the Italian
iron culture are: (i) the northern cultures of Golasecca
(Liguria, Piedmont, and Lombardy) and of Este (Venetia),
(ii) the 'Villanovan' culture of Etruria and Aemilia, (iii) the
Latian culture, (iv) the 'eastern' culture of Umbria, Picenum
and Samnium and the Apulian culture, (v) the 'southern'
culture of Campania and Calabria, (vi) the Sicel culture.

The question of funerary rites is of particular interest to
the study of this period. Until then in Italy the dead were
buried in little grottoes or in graves. Towards the end of
the bronze age, corresponding with the last phases of the
terramara and 'Ausonian' cultures, there began to appear

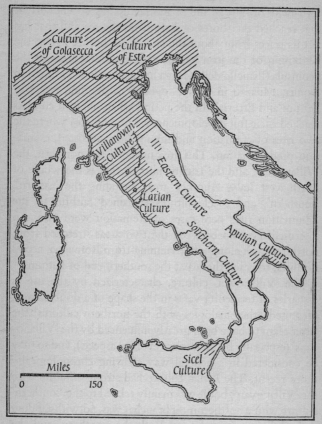

Figure 2 – THE CULTURES OF PROTO-HISTORIC ITALY
The cross-hatched areas are those where cremation rites prevailed;
areas left in white correspond to inhumatory customs.

groups of tombs with terracotta urns containing the ashes
of the cremated dead. They are not only met in the Po
valley, but also in the extreme south of Italy (Torre Castelluccia, in Apulia), and their presence proves the coexistence
of a cremation 'current' of continental origin related to the

Urn-fields of Europe and of another no less ancient current that reached the shores of Italy from the sea and that has left its traces from about the end of the bronze age to the beginning of the iron age in various coastal areas of the peninsula (Pianello della Genga in the Marches, Timmari in Apulia, Milazzo in Sicily, together with some traces in Latium and Etruria). In the period when the iron cultures reached their full development, we find an area where the two rites of cremation and inhumation coexisted, cremation predominating. This area included the northern, the 'Villanovan', and the Latian cultures, that is the whole of north-west Italy. Another area, including the 'eastern', 'southern', and Sicel cultures remained faithful to the inhumation rite; here cases of cremation were rare. An intermediary strip between the two areas stretched from north to south along a line running from Romagna, across Umbria, to reach the sea at the southern end of Latium.

The 'Villanovan' culture, characterized by the use as ossuaries of terracotta vases in the shape of a double cone, presented other analogies with the northern cultures; the latter seem to have been greatly influenced by the 'Villanovans' (especially by their more evolved aspects), and so may be considered in a general way as being chronologically more recent. The Latian culture had strong affinities with the 'Villanovan', but it was mainly related to the 'southern' culture whose northernmost branch it was, notwithstanding their different funeral rites. Both the 'southern' and the Sicel cultures developed when Hellenic influences first made their appearance, either at the same time as, or immediately preceding the earliest colonizations of southern Italy and Sicily. Finally, the 'eastern' culture, the most widespread of all, presented a great many similarities to the Apenninic bronze culture that preceded it; it occupied most of its territory and in certain aspects represented a local development. It was prolonged to the south into the Apulian culture which, however, possesses characteristics of its own and appears to be related to cultural manifestations on the opposite shore of the Adriatic. 'Oriental' cultural influences may also be found on the Tyrrhenian shore, especially in the area where the 'Villanovan' culture met that of Latium (Tolfa)[23]; the Apulian culture on the other hand, with its characteristic painted pottery, tended to expand towards the Tyrrhenian coasts of Lucania (e.g. Palinuro).

The transformation of the iron cultures into the full civilization of historical times was accompanied by a process of internal development which stood out most clearly in Etruria. For it was here that a great flowering of civilization occurred, ushered in by favourable economic and social conditions and by the influence of the highly-evolved societies of the eastern Mediterranean. In southern Italy and in Sicily the mature civilization of Greek colonists superimposed itself on the native one without however destroying it, but transforming it little by little. Elsewhere and especially in northern Italy, in the Apennines and on the shores of the Adriatic, iron age cultural conditions persisted for a long time, with few innovations, right up to the time of the Roman conquest during the fourth and third centuries B.C.

The Problem of Chronology

Closely related to the review of archaeological data belonging to Italian protohistory is the problem of chronology. Except in the case of the more recent facts, chronology can only utilize, owing to the lack of written documents, elements provided by the comparison of types of objects and patterns belonging to other civilizations to which an approximate date at least can be given, i.e. the Egyptian and Aegean civilizations of the eastern Mediterranean. There are in fact many cases of isolated influences, even at times of direct importation of objects from the East; and during the later phases of the iron age culture these influences became more and more frequent till they produced the characteristic 'orientalizing' civilization, that spread from southern Etruria.

According to calculations that are still generally accepted (based for the older period on the chronology of the Aegean civilization and for the more recent one on that of archaic Greece), the first stages of the bronze age in Italy have been assigned to the beginning of the second millennium B.C., those of the iron age to about the year 1000, and the establishment of the orientalizing civilization in Etruria to about the year 700 B.C. The latest studies and investigations have proved that the flowering of the Apenninic and Sicel bronze cultures coincided with the later phases of the Mycenaean civilization in Greece.[24] This probably means that the aeneolithic culture lasted in many parts of Italy till the second half of the second millennium and that the full establishment and final phases of the bronze culture should be assigned to the centuries immediately preceding and following the year 1000 B.C. The appearance of the iron cultures in central and southern Italy may be placed between the end of the ninth and the beginning of the eighth century; their eastern and northern diffusion probably took place during the eighth and seventh centuries. The first evidence of cremation as a funeral rite in Italy is also attributed to the beginning of the first millennium. And by the seventh and sixth centuries appeared the first inscriptions; these bear certain witness to the presence of the peoples of ancient Italy in those centres they occupied in historical times.[25]

Formation of Historical Peoples

We have now examined in the light of the newest discoveries and criteria the linguistic and archaeological data of the problem that confronts us, and we can without more ado establish a certain number of points. There is first of all no possibility of identifying the Italic peoples with northern invaders introducing cremation as a funeral rite. In Italy the Indo-Europeanization movement travelled from east to west and its beginnings must have been, without a shadow of doubt, older than the diffusion of the new rite. But of far greater import is the singular and incontrovertible fact that *the two linguistic and cultural maps of proto-historic Italy* (cf. p. 26 and p. 35) *do roughly coincide along the longitudinal line that divides the peninsula into two, from Romagna to Latium, leaving to the east an Indo-European linguistic area with inhumation as its prevalent funeral rite, and to the west a non-Indo-European linguistic area where it was cremation that prevailed*. This fact radically invalidates the equation Italic peoples=cremation peoples. It is harder to explain why the new rite should have been adopted mainly in a region inhabited by peoples belonging to the oldest linguistic stock. This may have been due to peculiar social and religious conditions or crises, to external influences or internal migrations. In any case the problem very closely concerns the question of the origin of the Etruscans, to be dealt with in the next chapter.

If the peoples of Italy may be considered as already established in their historical centres at the time of the spreading of the iron age cultures (as is proved by inscriptions belonging to a slightly later date), it is obvious that the Indo-Europeanization of Italy belongs to a very remote age. Now it is worth noting that the areas in which the Italic Indo-European languages first established themselves (i.e. south-eastern Italy) possessed a distinctive cultural unity not only during the iron age, with its 'eastern' culture and the inhumation rite, but even in the bronze age, with the Apenninic culture whose most important centres were in the heart of the peninsula and on its Adriatic slopes, and the succeeding 'Ausonian' culture dominant in the south. The picture of an Apenninic bronze culture slowly conquering Italy and spreading its influence towards the Tyrrhenian shores coincides remarkably well with the picture we may draw of the east-to-west advance of Indo-European speakers. Everything leads us to believe with the latest supporters of the anti-Pigorinian reaction, that the Apenninic culture mirrors, in the domain of external historical manifestations, the formation of an Italic *ethnos*.

But at this point to identify the cultural phenomena with the linguistic phenomena in question (i.e. to believe that the manifestations of the Apenninic culture mark the appearance of Indo-Europeans in Italy) would mean repeating the mistake made by the old theorists, though in a different direction. It has been proved that in certain sites such as the great prehistoric centre of Matera in Lucania the development from aeneolithic to bronze culture was uninterrupted. On the other hand Sicily showed a cultural dichotomy between its eastern and western halves (the two areas inhabited in historical times by – probably – non-Indo-European Sicans and by Indo-European Sicels) while still at the aeneolithic stage. It is likely that the diffusion of the oldest ('proto-Latin') Indo-European wave took place before the appearance of the bronze culture in Italy: it may even go back to before the beginning of the second millennium B.C. Towards the end of the bronze age, the region occupied by these peoples coincides fairly exactly with that of the so-called 'Ausonian' culture. The Umbro-Sabellic wave established itself most probably within the compass of the Apenninic culture.

This complex interweaving of linguistic and cultural phenomena and the long duration of the processes of penetration and establishment of the Indo-European languages on Italian territory are in a way sufficient to show that the obscure phenomenon of the Indo-Europeanization of Italy was substantially different from the rather over-simplified concept of a migration on the part of one or more peoples, so dear to the hearts of scholars of past generations. To come nearer to the truth, we have to imagine extremely varied, slow and complex changes, to whose final phases (the expansion of the Umbro-Sabellians) history is a witness. A reconstruction based on the analogy of such final phases may then perhaps be attempted: it should take into account the effect of various other possible factors such as conquests, partial displacements, cultural influences, etc., upon the broad picture presented by the attraction exerted by culturally more evolved territories upon more warlike and ruder peoples.

In any case the individuality of the various peoples of Italy was already evident in the main at the time of the diffusion of the iron cultures. The cultures of the Tyrrhenian coastal strips (Latian, 'southern', Sicel) doubtless belonged to the Latin-Sicel peoples.[26] The 'eastern' culture is proper to the Umbro-Sabellians, and its western ramifications correspond to the Umbro-Sabellic linguistic influences in Latium and in Campania, culminating later in historical times with the ethnic migrations of the Volsci, the Aequi and the Samnites towards the Tyrrhenian shores. The 'Villanovan' culture coincides broadly with the area inhabited by the Etruscans in historical times. The Golasecca culture was inherited by the Ligurians; that of Este, by the Veneti. To this period in fact may already be attributed the first settlements of speakers of Adriatic Indo-European dialects on the eastern shores of Italy; to the very flourishing culture of the Marches there corresponded the Picenes, while the Apulian culture together with its variants belonged to the Iapygi (Daunians, Peucetians, and Messapians).

NOTES

1. *Römische Geschichte*, 7th edition, 1881, pp. 44 ff.

2. *Die vorklassische Chronologie Italiens*, 1912.

3. For more details see especially W. Helbig, *Die Italiker in der Po-Ebene*, 1879.

4. To mention only more recent works, cf.: E. Täubler, *Terremare und Rom*, 1926; V. Basanoff, *Pomerium palatinum* (in *Memorie della R. Accademia dei Lincei*, 1939). The theory is exhaustively criticized by P. Barocelli in *Bullettino della Commissione Archeol. comunale*, LXX, 1942, pp. 131 ff.

5. On this subject as a whole, see U. Rellini, *Le origini della civiltà italica*, 1929; *Recenti studi sulla civiltà enea in Italia* (*XXVIII Riunione della S.I.P.S.*, vol. IV, pp. 343 ff.); M. Pallottino, *L'origine degli Etruschi*, 1947, pp. 108 ff.; G. Patroni, *La preistoria* (*Storia politica d'Italia*), 2nd ed., 1951, pp. 612 ff. On the subject of the *terremare* and their chronology, see G. Säflund, *Le terremare delle provincie di Modena, Reggio Emilio, Parma, Piacenza* (*Acta Instit. Rom. Regni Sueciae*, VII, 1939): his conclusions however are not wholly acceptable: cf. U. Rellini in *Bullettino di Paletnologia*, new series, III, 1939, pp. 114 ff.

6. On the ancient peoples of Italy, see J. Whatmough, *The Foundations of Roman Italy*, 1937; A. Furumark, *Det äldsta Italien*, 1947; M. Pallottino, *Popolazioni storiche dell' Italia antica*, in *Guida allo studio della civiltà romana antica*, 1952, pp. 71–90; L. Pareti, *Storia di Roma e del mondo romano*, 1952, pp. 63 ff.

7. The elements for such a reconstruction are now gathered in V. Pisani, *Le lingue dell' Italia antica oltre il latino*, 1953; the reader is referred to the bibliography of this work for both ancient and recent publications on the single languages, with the exception of a few additions which will be found in our notes.

8. Cf. P. Kretschmer, in *Glotta*, XXX, 1943, pp. 203 ff.; on the Lugurians in general, both as to their language and history, and their relations with the other ancient peoples of Italy, see also M. Pallottino, *Il problema dei liguri nella formazione dell' ethnos italico*, in *Atti del I Congresso Intern. di Studi Liguri*, 1952, pp. 83 ff.

9. V. Pisani and P. Kretschmer consider Raetic to be a pre-Indo-European language distinct from Etruscan though related to it. On the other hand C. Battisti (in *Studi Etruschi*, XVIII, 1944, pp. 199 ff.; XIX, 1946–7, pp. 249 ff.) tends to see in it the direct and late influence of historical Etruscan, thus following tradition as stated in Livy V,

33 (Livy's quotation is given in Chapter IV). Other authorities (cf. E. Vetter, in *Glotta*, XXX, 1943, pp. 75 ff.) attempt to include Raetic within the Indo-European framework.

10. E. Vetter, *Handbuch der Italischen Dialekte*, I, 1953.

11. V. Pisani, in *Sulla lingua dei Siculi*, in *Bollett. del Centro Studi Filol. e Linguistici Siciliani*, I, 1953, pp. 5 ff., now confirms the doubts already expressed elsewhere on a specific Siculo-Latin relationship commonly accepted by scholars.

12. For Sardinia, see M. Pallottino, *La Sardegna nuragica*, 1950, pp. 22 ff., and bibliography, p. 28.

13. In addition to the works mentioned on p. 42, notes 6 and 7, see especially, G. Devoto, *Gli antichi Italici*, 2nd ed., 1951, pp. 41 ff., with bibliography on pp. 62 ff.

14. F. Altheim presupposes the existence of a primitive Latin substratum that extended from the Euganean region to the Val Camonica; this would later have been covered by the Venetic stratum of Illyrian origin (*Römische Geschichte*, I, 1951, pp. 14 ff., where references to previous studies will be found). This hypothesis rests upon no serious foundations.

15. See G. Devoto in *Studi Etruschi*, XIX, 1946-7, pp. 296 ff., and *Gli antichi Italici*, 2nd ed., pp. 51 ff., and pp. 65 ff.

16. Cf. G. Devoto, *Storia della lingua di Roma*, 1940, pp. 37 ff.; B. Gerola, *Substrato mediterraneo e latino* (in *Studi Etruschi*, XVI, 1942, pp. 345 ff.); P. Kretschmer, *Glotta*, XXVIII, 1940, pp. 231 ff.; XXX, 1943, pp. 84 ff.

17. Whether it be considered as a penetration by way of land routes from the Danubian region (P. Kretschmer, *Glotta*, XXX, 1943, pp. 104, 199, 168 ff., 213 ff.), or whether it be admitted as a coastal infiltration from the Eastern Mediterranean basin, in which case it would partly link up with the tradition and belief of an Aegeo-Asiatic origin of the Tyrrhenians and the Pelasgians, a theory that will be found discussed on pp. 53-63.

18. The hypothesis of a slow cultural infiltration (of 'linguistic ferments', as its author designates them, contrary to the old theory of invasion) is mainly due to G. Patroni (*Espansioni e migrazioni*, in *Archivio Glottologico Italiano*, XXXII, 1940, pp. 21 ff.). A critical examination of this hypothesis may be found in G. Devoto, *Studi Etruschi*, XVI, 1942, pp. 409 ff., and in *Gli antichi Italici*, 2nd ed., pp. 67 ff. The idea of a political influence on the other hand has been elaborated on the basis of C. Jullian's theories by L. Homo, in his work *L'Italie primitive et les débuts de l'impérialisme romain*, 1925, pp. 58 ff. The traditional 'invasion' theory is substantially restated by

F. Matz in *Neue Jahrbücher für Antike und deutsche Bildung*, I, 1938, pp. 367 ff., II, 1939, pp. 32 ff., and *Klio*, XXXV, 1942, pp. 299 ff.; by H. Krahe, *Die Indogermanisierung Griechenlands und Italiens*, 1949; by F. Altheim, *Römische Geschichte*, I, pp. 13 ff. and by other, but especially German, scholars.

19. On the historico-cultural method, cf. G. Montandon, *Traité d'ethnologie culturelle*, 1934, pp. 26 ff.; W. Schmidt, *Handbuch der Methode der kulturhistorischer Ethnologie*, 1937. On its applications in the field of pre- and proto-history, see P. Laviosa Zambotti, *Origini e diffusione della civiltà*, 1947; B. Pace, *Dubbi metodologici e ipotesi di lavoro per la cronologia delle civiltà protostoriche*, in *Atti del I Congresso Intern. di Preistoria e Protostoria Mediterranea*, 1952, pp. 265 ff. On Italy in particular, see B. Pace, *Arte e civiltà della Sicilia antica*, I, 1935, pp. 142 ff.; M. Pallottino, *Sulle facies culturali arcaiche dell' Etruria*, in *Studi Etruschi*, XIII, 1939, pp. 85 ff.

20. L. Bernabò Brea, *Civiltà preistoriche delle isole eolie*, in *Archivo di Preistoria Levantina*, III, 1952, pp. 69 ff.

21. On the manifestations of the iron cultures of Italy, cf. F. v. Duhn, F. Messerschmidt, *Italische Gräberkunde*, I, 1924; II, 1939. Cf. also F. Messerschmidt, *Bronzezeit und frühe Eisenzeit in Italien*, 1935, and U. Rellini and G. Säflund in *Studi Etruschi*, XII, 1939, pp. 9 ff.

22. We are still a long way from a definite settlement of the chronological relations between the first manifestations of the iron cultures of Italy and the northern and north-eastern civilization areas of the late bronze age (a so-called transitional phase: Lausitz, *Urnenfelder*) or of the iron age (Hallstadt, Danubian cultures, etc.). Many scholars, the Germans in particular, believe in the derivation of the culture of the Italian cremation peoples from transalpine cultures. In fact, however, we possess no definite evidence by which to determine the absolute chronology of transalpine cultures and thereby establish definite priority over the Italian parallels. The recentness of Hallstadt is now universally accepted (N. Åberg, *Bronzezeitliche und Früheisenzeitliche Chronologie: Italien*, 1930). In southern Gaul, the 'transitional' manifestations of the *Urnenfelder* (urn fields) culture now appear to be contemporary with the beginnings of Ionic colonization (sixth century B.C.): cf. *Gallia*, I, 1943, pp. 5 ff. For European and Italian cultures of the late bronze age and early iron age and their inter-relations, cf. E. Dunareanu-Vulpe, *L'espansione delle civiltà italiche verso l'oriente danubiano nella prima età del ferro* (in *Ephemeris Dacoromana*, III, 1925, pp. 58 ff.) as well as Åberg's work referred to above; G. von Merhart, *Donauländische Beziehungen der früheisenzeitlichen Kulturen Mittelitaliens*, in *Bonner Jahrbücher*, 147,

1942, pp. 1 ff.; C. F. C. Hawkes, *From Bronze Age to Iron Age: Middle Europe, Italy and the North and West,* in *Proceedings of the Prehistoric Society for* 1948, pp. 196 ff.; G. Kossack, *Problemi cronologici della prima età del ferro in Italia e nell' Europa Centrale,* in *Atti del I Congr. Intern. di Preistoria e Protostoria Mediterranea,* 1952, pp. 368 ff. (with divergent views on the subject).

23. Such cultural influences, which often possess an archaic flavour, have been considered (most probably in error) as manifestations of a chronological 'transition' from bronze to iron age: cf M. Pallottino, *Sulle facies culturali arcaiche dell' Etruria,* in *Studi Etruschi,* XIII, pp. 85 ff.

24. B. Pace, *Arte e civiltà della Sicilia antica,* I, 1935, pp. 142 ff.; G. Buchner, *Nota preliminare sulle ricerche preistoriche nell'isola di Ischia,* in *Bulletino di Paletnologia,* 1936–7, pp. 78 ff.).

25. For the chronology of the beginnings of the iron age in Italy, see (in addition to the studies quoted on p. 44, notes 21 and 22): Å. Åkerström, *Das geometrische Stil in Italien,* 1943; M. Pallottino, *Nuovi orientamenti sulla cronologia dell' Etruria protostorica,* in *Rendic. della Pontificia Accad. di Archeologia,* XXII, 1946–7, pp. 31 ff.; C. F. C. Hawkes, *Chronology of the Bronze and Early Iron Ages, Greek, Italian and Transalpine,* in *Atti del I Congr. Intern. di Preistoria e Protostoria Mediterranea,* 1952, pp. 256 ff.

26. Cf. M. Pallottino, *Appunti di protostoria latina ed etrusca* in *Studi Etruschi,* XIV, 1940, pp. 27 ff.; G. Devoto, *Protolatini e Tirreni,* in *Studi Etruschi,* XVI, 1942, pp. 409 ff.

CHAPTER TWO

THE PROBLEM OF ETRUSCAN ORIGINS

The Present State of the Question

THE problem of the origin of the Etruscans was first formulated by Dionysius of Halicarnassus, a Greek historian of the Augustan age, who devoted six chapters (xxv–xxx) of the first book of his *Early History of Rome* to a treatment of the question. With the critical means at his disposal he refuted the theories that identified the Etruscans with the Pelasgians or with the Lydians and declared himself favourable to the hypothesis that they were a people 'who had not come from outside, but were indigenous', and whose name was supposed to be Rasenna.

Before him, opinions current as to the origin of the Etruscans did not, so it seems, possess a scientific basis. Like all views on the origins of peoples and cities of the classical world they were on the border-line between history and myth, for the most part seeking their justification in etymological and onomastic similarities: thus the origins of Rome and of the Latins were taken back to the Trojans by way of Aeneas' wanderings. In the case of the Tyrrhenians (i.e. the Etruscans), there had been talk of an eastern origin – Lydia, in Asia Minor – and of an oversea migration led by Tyrrhenus, the son of King Atys of Lydia, to the Italic territory of the Umbrians (Herodotus, I, 94); they had also been identified with those mysterious nomads the Pelasgians (Hellanicus, in Dionysius, I, 28); or again there had been the theory of a migration of Tyrrhenus with the Pelasgians, who had already colonized the Aegean islands of Lemnos and Imbros (Anticleides in Strabo v, 2, 4). The Lydian origin of the Etruscans was accepted without difficulty, and became a common motif in classical literature: Virgil speaks indiscriminately of Lydians or Etruscans. Dionysius of Halicarnassus also stated that some authorities suspected them of being indigenous to Italy. But only Dionysius gathered the various opinions together, sifted them, and sought to prove that the Etruscans were autochthonous, basing his contention on their extreme antiquity and on their cultural and linguistic isolation amongst the various peoples of whom he had knowledge.

The problem has been taken up again in modern times with particular sharpness and polemic vigour, degenerating at times into sterile debates on preconceived theses. At first only classical texts were used as a basis for discussion; later, archaeological and linguistic data were also enlisted.[1] The first stage of the discussion occupied the whole of the eighteenth and the first half of the nineteenth century and was led by N. Fréret, B. G. Niebuhr, and K. O. Müller, who supported Dionysius of Halicarnassus' theory against the Asiatic origin tradition transmitted by Herodotus. But whereas Dionysius had given positive arguments in support of his theory, modern scholars particularly stressed the negative aspect of his criticism and, basing themselves on the analogy of the name Rasenna (which Dionysius had attributed to the Etruscans) with that of the Alpine Raetians, imagined the Etruscans to have originally descended from the Alps. It is interesting to note that right from this moment the problem of Etruscan origins was considered as being one of *provenance*, and not of *ethnic formation* as is usual when nations belonging to historical times are being studied. This polarization of the problem weighed heavily (except in a few rare cases) upon the whole future development of the discussion.

The success of comparative linguistics in establishing the relationship of a group of languages which it called Indo-

European; the discussions on whether Etruscan did or did not belong to the Indo-European group and, more particularly, to its Italic sub-group; the attempts to relate Etruscan with the non-Indo-European languages of the Caucasus and of Asia Minor; the discovery on the island of Lemnos of an inscription written in a dialect remarkably close to Etruscan; the identification (based chiefly upon toponymic data) of a Mediterranean linguistic substratum over which the Indo-European languages are thought to have spread, leaving here and there linguistic islands belonging to older stocks: these were the stages of linguistic research that added gradually more and more weight now to one now to the other thesis that sought to explain the origin of the Etruscans.

The same may be said for the data provided by archaeological discoveries. At first, these were largely fortuitous, but after the first half of the nineteenth century they were the result of excavations conducted with increasing enthusiasm in the territory of Etruria and in neighbouring areas. They revealed the existence of an Etruscan civilization, ethnically defined by inscriptions in Etruscan, that began to appear in the seventh century B.C. and lasted up to the beginning of the Roman Empire. Its area included Etruria itself (northern Latium and Tuscany), Campania, and the eastern half of the Po valley. The oldest phase of this civilization, characterized by a strong influx of oriental elements and known as a result as the 'orientalizing' period, merged at first with the 'Villanovan' iron culture. We have already described in Chapter One the manifestations in Italy of the iron age and of the preceding bronze age. As for the funerary rite in Etruria, the prehistoric period (aeneolithic and bronze cultures) is exclusively inhumatory, the subsequent 'Villanovan' iron culture predominantly crematory, and the orientalizing phase that followed in southern and coastal Etruria again inhumatory. The subsequent stages of the Etruscan civilization saw the coexistence of both rites, but inhumation predominated in the south and cremation in the north. It is worth recalling that in Rome too both rites lived side by side, strongly linked to family traditions: the great prevalence of cremation at the end of the republic and during the first century of the empire was followed in the second century A.D. by the general adoption of inhumation, though no ethnic transformation accompanied this change.

On the basis of the data provided by literary tradition, linguistic comparison, and the interpretation of archaeological discoveries, a great many theories have been put forward since the end of the last century. These may be grouped within three main systems: the first takes up and develops the traditional thesis of antiquity and ascribes an eastern origin to the Etruscans; the second follows the teachings of Niebuhr and Müller and believes the Etruscans to have descended from the north; and the third, the most recent, attempts to uphold Dionysius of Halicarnassus' theory on Etruscan autochthony by seeking their origin amongst the oldest ethnic substrata of Italy.

Of the three theses – which we shall respectively label oriental, northern, and autochthonous – the best known and most accepted is undoubtedly the first. It has been especially dear to those numerous archaeologists who have devoted themselves to the study of the antiquities of protohistoric Italy. These scholars have been greatly struck by the coincidence of traditional data with the orientalizing phase of the Etruscan civilization that appeared on the Tyrrhenian shores between the eighth and seventh centuries B.C. as a sudden flowering of civilized life in great contrast with the apparently backward manifestations of the preceding 'Villanovan' iron culture. They were also struck by similarities in religious rites, such as the changeover from cremation to inhumation. Edoardo Brizio in

1885 was the first to formulate this theory on a scientific basis: he identified the Etruscan invaders with the importers into Tuscany and Aemilia of the orientalizing and later of the Hellenistic civilization, and recognized in the 'Villanovan' cremation peoples the Umbrians of Herodotus, i.e. the Indo-European Italic peoples. Amongst the most important followers of Brizio's thesis were O. Montelius, B. Modestov, G. Körte, G. Ghirardini, L. Mariani, A. della Seta, P. Ducati, G. Patroni. The oriental thesis also appealed to many non-specialists . . . (archaeologists and linguists) who were attracted by the authority of tradition, the simple explanation of certain 'oriental' characteristics of the Etruscan civilization, the remarkable onomastic similarities between Etruscan and the languages of Asia Minor (first noticed by G. Herbig), and by the still plainer linguistic relationship linking Etruscan with the pre-Hellenic language of Lemnos. Slightly different theories were put forward by E. Pottier, who believed in the arrival of the Etruscans by sea, but by way of the Adriatic instead of the Tyrrhenian; and by F. Weege, who though also of the opinion that the Etruscans had reached Italy via the Adriatic dated their arrival during the second millennium B.C. F. Schachermeyer and E. Bulanda held that the Etruscan invasion from the East did not correspond exactly to the orientalizing period but took place in several waves, the oldest of which they ascribed to about the year 1000 B.C. The thesis of a Tyrrheno-Pelasgian migration to Italy during the bronze age (and of a partial return by sea towards the Aegean) has been recently taken up by J. Berard.[2] A confirmation of these oriental connexions might be the identification of the Etruscans or Tyrrhenians with the *Trš.w* mentioned in Egyptian hieroglyphs, i.e. with one of the seafaring peoples who attempted an invasion of Egypt under the Pharaohs Amejnoptah and Rameses III, between the years 1230 and 1170 B.C.

The 'northern' theory, though continuing Niebuhr's and Müller's hypothesis, based itself principally upon the archaeological discoveries that brought to light the bronze age *terramara* culture, linking it to the cremation cemeteries of northern Italy and to other iron cultures with cremation rites in central Italy. As we have already seen, they suggested to the archaeologist W. Helbig and to the Italian palethnologist L. Pigorini the idea of peoples descending from the north and of their subsequent historical development in central Italy. These tribes were thought to have included both the Italic and the Etruscan peoples, for no clear ethnic or linguistic distinction had yet been made between them. This theory was further strengthened by the fact that authoritative linguists such as W. Corssen and E. Lattes were convinced supporters of the Italic nature of the Etruscan language. Helbig thought there was a direct continuity, with no important breaks, from the *terramara* culture to the Etruscan civilization of historical times, via the 'Villanovan' and the 'orientalizing' phases.

The 'northern' theory greatly appealed to many archaeologists and historians, some of whom however (e.g. F. von Duhn and G. Körte) later went over to the 'oriental' theory. But the profound ethnic and linguistic differences between the Italic and the Etruscan peoples could no longer be ignored. This led the historian Gaetano De Sanctis to modify Helbig's thesis: he saw in the Etruscans the new northerners that had brought over with them the cremation rite, and in the Italic peoples the aeneolithic groups that had already settled in the centre of the peninsula. Luigi Pareti on the other hand distinguished an early Indo-European wave (the native aeneolithic inhabitants of Italy), a late Indo-European wave (the iron age cremation peoples other than the 'Villanovans', i.e. those possessing the 'eastern' Italic and the Latian cultures, which Pareti connects with the culture of Pianello della Genga), and finally the ethnic nucleus of the Etruscans (the actual 'Villanovans' who derived their culture from that of the *terramara* and the pile-dwellings of northern Italy). On the linguistic plane, an examination of the 'northern' theory should also take account of P. Kretschmer's hypothesis that the Etruscans belonged to an ethnico-linguistic 'Raeto-Tyrrhenic' or 'Raeto-Pelasgic' group that originally spread from the Danubian region of the Balkans towards Greece and Italy.[3]

The third, or 'autochtonous' theory, foreseen by the historian E. Meyer, was elaborated in the field of archaeology by Ugo Antonielli; during the last decades it has been especially well received by linguists as eminent as Alfredo Trombetti and Giacomo Devoto, who expounded it in detail in the first edition of his book *Gli antichi Italici* (1931). It does in fact rest upon a linguistic concept of the Etruscan nation: the links that connect Etruscan with the pre-Indo-European languages of the Mediterranean tend to make it appear rather as a relic, as an ethnic island of very ancient peoples isolated by the flood of Indo-European speakers, just as the present-day Basques of the Iberian peninsula represent the last-surviving remnants of primitive Hispanic populations in a sea of Romance speakers. And in fact, as we have seen in our preceding chapter, the toponymy of our area seems to bear evidence to the existence in the peninsula of a linguistic stratum older than the Italic dialects and akin to Etruscan and to the languages of Asia Minor, a stratum conventionally defined as 'Tyrrhenian'. The Etruscans would then have been a western concentration, under the pressure of Italic invaders, of elements belonging to this primitive layer. They would also naturally have received important racial and linguistic Indo-European contributions. From the archaeological (i.e. cultural) point of view, the earliest ethnic layer would have been that of the aeneolithic inhumators; these would then have been submerged by the Italic or proto-Italic cremation peoples, giving rise to the Etruscan nation of historical times, i.e. the consolidation of the original elements of the primitive stock under the cultural influx of the East.

The Theory of Oriental Provenance

Each of the theories outlined above seeks to explain satisfactorily the data obtained from tradition, from linguistic research, and from archaeological discoveries, so as to reconstruct the sequence of events that led to the establishment and development of the Etruscan people. They are in fact ingenious combinations of the various known elements, but satisfy only partially the requirements that a full critical evaluation of these elements demands. Each one of the three systems and their variants leaves something unexplained, comes up against well-established facts, without however helping in any way the other two reconstructions. Had this not been so, the discussion would have ended long ago with a working agreement amongst scholars; the debate would not have arrived at a dead end.

Let us consider the 'oriental' theory first: it rests upon the correspondence of traditional data (that agree in stating that the Etruscans came from the Aegean East, whether they be Pelasgians, Lydians, or inhabitants of Lemnos) with archaeological data (i.e. the presence of an orientalizing cultural phase). Moreover, there is the close resemblance of Etruscan with Lemnian, as well as the relationship that is thought to exist between Etruscan and languages in Asia Minor (Hittite, Lycian, Lydian, etc.). Let us try first of all to establish the actual value of each of these elements taken separately.

Concerning the migrations and ethnic relationships which tradition, in the mouths of Greek poets and logographers, has passed on to us, modern criticism is either definitely sceptical or extremely cautious. We are all well aware of the legendary nature of the tradition concerning the arrival of Aeneas in Latium, and hence the descent of the Romans from the Trojans, a legend that formed such an important part of the mythico-historical inheritance of late republican and imperial Rome. Equally baseless historically for the most part is the whole series of traditions concerning the Pelasgians, a people of Thessaly who were thought to have emigrated in post-Homeric times to various regions of the Aegean and even to Italy on the grounds of certain similarities in the form of place-names in Thessaly and in the countries that were thought to have been the goal of these migrations. Thus all those areas where the name Larissa appeared were called Pelasgic, because of Larissa in Thessaly: e.g. Attica, Argolis, Achaia, Crete, Lesbos, Troas, Lydia, southern Italy. The same may be said of names resembling that of the Thessalian city of Gyrton, such as Gortyna in Crete, Gortynia in Macedonia, Gortys in Arcadia, Croton in southern Italy, and Cortona in Etruria. That Hellanicus' identification of the Tyrrhenians of Italy, i.e. the Etruscans, with the Pelasgians was largely a learned hypothesis based on toponymic similarities and due to the mania for looking everywhere in the world around Greece for traces of the Pelasgians, is proved by the fact that other writers did speak of a Pelasgian occupation of Etruria, but earlier than, or, in any case, distinct from that of the Tyrrhenians, and that geographers vaguely refer to a land of the Pelasgians somewhere in Italy close to the land of the Etruscans.[4] This does not exclude, however, the possibility that ancient tradition, recorded by Herodotus himself (I, 57), as to the presence in Italy (at Cortona?) and in the Aegean (Hellespont) of Pelasgians speaking the same tongue, cannot be based upon observed affinities between the pre-Hellenic ethnic substrata of the two areas in question.[5]

Of a more complex nature is the problem concerning the migrations of the Tyrrhenians from Asia Minor or from

the Aegean isles. It is very probable that, according to
Pareti's criticism, Herodotus' well-known relation of the
arrival of the Lydians in Italy under the leadership of
Tyrrhenus should also be relegated amongst the learned
fables of Ionic logographers, attracted by the similarity of
the name Tyrrhenian (*Tyrrhenòi*, *Tyrsenòi*) with that of the
cities of Tyrrha or Torrhebus in Lydia. Tradition knew of
peoples bearing the name of Tyrrhenians in the east as well.
But it is unlikely that ancient writers had notice of other
Tyrrhenians, besides those of the west (i.e. the Etruscans),
before the fifth century B.C., for otherwise the silence of
Herodotus and Hellanicus on the matter would be difficult
to explain. It is possible that the localization of Tyrrhenians
at Lemnos, in the Aegean and in Asia Minor (frequent
among later writers) followed on learned elaborations of
the Ionian historians: i.e. of the identification of the Tyrrhenians with the Pelasgians (well known as the primitive
inhabitants of Lemnos) and with the Lydians.

The question of the *Trš.w*, mentioned in Egyptian monuments as a people that came from the sea, does not vitally
affect the Etruscan problem, though it has often been
brought into the field especially in support of the 'oriental'
theory. The first difficulty arises in reading the word, which
in the hieroglyphic inscriptions is literally rendered as
Twrwš.w (with the variants *Twrjš.w*, *Twjrš.w*). The spelling
is a syllabic one adopted for foreign names, where the semi-
vowels *w* and *j* may represent vowel sounds (the pro-
nounciation would thus be *Toorooshah*, *Tooreeshah*, or
Toorshah). Amongst the various assailants of Egypt there
are also mentioned the *Rk.w* (or Lookah, Lookoo), the
Jqjwšw. (or Aqajwahshah), the *Drdnj.w* (or Dardnooey), the
Prst.w (or Pooloosaht), the *Šrdn.w* (or Shardeenah, Shar-
dahnah), the *Šqrš.w* (or Shahqahlooshah), respectively
identified with the Lycians, the Achaeans, the Dardanians,
the Philistines, the Sardinians, the Sicels. Some of these

identifications (such as the Achaeans and the Philistines) are
by now undisputed; others, like the Sardinians and the
Sicels, are still weak and uncertain. In equating the *Trš.w*
with the Tyrrhenians, scholars had in mind the ancestors of
the Etruscans while still in the Aegean or wandering over
the seas in search of new lands. The thematic identity of
Trš.w with *Tyrsenòi* is possible and even probable. But the
frequency of analogous forms attested in ancient Mediterranean proper names deprives the comparison of any
specific value it may have. We are therefore unable to
demonstrate for the moment the identity of the Mediterranean people mentioned by the Egyptian monuments of
the end of the second millennium B.C. with the Etruscans,
called Tyrrhenians by the Greeks and whose national life
developed in Italy during the first millennium. Similarly
we cannot definitely exclude the possibility that the *Trš.w*
that attacked Egypt were a people who came from the
West.[6]

Let us now consider the archaeological aspect of the problem. We should point out straightaway that the manifestation of the Etruscan orientalizing civilization did not take
place in such a way as to justify the hypothesis of the landing of a foreign people bringing their own culture with
them; whereas unmistakable manifestations accompanied
the arrival of Greek colonists in Sicily and southern Italy
and of Carthaginian colonists in Sicily and Sardinia. In the
more evolved phases of the 'Villanovan' iron culture there
began to appear noticeable changes in the form and decoration of monuments (e.g. tombs) and objects (e.g. vases,
weapons, etc.). These changes anticipated the splendour of
the subsequent orientalizing phase: the use of iron became
general, precious metals (gold and silver) were more frequent and at the same time there was a greater number of
objects and patterns of foreign extraction (scarabs and
amulets from Egypt, imitations of Greek painted pottery,

etc.). But these exotic features were not exclusively and specifically the essential elements of the orientalizing civilization. The great architectonic tombs, black *bucchero* and *impasto* pottery, vases and weapons in laminated bronze, the shape of jewels and especially of *fibulae*, were well within the scope of the indigenous culture, even though activated by external ferments and the stimulus of economic prosperity. Other Mediterranean cultures of the same period offer only vague parallels to these manifestations. There was as already stated no lack of objects imported from the Syro-Egyptian and Greek worlds, but they were relatively limited in number; on the other hand there was a characteristic type of decoration where Egyptian, Mesopotamian, Syriac, and Aegeo-Asiatic motifs mingled at times in hybrid compositions; its original inspiration has been sought in the cities and ports of mixed culture such as those of Phoenicia and Cyprus, but its spread and elaboration was largely due to the Greeks themselves in the course of the seventh century B.C.[7] The main impression gained when considering Etruscan tombs of the orientalizing period, and their sumptuous fittings, is that their structure and the essential forms of the culture they represent were a development of local tendencies, whilst the spirit and characteristics of the decorative elements were external and acquired, and may be attributed to the oriental 'fashion'. If we ignore for the moment the composite character – indigenous and exotic – of this orientalizing civilization, and examine only its exotic elements, it becomes clear that they are no longer exclusive to Etruria, but appear in approximately the same forms in many contemporary Mediterranean lands, as in Punic Sardinia, southern Italy, the sanctuaries of the Greek world, Crete, etc., in those places in fact where no Tyrrhenian immigration could possibly be suspected.[8]

During the two centuries that followed the orientalizing fashion of the seventh to sixth century B.C., Etruria received in large measure cultural and artistic influences from Greece (Ionia at first and later Attica). A much more decisive alteration of the old indigenous culture took place under this influx: it even affected religion and everyday customs, as is clearly shown by the Hellenic deities and myths that penetrated Etruria. No one of course would dare put forward the historical absurdity of a sixth-century Greek colonization of Etruria, although we have actual proof of the presence of Greek trading colonies in Etruscan ports. Though the value of this argument is only indirect and analogical, it may help to reject the hypothesis that would make the Etruscan orientalizing civilization coincide with a presumed arrival of the Etruscans from the East.

As for the funeral rite, we should bear in mind that though it is true that cremation tombs were predominant during the 'Villanovan' phase whereas inhumation tombs were more numerous during the succeeding orientalizing period, the fact is of extremely limited value. We find iron age cremation cemeteries spread along the coast, backed by a compact area of inhumation peoples in the centre of Italy. These coastal cemeteries are seldom entirely devoted to cremation, for they are often found scattered with inhumation tombs. The latter, consisting mostly of poorly furnished graves, are difficult to date; but when it is possible to demonstrate that the funeral deposits are contemporary (as in the later phase of the 'Villanovan' culture and especially in southern Etruria: Tarquinii, Caere, Veii), we are immediately struck by the fact that the frequency of burial graves is as great as, if not greater than that of incineration tombs. There is no sudden change from one rite to the other. It is probable that in lower Etruria, already predominantly given to inhumation and exposed to the most direct cultural influences from central Italy, inhumation triumphed as early as the seventh century B.C.; in inner northern Etruria however (e.g. Clusium), the advent of the orientalizing civilization was marked by no change in the cremation rite, which continued uninterruptedly up to the days of Imperial Rome. Now Clusium was just as Etruscan as Tarquinii and Caere. Should an explanation for this phenomenon be sought, it will be found only in the progressive reconquest on the part of inhumation of the originally much greater area where cremation was practised, and not in the advent of a new rite introduced by a new people.

In spite of objections to the contrary made by Lattes, Pareti, and other scholars,[9] a close relationship unites Etruscan with the dialect spoken at Lemnos before the Athenian conquest of the island at the hand of Miltiades in the second half of the sixth century B.C.

There are precise agreements in flexional endings (-*z*, -*eiz*, -*zi*, -*ai*, -*aiδ*, -*ale*, -*ial*, etc. in Lemnian, and -*s*, -*eis*, -*si*, -*ai*, -*aiδ*, -*ale*, -*ial* in Etruscan inscriptions); in roots and in words (*naφoδ*, *ziazi*, *maraz* and *marazm*, *aviz*, *zivai*, *zeronai* and *zeronaiδ*, *morinail*, *haralio*, *arai*, etc. in Lemnian, and *napti* or *nefts*, *zia*, *mar* and *maru*, *avils*, *zivas*, *zeri*, *murinasie*, *harc*, *are* and *aras* in Etruscan inscriptions); and even in whole expressions (*holaiezi φokiasiale* and *larδiale hulχniesi; aviz sialχviz* and *avils . . . sealχlsc*). These agreements are all the more remarkable since we are only able to utilize a single Lemnian document of some importance, the funerary stele found at Kaminia.[10] This does not mean however that Lemnian and Etruscan were the same language, or even two dialects of the same language. Many words and forms have no equivalent in the opposite language, and the concordances so far observed have not helped to explain definitely the lexical and grammatical forms of the Lemnian inscriptions. As for Lydian and the other hitherto known languages of Asia Minor, their relationship with Etruscan within the compass of the pre-Indo-European Mediterranean linguistic units appears to be still more remote. Further, the onomastic agreements between Etruscan and the Asian languages carry no great weight (as Miss Fiesel correctly pointed out) when we consider that they are based upon material collected from Asian languages of great diversity, and that the onomastic agreements linking Etruscan with the Italic languages, for example, do not prove any common relationship between the two.[11] In the case of Lydian, these facts definitely exclude the possibility that the Etruscans, according to the letter of Herodotus' relation, were an ethnic group that had split from the main body of the Lydian nation.

Let us now examine arguments in support of the oriental hypothesis, not in isolation, but in the light of their reciprocal geographical and chronological relations. Classical sources agree in placing the original home of the Etruscans within the Aegean or on the Asiatic coast, and the linguistic analogies with Lemnian and the Asian languages partly concur with them. But those foreign elements that went to make up the orientalizing civilization lead us to a southeastern cultural area, i.e. to Syria and Egypt, and not to the Aegeo-Asiatic area as would be expected if the Etruscans had brought these elements over from their presumed home. The principal vehicle for the orientalizing influx must therefore have been the Phoenician and Greek navigators: they influenced in much the same way various other regions of the Mediterranean basin. The counter-proof to these statements is obtained from an examination of the Asian culture of the eighth century B.C., i.e. of the period when the migration is said to have taken place; and this despite the small number of protohistoric excavations made on the Aegean coast of Asia Minor.

The discoveries made in Lemnos, at Smyrna (Bayrakli) and at other coastal points of Ionia and Asiatic Aeolis, at Sardis and in the interior of Anatolia (Alishar, Pozarli, etc.) have not brought to light any elements common to the orientalizing civilization of Etruria (if we except those of a rather vague and generic nature, such as tumuli, rock tombs, etc.) for the period termed 'Phrygian' in Asia Minor (eleventh to seventh century) and 'Tyrrhenian', but improperly, at Lemnos ('Pelasgian' would be a better term, on the basis of the oldest and most authoritative historical tradition).[12] Pottery continues to feature Anatolian geometric patterns or Mycenaean elements in its painted decorations, and the vases differ in shape from traditional and typical Etrusco-Italic ware. No derivations, in either direction, need be postulated between the black and grey ceramic of Anatolia and the characteristic *bucchero* of Etruria. The typical Asiatic *fibula*, extremely common everywhere, consisted of a semicircular rigid bow with pearl ornamentations, or was shaped like a magnet. It seems impossible that it should not have accompanied the migrations of an Asiatic people, and it is remarkable that it did not spread westwards, not even by way of commerce. And yet only one typical specimen has so far been found in central Italy: in the Riserva del Truglio, in Latium,[13] i.e. outside Etruria proper! The relations between Asia Minor and Etruria appear on the other hand to have become more and more close as we pass on to historical times, culminating in the preponderant Ionian influences in Italy during the sixth century. But this has nothing to do with the question of Etruscan origins as presented by supporters of the 'oriental' theory.

The identification of the orientalizing civilization with a presumed Etruscan immigration also appears to be invalidated for chronological reasons. The beginnings of the Etruscan orientalizing phase cannot be taken further back than the beginning of the seventh century B.C., i.e. the period during which Greek colonists were already firmly established on the coasts of Sicily and southern Italy. But Herodotus' relation on the Lydian migration should not on the other hand be detached arbitrarily from his chronological system that places it during the reign of King Atys of Lydia, i.e. (according to traditional mythical chronology) shortly after the Trojan war, between the thirteenth and twelfth century B.C. Such an important event occurring at the dawn of history and parallel with Greek colonization (and also competing with it) would not have been silently passed over by ancient historians nor transfigured, as in Herodotus, into a mythical event occurring half a millennium earlier. On the other hand as authoritative a source as the Greek historian Ephorus (quoted by Strabo, VI, 2, 2), when speaking of the founding in Sicily of Naxos – the oldest Chalcidian colony – during the eighth century, stated that before that time the Greeks would not venture on the western seas for fear of the Tyrrhenians. He therefore implicitly admits the presence of Tyrrhenians on the Italian shores.[14]

After breaking the link that was thought to unite the orientalizing civilization of Etruria with a possible Etruscan immigration, there is still the possibility that the latter might have occurred at an earlier period (as held by Bérard). In this case however no archaeological evidence can any longer be adduced in support of the theory, since there are no traces of eastern influences during the bronze age and the beginning of the iron age in Etruria (there is not even so far any evidence of relations with the Mycenaean world; so very plain in the south of the peninsula!). We should therefore have to limit ourselves to the data obtained from tradition with all their uncertainty and all their weakness. However, the linguistic evidence still remains: the similarities between Etruscan and Lemnian are certainly remarkable when considered in the light of the legends that give Lemnos as the original home of the Etruscans. This is the only argument in favour of the oriental theory that carries a certain weight, though the problem is rendered extremely intricate by it, and we are left without the possibility of defining either the character or the time of the relations between Lemnos and Etruria. These may find their place within the pre-Indo-European Aegeo-Tyrrhenian linguistic unit mentioned in the preceding chapter. Etruscan, forced to the extreme west by the Indo-European advance, and Lemnian, relegated to an island, would then represent conservative and marginal relics of such a unit, bound by certain similarities, in the sense of the Pelasgic ethno-linguistic 'islands' presupposed by the passage of Herodotus, I, 57, as outlined above. At any rate the known Lemnian inscriptions belong to the seventh or sixth century, that is to a period when the Etruscan nation was already formed in Italy. Moreover to isolate Etruscan from its geographical setting – as the supposition of a recent colonization of the Etrurian coast on the part of Lemnians would lead us to do –would mean going against the evidence of the presence of an ancient 'Tyrrhenian' toponymy in the regions of Italy that were later occupied by Indo-European-speaking peoples, and against the undoubted affinities that exist between Etruscan and other very ancient Italian dialects such as 'Raetic'.[15]

The Theories of Northern Provenance and of Autochthony

Let us now pass on to a review of the 'northern' theory. The old comparison of the name of Rasenna with that of the Raetians is puerile: the inscriptions found in the region of Trento and the upper valley of the Adige were written at a comparatively recent date (after the fourth century B.C.) and if they reveal very ancient ties or more recent relationships with Etruscan, they are quite valueless for the purpose of ascribing an Alpine origin to the Etruscans as a fully constituted people. From the archaeological point of view, the criticism already made of Pigorini's and Helbig's theories seriously invalidates the 'northern' hypothesis. The

Etruscan character of the Po valley was the result of a historically well defined conquest that took place between the end of the sixth and the beginning of the fifth century, as is proved by the nature of its culture and its inscriptions; here we may agree with Brizio and Ducati, though denying that the 'Villanovans' of the earlier Bologna phases were Italic Umbrians, whose appearance on the eastern slopes of the Apennines is more recent still.

Linguistic science has now definitely discarded any possibilities of a relationship between Etruscan and the Italic languages, so that even from this point of view Helbig's and Pigorini's theses of a single descent on the part of Etruscan and Italic peoples has lost all meaning. This explains the reaction of De Sanctis and Pareti who tend to identify the Etruscans with the 'Villanovan' cremation peoples, and the Italic peoples with the inhumators of the old aeneolithic stock (or, as we would say now, with the central Italian peoples possessing the Apenninic bronze culture). This identification is the only one that satisfies the correspondence we have already noted between the inhumation and cremation areas on the one hand and the Indo-European and non-Indo-European linguistic areas on the other.

The value of De Sanctis' and Pareti's observations is however mainly of a general order: they should not be taken as an identification of particular peoples. There is no proof of the existence of a 'Villanovan' ethnic unit, still less of its descent from the North. The simpler and more archaic 'Villanovan' cemeteries of Aemilia and Romagna do not attest a chronological priority in the strictest sense: they may equally well be explained as marginal or late manifestations. In any case these primitive atypical monuments suggest an Adriatic area of diffusion (Lozzo near Este, Pianello della Genga in the Marches) rather than a northern origin.[16] On the other hand, the fact that the Latins cremated their dead whereas the Umbro-Sabellians practised

inhumation cannot be explained by supposing with Pareti
that the Latin immigration took place later than the
Umbro-Sabellian (thus contrasting with the linguistic data).
The explanation lies rather in the fact that the Latins during
the protohistoric period lived close to the cremation area,
whereas the peoples of southern Italy and Sicily, thought to
be more closely related to the Latins from the linguistic
point of view, belonged culturally to the inhumating
civilizations.

A further argument disproving the northern theory is the
nature of Etruscan itself, a Mediterranean language more or
less closely related to the pre-Hellenic languages of the
Aegean. In order to admit that it belonged to a continental
rather than a southern ethnic group, we would have to
imagine a migration originating from the East and proceed-
ing across the Balkans; but we would still have to explain
those elements in the 'Tyrrhenian' toponymy of peninsular
Italy seemingly related to Etruscan. These reservations do
not however exclude the presence in Etruscan of linguistic
elements belonging to the north-western branches of the
pre-Indo-European substratum (such as 'Ligurian' or
'Raetic') or even to the Indo-European stock. If anything,
this points to a widespread mingling in the area of elements
of different origins due to the complex superposition of
linguistic strata.

The autochthonous theory is also open to justified attacks.
The linguistic conception of Trombetti, Devoto, Ribezzo,
etc., who saw in the foundations of Etruscan the relic of a
greater pre-Indo-European linguistic unit, is, methodo-
logically speaking, indisputable. It rests upon the Mediterranean affinities of Etruscan and the presence throughout
most of Italy of a 'Tyrrhenian' underlayer as revealed by
toponymy. *Vice versa* the archaeological reconstruction
attempted by Antonielli and Devoto comes up against very
serious objections. It presupposes a clear ethnic opposition

of aeneolithic inhumators to 'Villanovan' cremation peoples descended from the North, and identifies the former with the primitive 'Tyrrhenian' stratum, the latter with the Italic Indo-European invaders. Once again however the almost exact correspondence of the cremation and inhumation areas with those of non-Indo-European and of Indo-European dialects respectively is obviously opposed to this 'autochthonous' reconstruction. Can it be that Etruria, where the cremation peoples (or, according to the old Pigorinian conception, the Italic peoples descended from the North) were most typical and most numerous, and where the preceding cultures (aeneolithic and bronze) were of a rather secondary and marginal character – can it be that Etruria was the very corner of Italy where the primitive language had preserved its main features down to the fullness of historical times? Whereas the Italic languages should have triumphed in the eastern areas of the peninsula where only sporadic and insignificant traces exist of the passage of the presumed Italic cremation peoples! It is clear that linguistic autochthony cannot be constrained within the absurd limits imposed by archaeological reconstructions in which the mark of the old Pigorinian prejudice is still so very patent. At any rate a purely autochthonic origin reveals itself *a priori* as an abstract, unhistoric theory; it also clashes with the evidence of cultural developments that reveal European and eastern influences and also with the presence of deep-seated Indo-European elements in the Etruscan language.

Towards a Solution of the Problem

None of the three fundamental theories concerning the origin of the Etruscans may thus be invoked towards a definite solution of our problem. But in the review of each of these theories, there stand out, together with negative elements, several positive specific aspects that fit without difficulty all the factual data we possess, and which therefore may be used in our discussion; they are:

(i) the establishment of a certain link between the Etruscans of historical times and the inhabitants of pre-Hellenic Lemnos;

(ii) the identification of the cremation peoples of western Italy and particularly of the peoples of the 'Villanovan' culture with the ethnic stock of the Etruscans;

(iii) the definition of Etruscan in its fundamental nucleus as a linguistic relic of a vaster pre-Indo-European 'Tyrrhenian' unit that once occupied the peninsula, in a zone where south-eastern ('Tyrrhenian') and northern ('Ligurian' and 'Raetic') substratum areas met and were superimposed.

Having set down these data, we shall now use them as starting-points in attempting a satisfactory explanation of our problem. But first it is necessary that the problem should be correctly formulated. In the various theories that have been advanced so far, the complexity of a phenomenon as great and many-sided as that of the origin of an historical nation has been reduced to schematic, and at times oversimplified, formulae. The Etruscan people have been considered as a unit, a block, right from their inscrutable prehistory; and to explain their appearance in Italy it was necessary to have recourse to the external and over-simple concept of *provenance*: in a positive sense, by accepting the idea of an actual arrival from foreign lands (eastern or northern) and thereby merely shifting the problem in space without actually solving it; and in a negative sense, by excluding an actual arrival and identifying the Etruscans with the ancient inhabitants of the peninsula, and thereby shifting the problem back in time. Even when the idea of a mingling of peoples has been put forward (e.g. that of a mingling of Tyrrhenians from Asia with indigenous

Umbrians, or of Mediterranean aeneolithic peoples with Italic cremation peoples) the predominance given to one of the formative elements has had the effect of attributing to it by anticipation the name and characteristics of the Etruscan nation.

Now the methodological basis of our discussion must be as follows: we must consider the concept 'Etruscan' as well defined, limited, and attached to a controllable historical reality: that of a nation that flourished in Etruria between the eighth and first century B.C., possessing its own language and its own customs. Various ethnic, linguistic, political, and cultural elements contributed to the formation of this historical reality. We may discuss the origin and provenance of each of these elements; but a more appropriate concept for the comprehensive phenomenon determined by them, would be that of *formation*. So as to make our meaning clearer we would like to point out that no one would dream of asking where Italians or Frenchmen came from originally; it is the formation of the Italian and French nations that we study. We may however speak of the origin of the Celts, of their Roman conquerors, of the Franks that were later to invade Gaul: ethnical elements that all went to the formation of the French nation. The same may be said concerning its linguistic and cultural elements. An essential factor in the formation of a nation is the geographical: the actual territory of a nation is that in which its formative process has taken place.

The inadequacy of the theories on Etruscan origins is due to the fact that the problem has been considered as one of provenance, whereas there merely existed one of ethnic formation. There have been discussions on whether they came from the east, the north, or on whether they were actually autochthonous, whereas the Etruscans formed a complex of eastern, European, and Italian elements which must be isolated, weighed, and compared one with the other.

It is naturally far from easy to attempt a reconstruction of the facts and tendencies that determined the birth of historical Etruria; but we are meanwhile able to state without fear of going wrong that the formative process of the nation *can only have taken place on the territory of Etruria proper;* and we are able to witness the final stages of this process thanks to the rich archaeological documentation we possess for the period from the eighth to the sixth century. This point of view has recently also been adopted by the historian F. Altheim, who, though he postulates a fusion of eastern immigrants with indigenous peoples, identifies the origins of the Etruscan nation with the formation of a political and cultural κοινή of those peoples inhabiting Etruscan territory.

The linguistic elements point to eastern affinities within the compass of the pre-Indo-European 'Tyrrhenian' unit. But the theories of oriental origin and of autochthony end by merging if we suppose a Tyrrhenian east-to-west movement in prehistoric times; Etruscan would then have been the westernmost outpost of such a movement as well as its last surviving remnant in the Italian peninsula. Naturally this explanation would be different if direct historical contacts were supposed between Etruria and, say, Lemnos; we have however no archaeological evidence and insufficient historical documents concerning such contacts.

We have already seen how absurd it was to wish to dissociate the 'Villanovan' cremation peoples from the Etruscan *ethnos*. Their appearance is in fact marked by a remarkable progress in the cultural development of Etruria which until then had displayed quite primitive manifestations linked in their essentials to aeneolithic culture and only partly influenced by the Apenninic bronze civilization.

With the 'Villanovan' culture we begin to see the growth of considerable centres of population in those sites which were to become the great historical centres of Etruria: Veii, Caere, Tarquinii, Vulci, Vetulonia, Populonia, etc. From the beginning of the 'Villanovan' culture till the fullness of historical times, this civilization develops without any break or sudden transformation. This cultural horizon clearly represents the external aspect of the Etruscan people during their formation; this statement however does not imply its reciprocal, i.e. that the appearance of the 'Villanovan' culture marks the appearance of the Etruscans.

In the present state of our knowledge, we are faced with a very arduous problem when trying to explain the origin of the 'Villanovan' culture of Etruria. Its characteristics, quite revolutionary when compared with the cultural level preceding it, would justify the classical hypothesis of an immigration of peoples. But this does not mean that it had to appear suddenly; it is even probable that its formative process may have been quite long and complex. Certain factors – e.g. the very rite of cremation, with ossuaries made of rough pottery, spheroidal or with a tendency to be biconical – should be considered as imported from regions outside our area, perhaps even by way of more or less substantial migrations. One may postulate infiltrations from the continent by way of the land route, as a reflection of the spread of the 'urn-fields' of central Europe and connected with the cremation cemeteries that make their appearance in northern Italy towards the end of the late bronze age. But infiltrations may also have taken place from the south by coastal or sea routes, if account is taken of certain very archaic cemeteries, traces of which have recently been discovered in Etruria not far from the Tyrrhenian coast (in the neighbourhood of Ischia di Castro and at Sticciano, near Grosseto[17]) and of a number of the more primitive cremation tombs of the Villanovan cemeteries belonging to the great southern Etruscan cities. In both cases there are unusual affinities with the culture of those isolated centres of cremation peoples who, as has already been seen, make their first appearance between the end of the bronze age and the beginning of the iron age in Apulia (Torre Castelluccia, Timmari) and on the coasts of Sicily (Milazzo).

But the true 'Villanovan' civilization, considered as a whole, is an original phenomenon, wrought locally upon Apenninic bronze-culture foundations, some of whose characteristic elements it absorbs (e.g. the shape of the great biconical *hydria* of dark *impasto* with wave patterns on the necks[18]). It is unnecessary, therefore, to postulate a deep ethnic transformation at the beginning of the 'Villanovan' period; but rather an impulse, a determining ferment which would have brought about the crystallization of 'Tyrrhenian' ethnic elements into an Etruscan nation in those territories that lie north of the Tiber. Thus the 'Villanovan' culture of Etruria proper would already mirror in the main the dawning of an Etruscan *ethnos*, the 'eastern' iron culture would indicate the formation of Umbro-Sabellic Italic elements, and the southern and Latian cultures that of the Latins and kindred peoples.[19]

This picture of the formation of the Etruscan nation is not complete without the inclusion of the elements that accompanied its first historical stages. The intellectual and artistic contacts with the East and with Greece played a preponderant role: they occurred through oversea trade, but probably also through direct intercourse or contacts with commercial colonies on Etruscan territory. The impression received by the still fresh, primitive, malleable Etruscan mind from the mature oversea civilizations was probably such as to orientate decisively the spiritual bent of the nation and to justify the feeling of strong ethnic affinities with the eastern world, a feeling which perhaps the ancients themselves did not eschew. This does not mean however that the civilization of ancient Etruria grew entirely from foreign seeds;

even less does it mean that the Etruscan national entity should be estranged from the racial, linguistic, and cultural background of ancient Italy.

NOTES

1. A history of the problem will be found in P. Ducati, *Le problème étrusque*, 1938. The whole problem of Etruscan origins is also tackled in the monographs of L. Pareti, *Le origini etrusche*, 1926, and of F. Schachermeyer, *Etruskische Frühgeschichte*, 1929; their conclusions however do not agree. Cf. also M. Pallottino, *La origine degli Etruschi*, 1947; F. Altheim, *Der Ursprung der Etrusker*, 1950; where full bibliographical data will be found.

2. *Revue des Études Anciennes*, LI, 1949, pp. 201 ff.

3. *Glotta*, XXX, 1943, pp. 213 ff.

4. M. Pallottino, *Tradizione etnica e realtà culturale dell' Etruria, Umbria e Romagna prima della unificazione augustea* (in *Relazioni della XXVIII Riunione della Società Italiana per il Progresso delle Scienze*, v, 1940, pp. 81 ff.). See also note 1 on p. 82.

5. Cf. M. Pallottino, *Erodoto autoctonista?* in *Studi Etruschi*, XX, 1948–9, pp. 11 ff.

6. On the sources and problem of the *Trš.w*, cf. F. W. von Bissing, *Die Überlieferung über die Turuscha* (in *Wiener Zeitschrift für die kunde des Morgenlandes*, XXXV, 1928, pp. 177 ff.).

7. Cf. L. Pareti, *La tomba Regolini-Galassi e la civiltà dell' Italia centrale nel sec. VII av. Cr.*, 1947, pp. 520 ff. It should be remembered, however, that the Greeks responsible for the spread of the orientalizing civilization were unlikely to be Phocaeans, as thought by Pareti, but rather Chalcidians and Dorians: cf. *Studi Etruschi*, XX, 1948–9, pp. 335 ff.

8. F. Poulsen, *Der Orient und die frühgriechische Kunst*, 1912.

9. C. Pauli, *Eine vorgriechische Inschrift von Lemnos* (*Altitalischen Forschungen*, 1886, 1894); E. Nachmanson, *Die vorgriechische Inschriften von Lemnos* and G. Karo, *Die 'Tyrsenische' Stele von Lemnos* in *Atenische Mitteilungen*, XXXIII, 1908, pp. 47 ff.; L. Pareti, *Le origini etrusche*, pp. 89 ff.; S. P. Cortsen, *Die lemnische Inschrift*, in *Glotta*, XVIII, 1929–30, pp. 101 ff.; J. Friedrich, *Kleinasiatische Sprachdenkmäler*, 1932, pp. 143 ff.; B. Hrozny, *Die Inschrift von Lemnos*, in *Studi Etruschi*, IX, 1935, pp. 127 ff.; S. P. Cortsen, *L'inscription de Lemnos*, in *Latomus*, Brussels, II, 1938, pp. 3 ff.; P. Kretschmer, *Die*

tyrrhenischen Inschriften der Stele von Lemnos, in *Glotta*, XXIX, 1941, pp. 89 ff.

10. The other known inscriptions are only very brief and scratched on fragments of vases; they are practically useless from the linguistic point of view: cf. A. della Seta, in *Scritti in onore di B. Nogara*, 1937, pp. 119 ff.

11. A. Trombetti, *La lingua etrusca*, 1928; E. Fiesel, *Etruskisch*, 1931, p. 63. P. Meriggi (in *Osservazioni sull'Etrusco*, in *Studi Etruschi*, XI, 1937, pp. 129 ff.), re-examined the close relationship between Etruscan and Lydian but with negative results as far as the interpretation of Etruscan is concerned.

12. On Lemnos D. Mustilli, *La necropoli tirrenica di Efestia*, in *Annuario Scuola Ital. d'Atene*, XV, XVI, 1938. For Asia Minor, cf. H. Th. Bossert, *Altanatolien*, 1942; K. Bittel, *Grundzüge der Vor- und Frühgeschichte Kleinasiens*, 2nd ed., 1950, with relevant bibliography.

13. U. Antonielli, in *Bullettino di Paletnologia*, L–LI, 1930–1, pp. 191 ff.

14. Cf. E. Fiesel, *Etruskisch*, 1931, pp. 65 ff., who also quotes U. Wilamowitz' authoritative opinion on the subject.

15. G. Devoto, *Storia della lingua di Roma*, pp. 17 ff.

16. Cf. G. Patroni, *La preistoria*, 2nd ed., pp. 733 ff.

17. For Sticciano, cf. *Studi Etruschi*, XXI, 1950–1, pp. 297 ff.; for Ischia di Castro, see F. Rittatore, in *Rivista di Scienze Preistoriche*, VI, 1951, pp. 167 ff.

18. See M. Pallottino, *L'origine degli Etruschi*, pp. 113 ff.

19. Cf. note 26 on p. 45.

CHAPTER THREE

THE ETRUSCANS AND THE SEA

The Etruscan 'Thalassocracy'

THESE frequently sterile and interminable discussions on the origin of the Etruscans have generally led etruscologists and students of ancient history to lose sight of problems much more attractive and useful in the study of the ancient civilizations of Italy.

It has been said, for instance, that it was Carthage that taught the Romans navigation and how to be masters of the sea: just as Greece had been their teacher in the realms of art and poetry. There is a part of truth in both assertions, in the sense that on the high and universal level of Hellenistic culture the teachings of both Carthage and Greece played a decisive role in the growth of the civilization and might of Rome. But it would be a very serious mistake to imagine that republican Rome, like the Rome of the kings before it, was no more than a city of shepherds and semi-barbarous peasants, when she lived on the borders of, and greatly profited by the advanced civilization of Etruria. To the refined generations of Cicero and Augustus, the Roman of one or two centuries before could well have seemed *'ferus victor'*, *'arte rudis'*. But when we think that already towards the end of the sixth or the beginning of the fifth century such superb and mature works of art as the Capitoline she-wolf or the Ficoroni cist were being produced in Rome, we cannot help realizing the absurdity of a definition that many moderns have unfortunately accepted uncritically from the hands of ancient authors.

It was Etruria that first gave the Italic peoples the urge to conquer and dominate the sea. We cannot overlook the unanimous testimonies given by historical tradition: they all speak of a far-reaching domination of the sea on the part of the Tyrrhenians or Etruscans. Greek historians referred to this domination by the traditional name of 'thalassocracy'. From relatively ancient times Greek tradition took pleasure in representing the supremacy of the Etruscans both in eastern and in western seas as dreadful and unceasing piracy. In the 'Homeric' hymn to Dionysus, for example, the god is ravished by Tyrrhenian pirates whom he later succeeds in metamorphosing into dolphins. Under the name of Pelasgians, they were also held responsible for the stealing of Hera's statue on the isle of Samos (Athenaeus, XV, 12), for the rape of Brauron's wives in Attica and the conquest and sack of Athens (Plutarch, *de mul. virt.*, 8; *Aetia gr.*, 21; Eustathius, *Comm. Dion*, 591; Philochorus, 5).[1] The control and ceaseless threatening of the western seas, especially the Tyrrhenian, the Ionian, and the coasts of Sicily, were also attributed to the Tyrrhenians (Palaephatus, *Epist.*, XX; Strabo, VI, 2, 2; etc.). To this list should be added references to an Etruscan colonization of Corsica (Diodorus Siculus, V, 13), of Sardinia (Strabo, V, 2, 7), of the Balearic Isles and even of the coasts of Spain (Stephen of Byzantium, s.v. *Banaurides*; Ausonius, *Epist.*, XXXI, 326),[2] and the story of the conflict between Etruscans and Carthaginians for the possession of an Atlantic island (Diodorus Siculus, V, 19 ff.). Etruscan achievements in naval technique, first mentioned by Dionysius (I, 25), are confirmed by the mythological tradition concerning the Tyrrhenian origin of the *rostri* (Pliny, *Nat. Hist.*, VII, 56, 209).

As far as may be inferred from external remains, archaeology supports historical tradition as to the maritime power of the ancient Etruscans. Even without taking into consideration the very large, almost incalculable, number of foreign objects and motifs (Eastern, Sardinian, Punic,

Hellenic) that have been found in archaic Etruscan tombs, denoting intense maritime activity that cannot wholly be due to Phoenician and Greek shipping, there is no lack of evidence pointing to the spread of the Etruscan civilization along the shores of Italy, Sardinia, Corsica, North Africa, as well as in Greece, southern France, and Iberia.[3] This consists of *bucchero* vases, of wrought bronzes, and even of inscriptions in Etruscan (e.g. an ivory tablet bearing the effigy of a lion found at Carthage).[4] From the name of the Etruscan people and that of an Etruscan port, Adria, are derived the names of the two great seas surrounding Italy: the Tyrrhenian and the Adriatic.

When and how did the Etruscan supremacy on the seas become established? How should we interpret the data provided by classical and archaeological sources? It is obvious that such an ample, varied, but in the main unanimous historical documentation as that referring to Etruscan 'thalassocracy' and piracy cannot have been born from nothing and must have largely been due to a widespread feeling of admiration and fear on the part of the Greek world, though it too was much devoted to daring sea and colonizing ventures. A clear indication of such feelings is the core of legends on Tyrrhenian piracy, legends unknown to epic literature but which arose in time to be introduced in the last stages of the elaboration of Greek myths, between the sixth and fifth century B.C. They were obviously embroidered around the core of fearful tales told of these freebooters of antiquity in the coastal towns of Hellas and its colonies. The historical basis of tradition becomes more evident in those western sea areas that were the scene of the adventures of the Tyrrhenian pirates: we are told of the difficulties the Greeks had to face on the seas around Sicily and of the contests between Greeks and Tyrrhenians for the possession of the Lipari islands.

This picture of the Tyrrhenians as fearful and ferocious

bands of privateers fits in well with the tendency to over-simplify ethnic characteristics, both good and evil, that was so dear to classical antiquity; even we moderns cannot wholly free ourselves from it. Its origins must doubtless be sought in the sharp commercial and territorial competition between Etruscan navigators and Greek colonists around the coasts of Italy. Piracy is the most obvious facet of a keen maritime war; and since both the legendary and the histori-cal sources in our possession are Greek, we can easily under-stand the bad name given to the Tyrrhenians by ancient literature. And the great conflict between Greeks and Etruscans in historical times was to be the cause of other preconceived judgements on the moral character of the Etruscans: accusations as to their lasciviousness, sensuality, and refined cruelty were far from uncommon.

The fact that Homer is silent on the subject of Tyrrhenian piracy, whilst the later 'Homeric' hymns on the Dionysus myth refer to it, enables us to place the period of greatest development of Etruscan naval supremacy between the eighth and sixth centuries B.C. Archaeological evidence confirms this. If the passage ascribed to the historian Ephorus (probably derived from one of the Siceliot historians) and included in Strabo's *Geography* (VI, 2, 2) is trustworthy, we are able to state that in the eighth century, when the Greeks were beginning to establish their first trading outposts on the eastern shores of Sicily, the seas surrounding the island were already being ploughed by Etruscan ships. Now the eighth century offers us an apparently primitive picture of the cultural development of Etruria, for it corresponds to the development of the 'Villanovan' culture. But towards the end of this period oriental objects were already beginning to appear, and also the first scratched or painted reproductions of ships (see plate 3B).[5] It is not actually possible to have a clear idea of the capabilities and activities of a people merely from the

examination of their tombs, even when the latter show them
to be archaic: we only need think of the very daring naviga-
tional exploits of the Polynesians, whose culture is of a
neolithic type and relatively less advanced than that of the
iron age inhabitants of Italy. We cannot exclude therefore
that the first seafaring activities of the Etruscans went back
as far as the eighth century and that they did come across
the oldest Greek colonists.

The Etrurian coastline, jagged and rich in islands, with
alternate promontories and flat stretches of coast, must have
favoured an early development of coastal navigation for
fishing and barter. It is worth noticing that facing Etruria
there lay not only Elba with its iron deposits and other
small islands near it, but also the great lands of Sardinia and
Corsica; the former of the two being the seat of ancient
cultures and of a well-developed social organization.

In considering the earliest stages of the civilization and
seafaring activities of the Etruscans, we are faced with the
problem concerning the relations of Etruria and Sardinia.[6]
The legend concerning the foundation of Populonia by the
Corsicans (Servius, *ad Aen.* x, 172) is evidence of the presence on the coasts of Etruria of inhabitants from the islands
facing it. Strabo (v, 2, 7) explicitly refers to incursions on
the coasts of Tuscany by Sardinian pirates, and also attributes a Tyrrhenian origin to the Sardinians. We have much
evidence of the commercial relations between the Etruscans
of the mining areas and the Sardinians: some objects,
including a little bronze ship with animal figurines, found
in eighth- and seventh-century tombs at Vetulonia, seem to
be incontestably Sardinian. Here and there we also find
elements recalling characteristic types of the civilization of
the *nuraghi* (those Sardinian prehistoric monuments built
without mortar in the shape of a truncated cone): as, for
instance, long-necked vases whose occurrence at such an
early phase seems to be limited to the Vetulonia necropolis.

There is also the question of whether the technique used in building the typical pseudo-cupola constructions of the northern Etrurian coast is connected with that of the *nuraghi*. In Sardinia too, there are traces of Etruscan influence: these may include the name *Aesaronenses* belonging to one of the peoples inhabiting the eastern coast (cf. the Etruscan word *aisar*, 'gods'), the presence of *bucchero* vases, certain early Sardinian bronze statuettes of Etruscan type, etc. Similarly, a few rock-hewn tombs in the necropolis of S. Andrea Priu or at Fordongianus imitate architectural details found in the Etruscan sepulchres of Cerveteri.

It is interesting to note that the Etruscan area most closely linked with Sardinia is the northern one. This is due to geographical reasons: for even in the Middle Ages and in modern times sea-traffic between Sardinia and the peninsula followed the coasts of Corsica and the Elban archipelago in the direction of Pisa. But the mineral resources of the Populonia and Vetulonia regions must also be taken into account, for this most important factor closely unites Etruria and Sardinia and the characteristics of the two peoples, both equally skilled craftsmen in bronze. This mineral region is the only one in Etruria or, for that matter, in the whole of Italy. Though we would not overstress the economic factor in history, we should remember that, except for the Sardinian mines, the only great iron, copper, and argentiferous lead mines in the central Mediterranean were those of Etruria. From the moment when they first began to be worked (during the iron age, roughly corresponding with the beginnings of the Etruscan civilization), they must have been a centre of especial attraction to the seafaring nations on the shores of the great sea.

Amongst the most characteristic cultural phenomena of primitive Etruria is the passage from the simple iron age 'Villanovan' culture to the orientalizing civilization; as we have seen, this change has been explained by believers in the oversea origin of the Etruscans as a sign of the ethnic change resulting from the establishment of oversea colonists on the coasts of Italy. As far as we are concerned for the moment however, the important aspect of this phenomenon is the great display of wealth that accompanied it: a rapid rise in living standards and a great increase in purchasing power are both attested by large quantities of costly articles from far-off lands, and of precious imported raw materials such as gold, silver, and ivory. The following phase (occupying the sixth and the beginning of the fifth century) also displayed this feature, at least as far as the presence in Etruria of Greek wares is concerned: the cemeteries of the coastal towns of Vulci, Tarquinii, and Caere especially have restored them by the thousand; as a result of this, the present-day study of Attic pottery seems to be based almost exclusively on material extracted from Etruscan sites. It is also clear that in the commercial exchanges between Etruria and the East, Etruria played on the whole a buyer's role: the quantities of Etruscan articles found in other lands, especially in Greece,[7] cannot be compared with that of foreign articles found in Etruria. We are thus faced with a new problem: what was the nature of Etruria's purchasing power? Or, better, what products were exchanged for goods imported from Greece and the Orient? Everything leads us to believe that these products were crude and wrought metals from the Etruscan mines; we already know that a proportion of these metals was sent to Campania (Diodorus Siculus, v, 13), and that metal goods were prominent amongst the Etruscan products known in Greece.

The above statements appear to be obvious and they are in fact admitted by the majority of scholars. They are confirmed by the presence of Greek merchant colonies in the Etruscan ports of Caere and of Spina on the Adriatic. An important objection could however be raised against this over-simplified reconstruction of the facts: namely that those cities that were richest and most rapidly transformed by eastern ideas were in southern Etruria, not in the mining area at all. The answer to this might be that, at first, the exploitation of the great natural wealth of the Etruscan soil largely benefited centres that specialized in brokerage, centres of early political and cultural attainments, in direct contact with the great Mediterranean trade lanes, such cities in fact as Caere or Tarquinii; whereas it was only later that the cities that grew in the neighbourhood of the mining area seized the initiative in the commercial field. This explanation may agree with the late entry of Populonia into the alliance of the twelve Etruscan states (Servius, *ad Aen.*, x, 172), and with the fact that in the archaic culture of Vetulonia we find a great abundance of bronze objects, but no imported Greek products such as painted vases. It is certain however that throughout the centuries the mining area represented a constant goal for the Greeks, who during the fifth and fourth centuries sent naval expeditions in an attempt to conquer Elba, without however being able to set foot on the coast of Etruria. The lasting importance of the southern towns as markets for the exchange of Etruscan raw materials for manufactured articles from abroad is shown by the fact that Dionysius of Syracuse's expedition against the Etruscan mining territory began before Caere, with the capture and sack of the port of Pyrgos (Santa Severa) in 384 B.C.

Not only Greek and Phoenician, but Etruscan seamen too must have participated from the very beginning in this great commercial exploitation of the western Mediterranean. Hence the development of Etruscan shipping culminating in its dominance of the Tyrrhenian sea. The Greek colonization of the southern Italian and Sicilian coasts formed an obstacle to the free expansion of Etruscan naval and commercial activities; it gave rise to those conflicts whose echo has reached us by way of the historians of antiquity: Corsica (Herodotus, I, 166), the Lipari islands (Strabo, VI, 2, 10), Cumae (Diodorus Siculus, XI, 51); an explicit reference to an Etruscan naval expedition to Sicily is found in the *elogium* to a personage of ancient Tarquinii preserved in a Latin fragmentary inscription.[8]

The second stage of the Etruscan 'thalassocracy' was in fact characterized by this naval conflict with the Greeks, by the race for the possession of bases on the Tyrrhenian coast (as in Campania and Corsica), and finally by that policy of compromise typified by the alliance with Carthage against the Greek world, an alliance that was so close and so significant that Aristotle in his *Politics* (III, 9, 128a, 36) states that Etruscans and Carthaginians were as citizens of a single state. As a consequence the Etruscan naval sphere of action gradually became restricted during the sixth century, and during the fifth there developed the threat of an economic crisis that was going to hit central Italy with very serious repercussions. The most obvious and characteristic sign of this crisis was the sudden interruption of large-scale importations of Greek vases in the cities of southern Etruria. After this time, the Etruscan dominion of the seas was to be little more than a glorious memory, and the states of Etruria gradually assumed the character of small inland powers waiting to be absorbed by the political hegemony of Rome. When the latter prepared to fight her tremendous naval duel with Carthage, in the third century, not a trace remained of the Etruscan navy, and the allied cities of Etruria did no more than help provide materials for the construction of the Roman fleet.[9]

NOTES

1. The traditions concerning the adventures of the Tyrrheno-Pelasgians and the possibility of their being historically founded will be found discussed by J. Berard in *Revue des Études Anciennes*, LI,

1949, pp. 224 ff., and in *Studies Presented to D. M. Robinson*, 1951, pp. 135 ff.

2. The demonstration of a proto-Etruscan colonization of Spain attempted by A. Schulten (*Los Tirsenos en España*, in *Ampurias*, II, 1940; *Tartessos*, 1945) on the basis of toponymy, has however no reliable foundation. These hypothetical linguistic relationships and the analogies found between place-names in Lusitanian inscriptions and in the Tyrrheno-Pelasgic world (cf. *Glotta*, XVIII, 1930, pp. 106; *Klio*, XXXIII, 1940, pp. 83 ff.; *Glotta*, XXIX, 1941, pp. 90 ff.) may, if need be, be explained by referring back to older, prehistoric contacts (cf. my review of O. F. A. Menghin, *Migrationes Mediterraneae*, in *Doxa*, III, 1950, pp. 266 ff.).

3. For Greece, see G. Karo, *Etruskisches in Griechenland*, in *Archaiologike Ephemeris*, 1937, pp. 316 ff.; for Spain and Gaul: M. Almagro, *Los hallazgos de bucchero etrusco hacia occidente y su significación*, in *Boletín Arqueol. de la Sociedad Arqueol. Tarraconense*, XLIX, 1949, pp. 1 ff., with bibliography of previous studies; M. Pallottino, in *Archeologia Classica*, I, 1949, pp. 80 ff.; H. Rolland, in *Revue des Etudes Anciennes*, LI, 1949, pp. 90 ff.

4. E. Benveniste, *Notes étrusques*, in *Studi Etruschi*, VII, 1933, pp. 245 ff.

5. R. Vighi, *La più antica rappresentazione di nave etrusco-italica in un vaso della necropoli veiente* (in *Rendiconti della R. Accademia dei Lincei*, VI, VIII, 1932, pp. 367 ff.)

6. Cf. A. Taramelli, *Sardi ed Etruschi*, in *Studi Etruschi*, III, 1929, pp. 43 ff.; G. Lilliu, in *Studi Sardi*, VIII, 1948, pp. 19 ff.; M. Pallottino, *La Sardegna nuragica*, 1950, pp. 37 ff.

7. See note 3 above.

8. Discovered at Tarquinia, near the temple of the 'Queen's altar', and published recently with other historically interesting fragments in M. Pallottino, *Uno spiraglio di luce sulla storia etrusca: gli 'Elogia Tarquiniensia'*, in *Studi Etruschi*, XXI, 1950-1, pp. 147 ff.

9. For the historical problems concerning Etruscan maritime expansion and the relations with the Greek colonies and with Carthage, cf. M. Pallottino, *Gli Etruschi*, 1940, pp. 73 ff.

CHAPTER FOUR

THE ETRUSCANS AND ITALY

The Etruscan Expansion in Italy and its Starting Point

In Tuscorum iure pene omnis Italia fuerat: in the words of
Cato (Servius, *ad Aen.*, XI, 567), nearly the whole of Italy
had been under Etruscan domination. And Livy (I, 2; V, 33)
stresses the power, the wealth, the renown which the
Etruscans had acquired on land and sea, from the Alps to
the Straits of Messina: a clear proof that the Etruscans did
not merely hold the seas but had also extended their power
over the lands of the peninsula. We are sufficiently well
informed to-day as to which lands lay under Etruscan rule,
and which were only indirectly subjected to its influence.
But Cato's and Livy's statements are of real value, especially when we consider that before the domination of Rome,
the only power able to effect a partial ethnico-political and
a wider cultural unification of Italy was Etruria. In spite of
the loose political system that seems to have dominated
much of its history, Etruscan expansion, relying no doubt
upon the effective union of individual energies, must have
been so powerful (at least for the period that stretched from
the seventh to the sixth century B.C.) that it was able to
achieve a political, territorial, and linguistic unity, in the
Etruscan sense, over most of northern and central and part
of southern Italy as well as over the islands lying off its
Tyrrhenian shores. And there is no doubt that the cultural
mark left on Italy by the Etruscans went far beyond the
geographical and temporal boundaries of their national
life; their civilization radiated over the whole of the peninsula and even over northern lands beyond the barrier of the

Alps,[1] whilst it penetrated at the same time deep into the traditions and customs of Rome so as to survive the death of Etruria as a racially and linguistically distinct nation.

The stretch of land that may be considered as the original territory of the Etruscans lies between the Tyrrhenian and the rivers Tiber and Arno: this is Etruria proper or Tyrrhenian Etruria. To it belong the twelve cities which, according to tradition, make up the Etruscan nation; and here, from a very early age, Etruscan is written and, therefore, spoken. When presented with this rather simplified picture of an Etruscan national territory where the stock had its roots, it is only natural one should suspect the critical validity of the original Etruscan character of this region as a whole. According to the theory that ascribes an oversea origin to the Etruscans, for instance, the Tyrrhenian colonists would first have settled on the coastal strip, and this would have been the starting point for the gradual occupation of the territory. This view seems to be borne out by the difference in the funeral rites – mainly inhumatory in southern Etruria and crematory in northern Etruria: a sign of the predominance of Tyrrhenian immigrants in those regions nearest their landing points, and of pre-Etruscan (i.e. Umbrian) populations in the interior. This idea of an Italic substratum subjugated by a small number of Etruscan conquerors occasionally re-emerges on the margin of discussions or in the study of certain isolated phenomena: as, for example, in the study of the personal names of the Caere inscriptions. These appear to be strongly influenced by Italic elements; according to R. Mengarelli, who was in charge of the excavations, this proves the original 'Italicity' of the population.[2] These inscriptions are comparatively recent, however, for they belong for the most part to the period of direct Roman domination over the Etruscan city, when it actually was the Etruscan element that was disappearing. Just as fanciful, the hypothesis of an Italic origin of Veii has been thoroughly disproved by the discovery in a Veii sanctuary of an abundant crop of archaic Etruscan inscriptions, and by G. Q. Giglioli's studies on the subject.[3]

We cannot however exclude that within geographically Etruscan territory (i.e. on the right bank of the Tiber) there existed important groups of non-Etruscan speakers: the Faliscans for instance, who occupied the area within the curve formed by the Tiber between Orte and the territory of Rome. Though they had been politically and culturally dominated by the Etruscans, they always kept their ethnic and linguistic Italic individuality. The archaic culture of Visentium (Bisenzio) too is remarkably close to that of Latium, whilst 'eastern' cultural elements occur in the oldest manifestations of the Tolfa region. The whole of Etruria, not merely Caere, abounds in onomastic and toponymic elements of Italic origin that betray deep and ancient penetrations of peoples with Indo-European tongues. The fact that the growth of the population and the urban development in coastal southern Etruria occurred earlier and were more vigorous than in the vast inland areas, leads to the conclusion that the formative processes of the Etruscan nation did not occur simultaneously over the whole of Etruria proper, but only after a long struggle with Italic elements, especially in the inland areas of southern Etruria, and they must have ended in the ethnic assimilation or political conquest of such elements.[4]

The lack of authentic historical sources prevents us from attempting the reconstruction, even along the broadest of outlines, of the political and military position of the various Etruscan cities and of their reciprocal relations. The most vivid aspect of history – names of kings and rulers, revolutions, wars, alliances, dates, all those things, that is, that we know with a fair degree of certainty for archaic and classical Greece – remains steeped in darkness for us. We can only just make out an organization based upon city-states more or less independent of each other, but united (at least at the time of the Roman conquest) in a kind of confederation, and perceive their development from monarchical to republican institutions; a process that will be treated in more detail in Chapter VI. The only concrete events of which we have notice are those connected with foreign policy and recorded in Greek and Roman sources. We may even go so far as to presume, on the basis of archaeological data and certain evidence of a literary nature (of Graeco-Roman origin in every case), that the cities of coastal Etruria, and especially Caere, Tarquinii, and Vulci, did go through a phase of particular splendour (both on the seas and, perhaps, on land) during the seventh and sixth centuries. The text of one of the Latin *elogia* recently recovered at Tarquinii, though unfortunately in a fragmentary state, would tend to prove the breadth of Tarquinian interests in archaic times, for it refers on the one hand to some unknown political action with regard to Caere and on the other to a war fought on the territory of Arezzo.[5] Towards the end of the sixth century Clusium probably became dominant (as reflected by the legendary traditions concerning King Porsenna), and this hegemony coincided probably with the beginning of the decadence of the coastal towns. Once again archaeological evidence comes to our support, for it shows a gradual increase in the importance of central and northern centres (Chiusi and Orvieto at first, and later Arezzo, Cortona, Perugia, Volterra, etc.) as the Etruscan civilization drew on to its final phase (from the fifth to the first century B.C.).

The 'Etruscanization' of Italy followed two main directions: to the south, along the Tyrrhenian coast, over Latium and Campania; to the north across the Apennines and over the lower Po valley. As a result Etruscan ethnic and political continuity was established from the Gulf of Salerno to the Tridentine Alps. Outside it to the west we

have western Lombardy, Piedmont, and Liguria (all occupied by peoples of Ligurian stock);[6] to the east, Venetia,
the whole of the eastern half of Italy (inhabited by Picenians, Umbrians, and Sabellians), and, finally, the southern
extremity of the peninsula. It is interesting to note that
Etruscan expansion seems to have been most vigorous in
those areas inhabited during the iron age by predominantly
non-Indo-European peoples or by peoples who practised
the cremation rite, areas where ethnic individualities were
least marked and where a new amalgamation was therefore
less difficult to attain under the compulsion of a strong
political force. We may even go so far as to imagine an
ethnico-linguistic substratum fitted to receive the Etruscan
stamp; as far as the Po valley is concerned, believers in the
northern origin of the Etruscans also believed that its primitive inhabitants were Etruscans. The lack of written documents relegates all this to the realms of pure hypothesis.
We should not however exclude the possibility of remote
links uniting the Ligurians, the Raeto-Euganeans and perhaps even the inhabitants of northern Picenum with the
earliest inhabitants of Tyrrhenian Etruria on whose stock
the nucleus of the Etruscan nation of historical times was
later to form. These links would explain on the one hand
the affinities between the 'Villanovan' civilizations of
Aemilia and Etruria and on the other the later contrast, in
Aemilia itself, between 'Villanovan' and Etruscan civilizations, the latter having been introduced in historical times,
towards the end of the sixth century B.C.

The overland expansion of the Etruscans towards the
south (i.e. Campania) must have taken place at a very early
date. It should be considered in relation to the question of
Etruscan predominance over the southern Tyrrhenian and
of the opposition they met on the part of the Greek colonies.
As early as the eighth century colonists from Chalcis had
occupied outposts on the Campanian coast and founded

Cumae, a long way from their bases. Capua, the centre of
Etruscan rule in Campania, was built in direct opposition
to Cumae, and it seems that frequent attempts were made
to eliminate this dangerous Hellenic competitor but with
no success.[7] And in this connexion it is interesting to
remember that the same wave of Italic peoples from the
hills of Samnium who during the second half of the fifth
century overwhelmed the Etruscan cities of Campania, also
succeeded in dislodging the Greeks from the coast of
Campania by occupying Cumae.

Many problems are presented by the Etruscan southward
expansion. In the first place, whether the Etruscans had ever
in fact been in Campania; some doubts had been cast on
this point, soon dispelled however by the discovery of the
inscribed tile of Capua and by J. Beloch's arguments.[8]
Secondly there is the question of the route: according to
some authorities the sea route was used, according to others
the land route. A few supporters of the latter alternative
believe that the Etruscans followed the valley of the Liri.
This presupposes an Etruscan predominance over Latium,
which brings us to the problem of the Etruscans in Rome.
The existence of an Etruscan phase in the history of Rome
is admitted even by those who, like De Sanctis, are little
disposed to admit the truth of the Etrusco-Roman legends
on the kings of Rome and who refute the Etruscan origin
of the Tarquin dynasty.[9] Two recent discoveries have
brought this question to the fore, confirming more or less
directly the veracity of tradition. Ancient writers speak of
two Etruscan brothers, Aulus and Caelius Vibenna, who
lived during the last years of the Rome of the kings, and of
a certain Mastarna reputed to have been their friend and
ally and later identified with the king Servius Tullius of
Roman tradition (Varro, *de ling. lat.*, v, 46; Servius, *ad Aen.*,
v, 560; Festus 31/44, s.v. *Caelius mons;* Dionysius of
Halicarnassus, II, 36, 2 ff.; Claudius, in *C.I.L.*, XIII, 1668;

Tacitus, *Ann.*, IV, 65). In the François tomb at Vulci there is
a painting of a battle scene: one camp is composed of a
group of fighters amongst whom we find Aule and Cele
Vipina (the two brothers Vibenna) and Macstrna (Mastarna); the other, of warriors amongst whom is a Cneve
Tarchunies Rumach, who is undoubtedly Gnaeus Tarquinius Romanus, a member therefore of the Tarquin dynasty.
These paintings, though probably belonging to the end of
the second or beginning of the first century B.C., are accompanied by Etruscan inscriptions and represent the Etruscan
version of the tradition.[10] Again in the course of the excavation of a Veii sanctuary, a fragment of a *bucchero* vase has
recently come to light; it bears an Etruscan votive inscription, the dedicator being one Avile Vipiiennas, an archaic
Etruscan form of Aulus Vibenna or Aule Vipina (see plate
29B). The inscription has been dated around the second half
of the sixth century B.C., just at the time of the monarchy in
Rome and of the Tarquins. It is therefore a contemporary and
original document of the historical period referred to by
the above-mentioned legend. It is probable that Aulus and
Caelius Vibenna were real historical personages, Etruscan
leaders who participated in a political struggle whose object
was the domination of Rome, and that one of them made a
votive offering at the sanctuary at Veii, so very near Rome.
That close relations united Veii and Rome at this time is
borne out by the tradition concerning works of art
fashioned by Vulca and other Veii artists for the sanctuary
dedicated to Jupiter, Juno, and Minerva on the Capitol
(Varro in Pliny, *Nat. Hist.*, XXXV, 157; Plutarch, *Public.*, 13).
Even if the two Auli were not the same person, we would
still have proof of the existence during the sixth century of
a Vibenna family in southern Etruria.[11] Two other discoveries are perhaps more important: they consist in the
finding of two Etruscan inscriptions on *bucchero* vases on the
slopes of the Capitoline hill and on the top of the Palatine

(see plate 29A).[12] They confirm the presence of Etruscan speakers in Rome during the sixth century and, in contrast with archaic Latin inscriptions (such as that of the famous *cippus* under the *Lapis Niger*, the Duenos vase, etc.), place the city within the bilingual Etrusco-Italic zone, to which the Faliscan territory was also known to have belonged.

The Etruscan domination of Latium and Campania at first comprised a phase of expansion that may go back as far as the seventh century and ended with a fairly intensive colonization of Campania, where it gave rise to Etruscan cities such as Capua, Nola, Acerrae (Acerra), Nuceria (Nocera), and others as yet unidentified but whose names are known to us through coins (i.e. Uri or Urina, Velcha, Velsu, Irnthi).[13] Whether the Etruscans ever reached or even occupied Pompeii, as stated by Strabo (v, 4, 8), has been a long-debated question; it has now been resolved by the discovery of fragments of *bucchero* vases bearing inscriptions that are certainly in Etruscan.[14]

Political Domination and Colonization of Campania and the Po Valley

We know that the Campanian dominion was governed in the same way as the cities of the mother country: it was divided into twelve small allied states, probably under the rule of Capua. As for Latium, we probably ought not to speak of colonization in a demographic sense: Etruria, as likely as not, merely dominated the political scene with a view to controlling the trade routes to the South, and maintaining territorial continuity with its Campanian dominion. Rome must have been particularly important in this respect because of its controlling position over the Tiber fords.

The second phase of Etruscan political activity in the South is chiefly marked by the struggle against local nationalisms, against the arch-enemy of Etruria, the Greeks, and especially against the threat represented by the expansion of bellicose Italic tribes from the Apennines, the Umbro-Sabellians, who at that period began to spread over the plains of the Tyrrhenian shore. We are now at the end of the sixth and the beginning of the fifth century, and the threat of the great economic crisis that was to follow already loomed large over Etruria's maritime and commercial interests. An alliance between the Latins and the Greeks from Cumae (Livy, II, 14; Dionysius of Halicarnassus, VII, 5 and 6) resulted in the collapse of Etruscan hegemony over Latium. Within this series of events we must no doubt place the liberation of Rome from Etruscan rule and the traditions concerning the end of the Tarquin monarchy and the institution of the republic. Events are complicated by the descent over the greater part of Latium of Italic mountain peoples, the Volsci and the Aequi: an event also known to us from the accounts of Roman historians. For a few decades the Etruscan dominion of Campania survived the territorial separation from the mother country, but it too finally succumbed around the year 430 B.C., before the descending wave of the Italic Samnites (Diodorus Siculus, XII, 31, 1; Livy, IV, 37, 1).

Etruscan expansion towards the north occurred later than the southern expansion. Its points of departure were the cities of inner northern Etruria: Perugia, whence, according to a traditional legend, an Etruscan chief by the name of Aucno or Ocno moved to the conquest of the Po valley and founded Felsina (Bologna) and Mantua (*Interpr. Verg.;* Servius, *ad Aen.*, x, 198). In reality the oldest Etruscan tombs in Bologna (distinguished by the cremation rite, the presence of imported Greek vases and funerary inscriptions in Etruscan), only go back to the very last years of the sixth or the beginning of the fifth century. Thus we may not attribute the founding of Bologna to the Etruscans, for it had been an important centre before their arrival, probably a market for the exchange of products from Etruria and the south with goods from central Europe (e.g. amber[15]). In the direction of the Adriatic, the Etruscans founded and occupied the cities of Caesena (Cesena), Ravenna, Ariminum (Rimini), and Spina. The latter became an important emporium for trade with Greece, as the recently discovered tombs of its rich necropolis testify. Inland, there were the cities of Parma, Placentia (Piacenza), Mutina (Modena), and Melpum, perhaps in the vicinity of Milan; near the village of Marzabotto, in the valley of the upper Reno (near Bologna), an Etruscan centre has been discovered which is particularly important for its characteristic chess-board pattern (the 'gridiron' system), with straight streets rigorously laid at right angles to one another in the direction of the four cardinal points, thus following the rules for the planning of Etruscan cities later handed down to the Romans.

In northern Italy, Etruscan expansion was held up by the Veneti to the east and the Ligurians to the west. It lasted little more than a century, for towards the end of the fifth and the beginning of the fourth century Gaulish hordes swept down upon Italy, spread over the whole of the Po valley as far as Etruria proper and even succeeded in sacking Rome. It would be interesting to study which local Etruscan ethnic groups survived these Gallic invaders. The latter's tombs may be distinguished by the fact that they were more poorly furnished with objects belonging to the backward iron culture of the Gauls known as 'La Tène'. Town-dwellers were very likely mainly Etruscan and their position with respect to the Gauls was probably much the same as that of the Romans of late Imperial times with respect to the Germanic peoples. It is probable for instance that Mantua preserved its Etruscan traditions until conquered by Rome.

As for the Etruscan inhabitants of the Adige valley, the late 'Etruscoid' inscriptions that have been found in the locality may have belonged to ethnic groups that became severed from the main body of the Etruscan world and mixed with Alpine peoples. The following well-known passage in Livy (v, 33) is the main basis of this theory: *Alpinis quoque ea gentibus haud dubie origo est, maxime Raetis: quos loca ipsa efferarunt, ne quid ex antiquo, praeter sonum linguae, nec eum incorruptum, retinerent.* (The Alpine peoples too, especially the Raetians, have undoubtedly the same origin (i.e. Etruscan); but the very nature of their surroundings caused them to grow so wild that the only memory they preserved of their past was the sound of their language and it too not uncorrupted.) A more likely explanation may be that the above inscriptions belonged to indigenous speakers of a pre-Indo-European dialect presenting certain affinities with Etruscan.[16] In any case it is impossible to demonstrate that these peoples were remnants of an earlier Etruscan migration, as supporters of the theory of northern origin believed.

A final word on the question of Etruscan influence in Liguria. Ancient tradition speaks of an Etruscan domination along the Ligurian coast as far as the Val di Magra and of the founding by the Etruscans of Luna (Luni). Archaeology on the other hand reveals the Ligurian cultural horizon as extending as far south as the northern bank of the Arno, and the presence of Etruscan works of art in Luna only at a very late period. These regions were probably the object of violent struggles between the Etruscans and the fierce Ligurian tribes; Etruscan rule had probably a transitory character till Rome appeared upon the scene and finally established herself in the area.[17]

The Spread of Etruscan Culture and the Growth of the Etrusco-Italic Civilization

If the political rule and direct colonization of the Etruscans only extended over part of continental Italy, their commercial activities and their cultural influence reached much further afield. Situated at the centre of the peninsula, Etruria was in fact the only beacon to radiate its civilization from early times upon generally backward peoples. Its only rivals were the Greek cities of Sicily and southern Italy, though the latter's influence was scarcely felt at first. As for the influence of Carthage, its cultural importance was only secondary and limited in range to western Sicily and to Sardinia. When speaking of a pre-Roman Etrusco-Italic civilization we are involuntarily led to place upon equal historical and chronological footings the various peoples of ancient Italy: Etruscans, Ligurians, Veneti, Latins, Umbro-Sabellians, etc., whereas a careful study of the archaeological documents in our possession is sufficient to persuade us that both the predominant role and absolute chronological priority in the formation of the civilization of ancient Italy belong to Etruria. During the sixth century, at the time of the great expansion and of the greatest flowering of the Etruscan civilization, the peoples of Aemilia, of Venetia, and of Liguria were still living within the scope of a backward iron age; the Picenians and the Umbrians were elaborating ways of life in which barbaric orientalizing elements were to predominate for a long time, elements which Etruria had discarded long ago, or alternately were more or less directly affected by Etruscan influences; Latium and Campania revolved within the orbit of Etruria and Greece; the Samnites showed, and went on showing for many decades, late features of the eastern iron culture. In all these peripheral regions, with the only exception of the extreme south colonized by the Greeks, there mainly subsisted a rather archaic *village* culture; its definite transformation into an *urban* culture, into a true and proper civilization, was at first due to the political predominance and cultural radiance of Etruria, and, later, to the unification of the peninsula achieved by Rome, the bearer of civilized forms of life which themselves owed much to Etruria.

That close links united the religion and ritual of Etruria, Umbria, and Latium is clearly shown by the texts of the Iguvine Tablets and by the sacred Latin formulas given by Cato in his *De re rustica*. They reveal a close analogy with what we are able to make out of Etruscan religious literature, e.g. in votive formulas and prayers, the names of deities and liturgical expressions.[18] It is worth recalling that many Etruscan deities are identical with Latin and Italic gods, even to their names: *Uni* – Juno, *Menerva* – Minerva, *Neθun* – Neptune, *Selvan* – Silvan, *Satre* – Saturn, *Velχan* – Vulcan, *Maris* – Mars, *Vesuna* – Vesona. Even if there existed common elements going back to an earlier prehistoric cultural unity, there is little doubt that these close analogies developed as a result of the cultural and political hegemony of Etruria in central Italy.

The same may be said for personal names. The Etruscans, the Latins and the Umbro–Sabellians were the only peoples of antiquity possessing a dual system: the *praenomen*, or personal name, and the name of the *gens*, or family. The system has no parallel amongst other Indo-European-speaking peoples and must have been formed within the Etrusco-Italic world. It had already appeared in Etruria by the seventh century B.C., whereas there is ground for believing that in Latium at that same period the use of a single name predominated.[19] Together with the social system, the Etruscan political system was also adopted in varying degrees by the peoples of Latium and of its hinterland. The Umbrians adopted the Etruscan magistrature of the *maru*, while the Roman monarchy, even in its external symbols (the golden crown, the throne, the *fasces*, the *toga palmata*, etc.) was explicitly stated by Latin writers to have been of Etruscan origin.

The diffusion of writing is one more important aspect of Etruscan cultural influence on the Italian peninsula. It spread

in two directions. To the south the same Greek alphabet
adopted by the Etruscans was also used at an early stage by
the Faliscans and the Latins (although naturally including
variants determined by the presence of different sounds,
such as *o* and the voiced consonants, lacking in Etruscan).
The form of the alphabet is still the same in the seventh and
sixth centuries. Traces of a direct Etruscan influence are
common: e.g. the Latin use of the digamma symbol to
indicate, as in Etruscan, the unvoiced velar consonant *k*
instead of the voiced *g*. The Umbrians and the Oscans on
the other hand, directly adopted the Etruscan alphabet with
the same inevitable modifications: this occurred at a later
period, i.e. not earlier than the fifth to fourth centuries B.C.
The other direction in which the Etruscan alphabet spread
was to the north: the alphabets of the Veneti, the Raetians,
the Lepontians and of the other Alpine peoples were linked
to the so-called northern Etruscan alphabet adopted in the
Po valley during the fifth century. To-day there is a grow-
ing tendency to believe that the runic alphabets of central
and northern Europe were also derived, at least in part,
from the northern Etruscan alphabet.[20]

Let us finally consider the realms of art and culture.
Objects found in the culturally advanced Umbrian cities of
Vettona (Bettona) and Tuder (Todi) reveal a very marked
Etruscan influence: in some cases we may even speak of
articles imported from Etruria. Etruscan elements belonging to the orientalizing period are also present in Picenum.
The whole civilization of Latium and Campania from the
seventh to the sixth century B.C. was frankly Etruscan: we
only need think of the type and form of the temple, and of
its decorations in painted terracotta as seen at Falerii, Rome,
Satricum, Aletrium (Alatri), and Capua. Painted tombs
similar to those of Etruria have been discovered at Rome,
Capua, and Paestum: they were adopted by the Samnite
invaders of Campania who also took over other Etruscan

E–4

customs, e.g. the gladiatorial combats which from Capua later spread to Rome. Similarly, material elements of the Etruscan civilization spread over northern Italy: the Venetic culture of Ateste (Este) seems deeply impregnated with Etruscan elements which at first reached it via 'Villanovan' Bologna, and later through direct contacts with the Etruscan Po valley; the same may be said of coastal and inland Liguria.

Thus, despite the persistence of backward and archaic forms right up to the threshold of the Roman conquest, especially in the peripheral areas, despite the lingering regional characteristics of some of its cultures, a certain unity was arrived at in Italy well before the unification achieved by Rome. This unity was mainly due to the political dominance and cultural prestige of the Etruscans. These forces were exerted longitudinally along the whole peninsula from the Po to the southern Tyrrhenian. At the centre, a more clearly defined Etrusco-Italic cultural block grew up after the seventh and sixth centuries B.C.: the regions of Etruria proper, Latium and Campania. It became one of the two great historical poles of ancient Italy, in opposition to the Hellenic block of Sicily and Magna Graecia. The meeting of these two spheres was to form the basis of an Italian civilization under the imperial domination of Rome, and the starting-point for the development of ways of life destined to triumph in Western Europe.

NOTES

1. Cf. E. Genthe, *Über den etruskischen Tauschhandel nach dem Norden*, 1874; J. Gy. Szilágyi, *Zur Frage des etruskischen Handels nach dem Norden*, in *Acta Antiqua Hungariae*, I, 1953, 3–4, pp. 419 ff.

2. *Cere all' epoca della sua annessione a Roma*, etc. (in *Atti del II Congresso di Studi Romani*, 1931, pp. 411 ff.); L. Pareti, *La tomba Regolini-Galassi*, pp. 8 ff.

3. In *Notizie degli Scavi*, 1930, pp. 335 ff.

4. The ethnic unification of Etruria considered as the assimilation and incorporation of peoples belonging to different linguistic stocks is a fundamental concept of F. Altheim's synthesis *Der Ursprung der Etrusker:* cf. p. 72, note 1, and p. 69.

5. Cf. note 8 on p. 83. This is a different *elogium* from the one quoted there, and refers to a different personage. The mention of a 'king of Caere' ((C)*aeritum regem*) makes it almost certain that the personage lived in archaic times. For the possible hegemony of Tarquinia during the oldest phase of Etruscan history, see M. Pallottino, *Tarquinia* (*Monumenti Antichi dell'Accademia dei Lincei*, XXXVI, 1937), cols. 245 ff. and 367 ff.

6. The presence of Etruscan inscriptions in Piedmont (cf. M. Buffa, *Iscrizioni etrusche nel territorio del popolo ligure* in *Memorie dell'Accademia Lunigianese*, XV, 1934) has raised the question of an Etruscan colonization of the valleys of the Tanaro and of the Stura as far as the outskirts of Cuneo. On the frontier between Etruscans and Ligurians, cf. also N. Lamboglia, in *Studi Etruschi*, X, 1936, pp. 137 ff.

7. We should mention here the great expedition against Cumae of 524 B.C. mentioned by Dionysius of Halicarnassus, VII, 3 ff. The Etruscan army, reinforced with Umbrian and Daunian contingents, was defeated under the city walls.

8. *Campanien*, 1879.

9. G. De Sanctis, *Storia dei Romani*, I, 1906, pp. 371 ff.

10. The most recent discussions on the subject may be found in L. Pareti, *Studi Etruschi*, V, 1931, pp. 147 ff.; A. Momigliano, *L'opera dell'Imperatore Claudio*, 1932, pp. 30 ff.; M. Pallottino, *Studi Etruschi*, XIII, 1939, pp. 456 ff. and in *Gli Etruschi*, pp. 108 ff., p. 270; S. Mazzarino, *Dalla monarchia allo stato repubblicano: ricerche di storia romana arcaica*, 1945, pp. 184 ff.; in the above works the reader will find full bibliographical data. On the date of the François tomb, see M. Pallottino, *La peinture étrusque*, 1952, pp. 123 ff.

11. *Studi Etruschi*, XIII, 1939, pp. 455 ff.

12. M. Pallottino, *La iscrizione arcaica su vaso di bucchero rinvenuta ai piedi del Campidoglio* (in *Bullettino Archeol. Comunale*, LXIX, 1941; *Rivista di epigrafia etrusca*, in *Studi Etruschi*, XXII, 1952–3, pp. 309 ff. An Etruscan inscription had already been found at Satricum, in Latium (*Studi Etruschi*, XIII, 1939, p. 427 ff.).

13. On the subject of the Etruscan domination of Campania and particularly of Capua, cf. J. Heurgon, *Recherches sur l'histoire, la religion et la civilisation de Capoue pré-romaine*, 1942. The city of Uri is probably to be identified with Nola.

14. The find was made under the temple of Apollo near the Forum at Pompeii (cf. A. Maiuri, *Greci e Etruschi a Pompei*, in *Memorie della R. Accademia d'Italia – Classe scienze morali e storiche*, IV, 1943, pp. 121 ff.). On the question of the Etruscans in Pompeii, cf. A. Sogliano, *Pompei nel suo sviluppo storico*, I, 1927; A. Boëthius, *Gli Etruschi in Pompei* (in *Symbola Philologica O. A. Danielsson dicata*, Uppsala, 1932); G. Patroni, in *Studi Etruschi*, XV, 1941, pp. 109 ff.

15. On the question of amber in Italy and the doubts now entertained as to its northern origins, see *Studi Etruschi*, XVII, 1943, pp. 31 ff., 419 ff.

16. Cf. p. 42, note 9.

17. For more details see the recent and competent studies of L. Banti in *Studi Etruschi*, V, 1931, pp. 163 ff. and *Luni*, 1937.

18. Cf. K. Olzscha, *Interpretation der Agramer Mumienbinde*, 1939, pp. 3 ff.; M. Pallottino, *Sulla lettura e sul contenuto della grande iscrizione di Capua*, in *Studi Etruschi*, XX, 1948–9, p. 159 ff.

19. In the inscription of the Palestrina *fibula*, only the two single names *Manios* and *Numasios* occur, but the latter may be the name of a divinity.

20. Cf. D. Diringer, *The Alphabet*, 1947, p. 516; F. Altheim, E. Trautmann, *Vom Ursprung der Runen*, 1939 (to be consulted with caution); J. G. Février, *Histoire de l'écriture*, 1948, pp. 513 ff.

PART TWO

Aspects of the Civilization of Etruria

CHAPTER FIVE

CITIES AND CEMETERIES OF ETRURIA

The Resurrection of Etruria

THE history of etruscology is closely linked to the story of the resurrection of the dead cities of Etruria. For almost two centuries now, investigators of all kinds, impelled at first by greed for treasure or local pride and later by thirst for knowledge, have relentlessly worked at the remains of the great Etruscan cities and their cemeteries. Even so the immense field of excavations is to-day a long way from being exhausted, though a very great number of monuments of prime importance to art, history, and epigraphy have seen the light of day these last two hundred years. Those familiar with the terrain of Etruscan cities know well that only a tiny fraction of the sites likely to yield interesting remains has so far been touched by modern excavators: the majority of documents needed for the reconstruction of the civilization of ancient Etruria still lie below ground awaiting the pickaxe.

The tale of the resurrection of Etruria is varied, stimulating, at times dramatic. At first, oblivion and silence lay over these ancient cities, whether it was the fresh sap of medieval and Renaissance life and art that had extinguished all memory of Etruscan monuments in towns like Volterra, Arezzo, Cortona, Chiusi, and Orvieto (whose life has continued uninterruptedly since Etruscan days), or that the wild Mediterranean scrub had covered all traces of the abandoned cities:

> *Ricordi tu le vedove piagge del mar toscano*
> *Ove china su'l nubilo inseminato piano*
> *La torre feudal*

Con lunga ombra di tedio dai colli arsicci e joschi
Veglia de le rasenie cittadi in mezzo ai boschi
                    Il sonno sepolcral . . .?
            (CARDUCCI, *Avanti, Avanti!*)

(Do you remember the widowed shores of the Tuscan
sea, where the feudal tower bends over the virgin fallow
plain with long and dreary shadow and watches from
the dark, burnt hills over the sepulchral sleep of the
Rasenna cities buried deep amidst the woods . . . ?)

The very name of many a famous city has been lost.
Over the ruins of Tarquinii, near Corneto (now re-christened
Tarquinia), fabulous stories were told of a city by the name
of Corythus. The site of Veii was the subject of much discussion during the eighteenth century; in the nineteenth
that of Vetulonia. To-day, important centres whose cemeteries were unearthed near Marsiliana d'Albegna and Massa
Marittima, and the Etruscan city of Orvieto itself, still
remain hidden and nameless to us.

Little by little, from the darkness of the past, some of the
features of the civilization of ancient Etruria begin to emerge.
At first it was the peasant and the passer-by, marvelling at
the weapons and jewels the earth had unexpectedly brought
forth, or wondering at the strange paintings and unde-
cipherable inscriptions on the walls of mysterious and
intricate underground chambers. It was finds such as these
that inspired the humanist Lucius Vitellius to sing of the
palace of Corythus buried close to the walls of Corneto in
a delicate poem to Philelphus, and that prompted Michel-
angelo to draw the head of Aita, king of the Etruscan underworld. Then, at the height of the *cinquecento*, at the golden
age of Renaissance sculpture, came the unearthing of superb
Etruscan bronzes, the pride of the Florence Archaeological
Museum: the Chimaera and the Minerva of Arezzo, the
Trasimene 'orator' (see plates 16A and 17). Finally, when
interest in ancient Etruria had wakened and reached a

climax through the work of Dempster, Buonarroti, Gori, and Passeri, there followed in ever-quickening succession the discoveries of Etruscan tombs at Siena, Corneto, Volterra, Cortona, till the day when, parallel with the creation of an Etruscan Academy at Cortona, began the first systematic search for Etruscan remains.

The second phase in the resurrection of the dead cities of Etruria began with the nineteenth century. On the initiative of private individuals and of institutes, the great Etrurian cemeteries, particularly those lying near the sea, were intensively explored. We cannot yet speak of strictly scientific activity; nevertheless the greater part of the material we possess came to light during this period of enthusiasm. Excavations that had begun in the eighteenth century around the centres of northern Etruria were now mainly concentrated upon the cities of coastal Etruria, especially Caere, Tarquinii, and Vulci. For years and years the immense necropolis that surrounded the latter city became (chiefly through the enterprise of Lucien Bonaparte, Prince of Canino) an inexhaustible quarry of Greek and Etruscan vases that now enrich the museums of the principal cities of Europe. The interest of local authorities and landowners was joined by that of the newly founded Institute of Archaeological Correspondence and, within the borders of the Papal States, that of the Camerlingate on whose account excavations were undertaken.

The second half of the nineteenth century generally brought a pause in the resurrection of Etruscan cities. A greater interest in prehistorical studies resulted in a series of discoveries that served to illustrate and to locate the very first Etruscan sites. Thus, at first in Aemilia (Bologna, Villanova, etc.), and later in Etruria proper (Tarquinii, Chiusi, Volterra, Vetulonia), iron age sepulchres of a distant culture were revealed that received the label 'Villanovan'. During this period the Italian government began to take an active interest in the search and excavations of ancient remains, but it was only during the first decades of this century, with the creation of a *Direzione Generale delle Antichità e Belle Arti* and of its dependent organizations in Tuscany and Latium, that a new and intensive campaign of exploration began that has greatly enriched Italy's national and local museums. To-day, the exploratory phase has reached its peak, with large-scale excavations at Veii, Caere, Tarquinii, and Populonia. We should also note that most recent researches no longer tend merely to increase the stocks of our museums by the easy and less costly excavation of tombs (generally well supplied with funerary objects); they are directed at the exploration of city sites and especially of those where favourable circumstances have left them unencumbered by later constructions. This change of emphasis is due to the rigidly scientific criterium of filling the gaps in our knowledge of certain aspects of the Etruscan civilization and to the hope of meeting with non-funerary inscriptions of a certain length or even perhaps with a bilingual Etrusco-Latin text.

Cities of Southern Etruria

Let us now cast a rapid glance at the principal centres of Etruscan life, tell the story of their discovery and describe their most obvious characteristics.[1] Geographical and historical factors first require a fundamental distinction to be made between the cities of southern and those of northern Etruria. The approximate line of demarcation between the two regions is marked by the rivers Fiora, that flows into the Tyrrhenian sea, and Paglia, a tributary of the Tiber; it is substantially the modern frontier between Tuscany and Latium. Southern or Latian Etruria consists of volcanic or alluvial terrains and belongs to the volcanic hill and lake system of Latium; northern Etruria, larger in area, lies over

Figure 3 – THE CITIES OF ETRURIA PROPER

The modern Italian names are given in brackets after the Latin names.

the foothills of the Apennines, rich in rivers and vegetation. From the historical, and monumental, point of view the two regions are fairly clearly differentiated. The south developed far earlier, and comprises great and ancient cities, especially near the sea, and at a relatively short distance from one another: Veii, Caere, Tarquinii, Vulci; their decadence, in the final phase of the Etruscan civilization and under the Roman empire, was correspondingly quick, and was hastened by the spread of malaria in the Maremma region. The limited development of this area in medieval and modern times has done much to preserve its ruins in a wild and primitive landscape. The cities that stood along the Tyrrhenian shore to the north of the Fiora and of Monte Argentario (such as Rusellae (Roselle), Vetulonia, and Populonia), present much the same characteristics: the same precocious development and just as precocious decadence, the same Maremman landscape, etc. Altogether different is the case of the cities of inland northern Etruria: Clusium (Chiusi), Cortona, Perusia (Perugia), Arretium (Arezzo), Faesulae (Fiesole), Volaterrae (Volterra); these stood at a certain distance from one another and developed more tardily as compared with the cities of the south: they flourished during the final phase of the Etruscan civilization and in Roman times. Even more important however is the fact that they continued to live without a break through the Middle Ages; we should not speak of them as of dead cities, and it is in them that we should seek the links that unite the ancient Etruscan nation with the spirit of the Tuscan civilization of the Renaissance.

An ordered survey of the cities of Etruria should begin with Rome, the Etruscan form of whose name was *Ruma-*.[2] It is quite certain that for a period during the sixth century B.C. Rome was the centre of an Etruscan monarchy, with monuments, works of art, a constitution, and a religion under Etruscan influence. The people were of Latin and, partly, of Sabine stock; but the already mentioned recent finds of Etruscan inscriptions on vases within the area of the city testify to the presence of Etruscan inhabitants, according to tradition (Varro, *de ling. lat.*, v, 46; Livy, II, 14, 9; Dionysius of Halicarnassus, v, 36; Festus, 536/355, s.v. *Tuscum vicum*), in the Velabrum quarter, near the Vicus Tuscus. The political contingencies that led to the downfall of Etruscan supremacy in Latium, to the sweeping down of the Italic peoples, to the isolation of the city and, finally, to its spectacular political and military recovery, were such as to cause the future metropolis of the Mediterranean world to develop outside the orbit of the Etruscan nation if not actually of the Etruscan civilization. Thus it is that we have so very little left of the external, monumental features of the Rome of the sixth century. Only the excavation of the city's sacred sites (as for instance the three-cell Capitoline temple built according to the Etruscan manner and with the help of Etruscan artists, or the recently discovered sacred site of Sant'Omobono in the Forum Boarium) and the exploration of those few square feet of archaic cemeteries that escaped the upheavals of thousands of years of building activity, allow us to imagine the life of the city under Etruscan rule.

Within a few miles from Rome, on the right bank of the Tiber and at the confluence of the two branches of the Cremera, there stood upon a high and rocky spur the city of Veii. Veii was the only great city of Etruria that ceased to be such with the decline of the archaic period. This occurred as the result of a well-determined historical fact: the implacable life and death struggle with Rome, towards the end of the fifth and the beginning of the fourth century B.C. It ended with the capture and destruction of Veii in 396. We ought not to think however of total and instantaneous obliteration: at the time of the Gallic invasion, Camillus found refuge in the city and after the burning of Rome, the possibility of transferring the seat of government to Veii was seriously considered; there are also traces of monuments belonging to the republican and imperial age. That a great city should survive and grow at such small distance from the capital was clearly unthinkable; and at the beginning of the Empire, Propertius was able to write (IV, x, 27):

Heu Veii veteres! et vos tum regna fuistis
et vestro positast aurea sella foro.
Nunc intra muros pastoris bucina lenti
cantat, et in vestris ossibus arva metunt.

(Veii, thou hadst a royal crown of old,
And in thy forum stood a throne of gold! –
Thy walls now echo but the shepherd's horn,
And o'er thine ashes waves the summer corn.)[3]

The Augustan poet perhaps romantically overstressed the desolation of the ancient city; but it is significant that his description corresponds perfectly to the impression received by the modern sightseer. There is nothing to show that life continued there during the Middle Ages, and the growth of a little hamlet round the castle of Isola Farnese that dominates the Veii plateau is comparatively recent. The site of the city was discovered only at the beginning of the last century: it was thought at first to have been at Civita Castellana. The first great discovery was of a painted tomb named, after its finder, Campana, in 1842. After that time excavations were sporadically conducted in the necropolis, but with no great results. It was only during the second decade of our century that a systematic exploration of the sacred zone of Portonaccio (where the famous Apollo of Veii came to light – see plate 5) was undertaken. Much, however, remains to be done.

To the unsuspecting sightseer, Veii appears as one of the most suggestive spots in the neighbourhood of Rome: a picturesque tumble of rocks, torrents, cascades, and thick brushwood meets the traveller quite unexpectedly as he crosses the volcanic and rather monotonous plateau traversed by the Via Cassia. The millennial neglect of the site heightens the charm of its setting: here nature is once more the mistress of a landscape that long ago teemed with life.

From the hamlet of Isola Farnese, beyond the confines of the old Etruscan city, the visitor descends to the foot of the rocky cliff and crosses the foaming Cremera at the little bridge of La Mola set between two cascades; then up again, along a stretch of the old Roman road, till he reaches the level ground of Portonaccio, where the temple once stood. Excavations have revealed this area to be a complex sacred enclosure, an Etruscan sanctuary clearly connected with the cult of the health-giving waters emerging from the hillside. There stood the temple, of which only the foundations remain, built in tufo stone according to the Etruscan plan with three cells (or one cell and two wings) and a wide forecourt. Along one of the temple's sides there is a pool, in whose healing waters the pilgrims probably bathed. At a certain distance before the temple a rectangular altar has been found, with a square opening in the centre and traces of sacrificial burnings. The whole surrounding ground has yielded fragments of the painted terra-cotta decorations of the upper portion of the temple, and of other sacred buildings, as well as votive objects, statues, fragments of vases with Etruscan inscriptions, etc. The most important discovery, made in 1916, consisted of fragments of a series of large painted terra-cotta statues of archaic style, the most complete of which is one of Apollo. More recently, the greater part of a statue of a goddess (Latona?) bearing a child in her arms has been discovered: its technique and style are the same as those of the Apollo. These statues were *acroteria* placed upon the roof of the rich temple, and reveal the hand of an artist with a most original style who worked towards the end of the sixth and the beginning of the fifth century B.C. In other areas within the city, and especially in the locality known as Campetti, large quantities of votive objects have come to light, particularly terra-cotta statuettes. All this material is generally believed to be earlier than the fourth century B.C., and the same may be said of the objects found in the tombs. The rock-hewn 'Campana' tomb, painted with figured scenes and ornamental patterns, is attributed to the beginning of the sixth century.[4]

Upon one of the hillocks of the tufo plateau that lies between the Lake of Bracciano and the sea, stand the remains of another great and famous Etruscan metropolis: Caere (the Etruscan form of which was probably χaire). The little town of Cerveteri (i.e. old Caere) is its impoverished descendant. The city or rather the immense necropolis that surrounds it began to be excavated during the first half of the nineteenth century, when the famous discovery of an intact and wealthy tomb belonging to the orientalizing period was made. The material belonging to this tomb, named 'Regolini-Galassi' after its excavators, is of unique importance and may be seen at the Gregorian Etruscan Museum in the Vatican (see plate 28). The systematic excavation of the sepulchres of Caere and of a few monuments in the city, and the careful restoration of the grandiose tumuli are however quite recent. To this work we owe the precious material (vases in particular) that so enrich the collection of the Museum of Villa Giulia (the 'Museo di papa Giulio') in Rome. To-day, the Cerveteri necropolis is one of the most suggestive groups of monuments not only of Italy but of the whole Mediterranean world. Within the restored area may be seen a series of tumuli heaped on rock or stone plinths, whose diameter may reach the truly impressive figure of one hundred feet (see plate 1A). Carved out of the tufo at the base of the tumuli one or more groups of tombs may be found; these imitate the interiors of houses and consist of several rooms, with doors, windows, columns, and pilasters outlined on the walls, beamed or coffered ceilings, and including furniture, armchairs, funerary couches, etc. The impression one receives in some of these tombs is quite uncanny. One of the most recent, a hypogeum deep below ground level, possesses walls and pilasters decorated with painted stucco reliefs reproducing objects supposed to be hanging on them (see plates 30 and 31). These stuccoes provide us with an extraordinarily vivid picture of weapons and tools used in domestic life. The material found in the Cerveteri tombs covers without any interruptions a period that runs from the iron age to Roman times. Amongst the most characteristic objects found there are archaic terra-cotta sarcophagi with lids in the shape of reclining figures and painted panels that originally covered the walls of sacred or public buildings and tombs. A special type of painted vase – the so-called *hydria* of Caere – the probable local production of Ionic artists, has only been found in the Cerveteri necropolis. The city itself was protected by rocky cliffs and, in the more accessible places, by walls of square stone blocks and a wide ditch; within the city, temples abounding in votive objects have been excavated.[5]

The great quantity of objects of foreign manufacture brought over by sea from the East and from Greece show Caere to have been an important coastal city though actually a few miles distant from the sea. Its ports were Alsium (near Palo), Pyrgis (Santa Severa), and Punicum (corresponding perhaps to Santa Marinella). The period of Caere's greatest prosperity coincides with the seventh and sixth century B.C.; during this time, unless we are being misled by the nature and quantity of the tombs, it must have been an extraordinarily rich and populous centre, perhaps one of the most splendid of the world as then known. And in spite of the long struggles with the Greeks and, later, its submission to the Romans, life at Caere continued to be fairly prosperous up to imperial times.

Between the Cerveteri and the Tarquinia area stand the trachytic hills of La Tolfa, on the slopes and at the foot of which were many small Etruscan villages that deserve careful exploration; the whole of this area is as yet practically untouched by the archaeologist's pickaxe.[6]

The story of Tarquinii (in Etruscan: *Tarχ(u)na-*) is quite different: it lived on throughout the Middle Ages and up to modern times as the town of Corneto, one of the most sizeable of Latian Tuscia and of the whole Patrimony of Saint Peter. The heated controversy on the exact location of Etruscan Tarquinii (some scholars believed it to be on the hill of Corneto, next to the necropolis) may now be considered definitely solved in favour of another hill, parallel to it, the *colle della Civita*, abounding in ancient remains. Nevertheless Corneto may be considered as the modern descendant of ancient Tarquinii, and, as a result, its name has now been changed to Tarquinia. Already in the eighteenth century, but especially in the first half of the nineteenth, the site was famous owing to the discovery of painted tombs. Local authorities, private individuals, and, later, the Italian State, conducted excavations on the site of the necropolis huddled on the hill of Corneto. Objects found in the tombs went to build up the two rich collections of the Counts Bruschi-Falgari and of the local Commune; they are now gathered together in the Museo Nazionale Tarquiniense housed in the Palazzo Vitelleschi. Within recent years the systematic excavation of the ancient city site has begun with very promising results: not only has the grandiose wall of squared stone blocks dating back to the fourth century B.C. been brought to light, but the foundations of a majestic Etruscan temple as well, the so-called *Ara della Regina* (the Queen's altar), to which belong two terracotta winged horses which may be considered as among the greatest masterpieces of Etruscan art (see plate 7).

Instead of the tumuli and the rock-hewn tombs of Caere, carved to represent the interiors of houses, the Tarquinii cemetery is famous for its painted underground chambers.

These are generally small and scattered throughout the hill of the necropolis. Of the very great number of which we have some knowledge, only twenty or so are still open, accessible, and in a good state of preservation: in recent years, the paintings of two of the most famous tombs (the Tomb of the Chariots and the Tomb of the Triclinium), in serious danger of being irreparably damaged, have been detached and remounted in the Museo Tarquiniense.[7] This unique collection of monuments is as interesting to the art historian as it is to the archaeologist. The life which the Etruscans led at the most felicitous period in their history (the majority of tombs date back to the end of the sixth and the beginning of the fifth century B.C.) vividly unfolds itself before our eyes in realistic scenes: banquets, dancing, and musical scenes; hunting, fishing; circus games with their accompanying crowds of spectators; all partly connected with funeral ceremonies. In the most recent tombs however (from the fourth to the second century) the paintings tend more and more to deal with the underworld, with its gods and its mythical dwellers, and especially the frightening demons that symbolize death wrenching the souls of the dead from the joys of existence and the love of dear persons, to direct them towards the dark and hopeless kingdom of the nether regions. Amongst the most characteristic monuments found in the Tarquinii necropolis, we should mention archaic stone reliefs roughly decorated in oriental styles, and sarcophagi belonging to a later period in stone or in terracotta with the reclining figures of the dead reproduced on the lids, and figured reliefs sculptured on the sides. There is also a remarkable number of inscriptions painted on the walls of tombs or carved on the sarcophagi; some of these are of substantial length and are important to the study of Etruscan epigraphy.

About twelve miles to the north-west of Tarquinii, on the banks of the Fiora, there stood another great city of southern Etruria: Vulci (in Etruscan, *Velχ-*). The ruins of this city and of its boundless cemeteries stretch along a vast uninhabited area between the two small villages of Montalto di Castro and Canino, in one of the most picturesque districts of the whole of central Italy. As we have already seen, the golden period of the Vulci excavations occurred during the first half of the nineteenth century, and was mainly due to the interest shown by the Prince of Canino. During the second half of the century the necropolis was again intensively explored on the initiative of Prince Torlonia, who owned much of the site. Objects discovered during the initial excavations may mostly be found scattered in the Vatican, the Louvre, and the Munich and British Museums, etc.; those that came to light in the course of the Torlonia excavations are still for the most part in private collections. A few tentative excavations have been sporadically undertaken by the state or under its control during the last few decades: these later findings are preserved in the Museum of Villa Giulia in Rome. The tumuli and hypogea of Vulci do not differ much from those of Caere or of Tarquinii: amongst the most remarkable is the 'François' tomb, named after its discoverer: its mural frescoes have been detached and are kept at the Torlonia Museum in Rome. They probably belong to the last phase of Etruscan artistic production (second to first century B.C.) and feature a number of portraits and mythical and historical scenes, the latter referring to events that occurred during the earliest phases of Etruscan history (the exploits of the Vipina brothers and of Macstrna). Amongst the outstanding monuments of the Vulci necropolis, there is a grandiose tumulus comprising an intricate network of underground chambers and passages, termed *la cuccumella* (the little coffee-pot). Vulci was an important centre for the marketing of bronze products: its cemeteries have in fact returned many bronze articles: weapons, tools, tripods, etc. But even more remarkable are the large quantities of painted vases that have been found, mainly imported from Greece. There are also many samples of curious sculptures.[8] This city too appears to have reached its highest peak of prosperity during the second half of the sixth century B.C.

So far we have dealt with the cities of coastal southern Etruria. The inland towns are, generally speaking, smaller and of minor historical importance; this fact has naturally caused them to have been rather neglected by archaeologists. Many areas in the vicinity of the lakes of Bracciano, Vico, and Bolsena may thus be considered to be still virtually unexplored.

Within Faliscan territory (the country between the Sabatine and Cimine mountains and the Tiber), finds of a certain importance have been made. This fraction of Etruscan land was mainly inhabited by Italic peoples or, more precisely, by peoples speaking a Latin influenced by Sabine. It appears however to have been linked to Etruria by strong political and cultural ties.[9] Its principal centre was Falerii (now Civita Castellana) in a well-protected and picturesque setting, with its many sanctuaries (rich in figured terracottas) and a vast necropolis. The Romans, who finally subdued the city in 241 B.C., wished to transfer it to another, at a short distance from it: Falerii Novi (Santa Maria di Fálleri), whose imposing crown of walls is still standing. Other minor Faliscan towns stood on the sites of the modern Narce, Vignanello, and Corchiano.

Amongst the more truly Etruscan centres of the interior, we should record Nepete (Nepi); Sutrium (Sutri, in Etruscan, *Suðri-*), a bone of contention between the Etruscans and the Romans during the fourth century, with imposing city walls and rock-tombs belonging to a late period; Horta (Orte), on a high and dominating site in the valley of the Tiber, on the borders of Faliscan and Sabine territory; Polimartium (Bomarzo). Of greater importance are the monuments found in a band of territory in the hinterland of Tarquinii and Vulci: this comprises a number of small cities each surrounded by a characteristic necropolis whose principal feature consists of tombs hewn out of the rock face and sculptured so as to imitate the façades of houses or temples (San Giuliano, Blera (Bieda), Norchia, Castel d'Asso and, further north, Sovana, the Suana of old).[10] A few other centres in this same band of territory appear to have flourished particularly during the archaic period, between the eighth and sixth centuries B.C., as far as can be surmised from their cemeteries: e.g. Vetralla, near the lake of Vico; Visentium, now Bisenzio, near Capodimonte, on the southern shores of the lake of Bolsena; they appear to cluster especially thickly along the higher course of the Fiora, north of Vulci: Ischia di Castro, Farnese, Poggio Buco (probably corresponding to Statonia),[11] Pitigliano. Tuscania, on the other hand, appears to have developed late; its chief feature is a number of sculptured sarcophagi of the Tarquinian type.

Within this inner zone of southern Etruria, there rose one of the most important Etruscan cities, considered by the ancients to be the spiritual centre of the whole nation: this is Volsinii (in Etruscan, *Velzna-*). In its neighbourhood, in fact, there stood the famous sanctuary of Voltumna (the *Fanum Voltumnae*), where the yearly gathering of the twelve Etruscan *populi* took place, accompanied by feasts and celebrations. Recent excavations have definitely proved that Volsinii corresponds to modern Bolsena, as the latter name implies (an earlier hypothesis connected it with Orvieto).[12] A powerful girdle of city-walls crowned the acropolis dominating the lake, upon which the remains of a three-celled temple have been found. The site of the Sanctuary is still unknown; it has been variously located at Orvieto, Montefiascone, etc., but it may well have stood in the immediate vicinity of the city.

And so we come to Orvieto, upon its mighty pedestal of red tufo stone, watching over the valley of the middle Tiber, about eight miles, as the crow flies, north-east of Bolsena. Its Etruscan origins have been confirmed by an imposing series of discoveries of sacred buildings and depositories made within the city enclosure, as also by the cemeteries that surround it, that include tombs both of the chamber and of the painted varieties (Sette Camini, Porrano). It appears that this great centre flourished especially between the sixth and the fourth centuries B.C. The first direct references to it, however, only go back to the Byzantine age (Procopius, *De bello Gothico*, II, 20), when the city is referred to as *Ourbibentos*, a name that may perhaps be related to *Urbs vetus* (whence Orvieto). Its true ancient name remains therefore a mystery, and Orvieto is the only city of Etruria of any size and importance whose ancient name is still unknown to us. For various reasons, carrying more or less weight, identifications with Etruscan Volsinii or with the Voltumna sanctuary must be rejected; for what it is worth, the hypothesis may be put forward of a connexion with the Salpinum mentioned by Livy, V, 31–2, as an autonomous and militarily powerful centre situated at not too great a distance from Volsinii.

Cities of Northern Etruria, Campania, and the Po Region

In passing from southern to northern Etruria, we should begin by mentioning those coastal sites that continue to the north of Vulci the constellation of cities dotted along the Tyrrhenian shore. At a short distance from the Lake of Orbetello, there rise the ruins of Cosa, with its famous girdle of polygonal walls, its temples, its public buildings, a town wholly built by the Romans as a military colony in the year 273 B.C.:[13] its Etruscan origins are as yet uncertain. Beyond Monte Argentario lies the small sea town of Tela-

mon (Talamone) where remains of a temple and a collection of votive objects have been found: they may be connected with the battle fought in this area by Romans and
Gauls in the year 225 B.C. Further inland, in the neighbourhood of Marsiliana d'Albegna, a large archaic necropolis
was discovered and excavated: it has been hypothetically
related to Caletra, whose site is unknown.[14] Other Etruscan cities in the same region with some remains of interest
to archaeology include Heba (the Magliano of to-day) and
Saturnia.[15] In the Grosseto area there are the ruins of a
city that was one of the greatest in Etruria: Rusellae
(Roselle). Here too, traces of a city wall, of a temple and of
a few tombs have been found, but the site awaits large-scale
systematic excavations.[16]

Still within the Grosseto area but nearer to the sea stood
Vetulonia (or Vetulonii, the Etruscan name of which was
Vetluna, Vatluna). The site of this famous city was sought
all along the Etruscan coastal belt, and was, till the last few
decades, the object of heated arguments between scholars
who placed it at Poggio Colonna and others who identified
it with Poggio Castiglioni near Massa Marittima. There
can no longer be any doubt that the first is the correct site:
there, in fact, remains of city walls and of houses have been
found. But the importance of the city is mainly revealed to
us by the vast necropolis that surrounds it. A systematic
excavation of the site was conducted with ample means
towards the end of the last century: the abundant material
found there became the nucleus of the collections now at
the Museo Archeologico in Florence. The most important
tombs are marked by stone circles or are in the shape of
tumuli, and the funerary furnishings, consisting for the
most part of bronze objects, have been attributed to the
period stretching from the eighth to the sixth century B.C.
After this period, as far as we can tell from archaeological
data, the city must have fallen into rapid and complete

decline, for there remain no traces of life after the beginning of the Roman age.[17]

Further to the north there stood Populonia (or Populonium, the Etruscan form of which was *Pupluna*, *Fufluna*) on the site of Porto Baratti, near Piombino. It is the only important Etruscan city built right on the sea shore. Its discovery is quite recent. Great excavations have been conducted in its necropolis since the beginning of this century under the direction of the *Soprintendenza dell' Etruria*, and are still continuing. The most characteristic sepulchres of Populonia are great tumuli comprising chambers with false cupolas or vaulted ceilings; within these chambers objects have been found dating from the archaic period up to the late sixth century.[18] An important feature of the site is the presence round the city of vast fields of iron slag, the result of the smelting of iron ores extracted from the Elba mines in Etruscan and Roman times. For Populonia was one of the most important iron centres of the ancient world. The earliest tombs were found under the slag: this is now being removed and made to undergo a new industrial process of extraction with excellent results. More traces of Etruscan mining activity may be seen on the slopes of the metal-bearing hills nearby, where numerous ancient shafts have been discovered.

Let us now examine the inland cities, found scattered mainly along the banks of large rivers. Here, we should first mention Clusium (Chiusi; the Etruscan name was in all probability *Clevsin-*, but the town also appears under the name of *Camars*). This city, famous for its part in the history of both Etruria and Rome, never ceased to be an important centre throughout the Middle Ages and up to modern times. This fact explains the almost complete disappearance of all Etruscan buildings on the one hand, and on the other, the early and frequent discoveries made in the vicinity. A characteristic feature of Clusium and of the surrounding region is the presence of a large number of cemeteries distributed near the city and neighbouring towns (Pania, Poggio Gaiella, Poggio Renzo, Dolciano, Sarteano, Chianciano, Città della Pieve, Montepulciano). All these small towns possessed a substantially similar type of civilization: their presence shows that the territory was occupied by a number of small inhabited centres under the aegis of the metropolis. Excavations, made at varying times according to the site, have brought to light much material now mostly kept at the Museo Archeologico of Florence and the Museo Civico of Chiusi (a small number of objects, belonging to the late Casuccini Collection, may be seen in the Palermo museum). The earliest cultural phase of Clusium is characterized by cremation tombs and the presence of so-called 'canopics', i.e. ossuaries with a lid in the shape of a human head and roughly imitating the human form. A few chamber tombs in the environs of Chiusi have painted scenes from daily life, as in Tarquinii, and largely belong to the fifth century B.C. Stone cippi and cinerary urns decorated with reliefs of banquets, games, funerals, etc. are typical of the phase that stretched from the end of the sixth to the end of the fifth century B.C. This artistic production is representative of the most flourishing period in the history of the town, a period that coincides with the beginning of the decadence of the coastal cities. We may remember, in fact, that tradition ascribes to the end of the sixth century the reign of King Porsenna, the attacker and, according to some sources, the conqueror of Rome, indicating a period of expansion in the history of Clusium. Later, the end of the fifth century and the beginning of the fourth witnessed the production in and around Clusium of sarcophagi and funerary statues; to the Hellenistic period, on the other hand, there belongs a rich collection of small cinerary urns of painted terracotta, with the dead person's image on the lid and mythological reliefs on the front.[19]

Perusia (Perugia) was one more great centre of ancient Etruria destined to acquire an ever-growing importance through the centuries of the Roman Empire, the Middle Ages, and the modern era. This continuity of life was not sufficient however to erase all traces of the most glorious period in the life of the Etruscan city, a period that lasted from the third to the first century B.C., and thus coincided with the final phase of the Etruscan civilization. The many remains include long tracts of the city wall built with large squared blocks of travertine, the grandiose arched gateway that came to be named after Augustus, and the handsomely sculptured design of the Porta Marzia, adorned with sculptured deities which, with humanistic foresight, the Renaissance architect Sangallo succeeded in incorporating into one of the bastions of his Rocca Paolina. As the main centre of etruscological studies during the nineteenth century, Perugia was the subject of intense research on its urban and suburban monuments; occasional discoveries led to the creation of the valuable Etruscan collection in its Museo Civico. So far however, there has been no organic plan for the exploration of its foundations and its cemeteries. A monument particularly worthy of notice is the Volumni Hypogeum in the Palazzone necropolis, quite near the town: a tomb hewn out of the rock and consisting of several chambers containing reliefs and cinerary urns with figured decorations and Etruscan and Latin inscriptions belonging to the first century B.C. Typical of Perugia and its surrounding area are the small travertine and terracotta urns decorated in relief. Amongst the numerous inscriptions which may be seen in the Perugia Museum, there is a cippus, perhaps a boundary-stone, inscribed with the longest Etruscan epigraphic text on stone in our possession.[20]

The role of Perugia as a centre of research on ancient Etruria during the nineteenth century was previously filled in the eighteenth century by Cortona (in Etruscan, *Curtun-*).

Here isolated discoveries and excavations were made in the neighbourhood of the town. Of the old city there remain a few traces of its walls; of the cemeteries surrounding the town, isolated tumuli (locally known as 'melons') and a circular mausoleum of later date, known as '*la Tanella di Pitagora*' (Pythagoras' little den). In the Museo dell' Accademia Cortonese is preserved a famous bronze candelabrum with rich figured decorations (see plate 19A).[21] At Arretium (Arezzo) sections of the famous brick wall protecting the city have been unearthed, and a part of the old Etruscan city level may still be recognized; here, during the sixteenth century, were found the Chimaera (see plate 16A) and a bronze statue of Minerva. We should also mention the figured terracottas in Hellenistic style discovered in the course of the exploration of the city walls and now kept at the Archaeological Museum in Florence. Another important Etruscan centre was situated on the hill of Faesulae (Fiesole) dominating the valley of the Arno and the Florentine plain. The excavation of this vast archaeological site has brought to light the foundations of a three-cell temple and of an altar in front of it, together with a fine stretch of city wall. Typical of Fiesole are stone funerary steles in the shape of a horseshoe with figured reliefs, many of which are kept at the local Museo Civico.[22] The Florence site, though already inhabited in archaic times (as shown by some iron age graves discovered in the heart of the city) only re-emerged as a centre of life during the Roman period.

We should finally mention the city of Volaterrae (Volterra, in Etruscan *Velaδri*) that stands upon a high hill dominating the valley of the Cecina. Like the other centres of northern Etruria it survived the end of the ancient world, though in medieval and modern times the city has occupied a far more reduced area than the one indicated by its powerful girdle of Etruscan walls. Of the old city's monuments, the gate known as the *Porta dell' Arco*, embellished with sculptured heads of Etruscan deities, is perhaps the most remarkable. Like Cortona, Volterra was a centre of etruscological research during the eighteenth century, when excavations of its tombs were begun, excavations that have often been taken up again in brief and successful campaigns. The greater part of the archaic necropolis of the city was destroyed in the huge landslide of the *Balze*. Volterra's most characteristic yield belongs to the later phases of the Etruscan civilization; it consists of alabaster cinerary urns with decorations in high-relief, a large number of which may be seen in the local Museo Civico Guarnacci.[23]

To this review of the principal characteristics of the cities of Etruria proper should be added a mention, however brief, of the Etruscan centres in Campania and the Po valley. The capital of the Etruscan dominion in Campania was Capua (known also as Volturnum) which later became one of the greatest and most populous cities of both the Italic and the Roman worlds. It stood upon the present site of Santa Maria di Capua Vetere. Amongst the most characteristic Etruscan remains found at Capua are the architectural terracottas and votive statues now gathered together in the local Museo Campano.[24] One of the most important finds was a terracotta tile bearing a lengthy Etruscan inscription, now in Berlin. Other Etruscan centres in Campania were Nola (in Oscan *Núvla* and in Etruscan *Nula*), Acerrae (Acerra), Pompeii (Pompei), and Salernum (Salerno).

The capital of northern Etruria was in all likelihood Bononia (Bologna, in Etruscan *Felsina*), a city founded in archaic times during the period of the 'Villanovan' iron culture, and conquered by the Etruscans towards the end of the sixth century. The very abundant material found in its Etruscan tombs (amongst which are some typical sculptured steles) is kept at the town's Museo Civico.[25] An interesting Etruscan city in the vicinity of Bologna was discovered in the valley of the upper Reno near the modern village of Marzabotto (its ancient name was probably Misa); it was built in chess-board pattern with paved streets and a fairly evolved water system; on the acropolis, the foundations of a number of sacred buildings may still be seen. Its excavation has yielded large quantities of material dating back to the fifth and fourth century B.C. and kept in the local Museo Aria, though the collection was much mutilated during the 1939 war.[26] The sea town of Spina was also important; its necropolis, rich in Greek vases, has been identified and excavated within the last decades: the funerary furnishings of its tombs have been used to create the new Archaeological Museum of Ferrara.[27] Other Etruscan cities to the north of the Apennines were Ariminum (Rimini, probably from an Etruscan *Arimna-*), Caesena (Cesena, probably cognate to the Etruscan *Keisna*, a family name found in Bologna), Mantua (Mantova, in Etruscan *Manδva-*?), Mutina (Modena), Parma and the city which the Romans rechristened Placentia (Piacenza); these towns all present merely sporadic evidence of Etruscan occupation, for they were early overrun by Celtic invaders.

NOTES

1. As a work of reference on the topography, history, and archaeology of the cities and sites of Etruria, G. Dennis' *Cities and Cemeteries of Etruria*,[3] 1883, would be difficult to replace, for its descriptions, its erudition and its considerable literary merits. See also A. Neppi Modona, *A guide to Etruscan Antiquities*, Florence, 1954; H. Nissen, *Italische Landeskunde*, 1883–1902; A. Solari, *Topografia Storica della Etruria*, I–IV, 1915–20, and the short introductory chapters to the collections, divided according to cities and territories, of inscriptions in the *Corpus Inscriptionum Etruscarum*.

2. On the Rome of the Etruscan period, with special reference to the archaeological data, see I. Scott Ryberg, *An Archaeological Record of Rome from the Seventh to the Second Century B.C.*, 1940.

3. The translation is from G. Dennis' *Cities and Cemeteries o Etruria*, 1883, i, p. 16.

4. There is no comprehensive work on Veii; particulars may be had in *Notizie degli Scavi*, 1919, pp. 8 ff.; 1929, pp. 325 ff.; *Le Arti*, i (xxvii), pp. 402 ff.; ii (xviii), pp. 17 ff.; *Monumenti Antichi della Accademia d' Italia*, xl, 1944, col. 177 ff.; *Bollettino d'Arte*, 1952, pp. 147 ff. Cf. also M. Pallottino, *La scuola di Vulca*, 1945.

5. On Caere, cf. R. Mengarelli, in *Studi Etruschi*, i, 1927, pp. 145 ff.; ix, 1935. pp. 83 ff.; x, 1936, pp. 77 ff.; xi, 1937, pp. 77 ff.; M. Pallottino, *La necropoli di Cerveteri (Itinerari dei Musei e Monumenti d'Italia)*², 1950. A series of accounts of Mengarelli's excavations are in course of publication in *Monumenti Antichi dei Lincei*.

6. Cf. S. Bastianelli, *Il territorio tolfetano nell'antichità*, in *Studi Etruschi*, xvi, 1942, pp. 229 ff.

7. M. Pallottino, *Tarquinia (Monumenti Antichi della Accademia dei Lincei)*, 1937; P. Romanelli, *Tarquinia. La Necropoli e il Museo (Itinerari dei Musei e Monumenti d'Italia*, 1940). For the most recent discoveries, see *Bolletino d'Arte*, 1948, pp. 54 ff.; *Notizie degli Scavi*, 1948, pp. 133 ff.

8. S. Gsell, *Fouilles de Voulci*, 1891; F. Messerschmidt, *Die Necropolen von Vulci*, 1930.

9. On the Faliscans: W. Deecke, *Die Falisker*, 1888; V. Pisani, *Le Lingue dell'Italia antica oltre il latino*, 1953, pp. 316 ff. For archaeological remains belonging to Faliscan territory (mostly kept at the Villa Giulia Museum in Rome), see especially A. Della Seta, *Museo di Villa Giulia*, 1918, pp. 37 ff.

10. G. Rosi, *Sepulchral Architecture as Illustrated by the Rock Façades of Central Etruria*, in *Journal of Roman Studies*, xv, 1925, p. 1 ff.; xvii, 1927, pp. 59 ff.; H. Koch, E. v. Mercklin, C. Weickert, *Bieda*, in *Mitteil. des deutschen Arch. Instituts Rom*, xxx, 1915, pp. 161 ff.; A. Gargana, *La necropoli rupestre di S. Giuliano (Monumenti Antichi dell' Accademia dei Lincei*, 1929); R. Bianchi Bandinelli, *Sovana*, 1929.

11. G. Matteucci, *Poggio Buco. The Necropolis of Statonia*, 1951.

12. R. Bloch, *Volsinies étrusque. Essai historique et topographique*, in *Mélanges de l'École Française de Rome*, 1947, pp. 99 ff.; *Volsinies étrusque et romaine. Nouvelles découvertes archéologique et épigraphique*, in *Mélanges*, etc., 1950, pp. 53 ff. For Orvieto: P. Perali, *Orvieto etrusca*, 1928; S. Puglisi, *Studi e ricerche su Orvieto etrusca*, 1934.

13. As shown by recent excavations undertaken by the American Academy in Rome: see F. E. Brown, *Cosa, I. History and Topography*, in *Memoirs of the American Academy in Rome*, xx, 1951.

14. A. Minto, *Marsigliana d'Albegna*, 1921.

15. A. Minto, *Per la topografia di Heba etrusca* in *Studi Etruschi*, IX, 1935, pp. 11 ff.; *Saturnia etrusca e romana* (*Monumenti Antichi dell' Accademia dei Lincei*, XXX, 1925).

16. R. Bianchi Bandinelli, *Roselle* (in *Atene e Roma*, VI, 1925, pp. 35 ff.).

17. I. Falchi, *Vetulonia*, 1891; *Studi Etruschi*, V, 1931, pp. 13 ff.; XXI, 1950–1, pp. 291 ff.

18. A. Minto, *Populonia. La necropoli arcaica*, 1922; *Populonia*, 1943.

19. R. Bianchi Bandinelli, *Clusium* (*Monumenti Antichi della R. Accademia dei Lincei*), 1925.

20. C. Shaw, *Etruscan Perugia*, 1939 (to be consulted with caution); A. M. Pierotti, M. Calzoni, *Ricerche su Perugia etrusca: la città e la necropoli urbana*, in *Studi Etruschi*, XXI, 1950–1, pp. 275 ff.; for the territory of Perugia, cf. L. Banti, in *Studi Etruschi*, X, 1936, pp. 97 ff.

21. A. Neppi Modona, *Cortona etrusca e romana*, 1925.

22. F. Magi, *Contributi alla conoscenza di Fiesole etrusca* (in *Atene e Roma*, X, 1930, pp. 83 ff.).

23. L. Consortini, *Volterra nell'antichità*, 1940 (to be consulted with caution).

24. J. Heurgon, *Recherches sur l'histoire, la religion et la civilisation de Capoue préromaine*, 1942.

25. A. Grenier, *Bologne villanovienne et étrusque*, 1912; P. Ducati, *Storia di Bologna, I tempi antichi*, 1928.

26. E. Brizio, *Guida alle antichità della villa e del Museo di Marzabotto*, 1886, reprinted in 1928; P. E. Arias, *Considerazioni sulla città etrusca a Pian di Misano* (*Marzabotto*), in *Atti e Memorie della Deput. di Storia Patria per le Provincie di Romagna*, III, 1953.

27. S. Aurigemma, *Il R. Museo di Spina*, 1935.

(A) Tumulus in the necropolis of Caere. *Cerveteri*

(B) Gate of Etruscan type at Falerii Novi. *S. Maria di Falleri*

I

(A) *Above*: Sepulchral urn in the form of a temple with winged goddess and panthers; from Chiusi. *British Museum*

(B) *Right*: Female figure on the lid of a Canopic ossuary; c. 600 B.C. Chiusi, *Museo Civico*

2

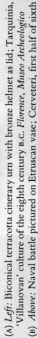

(A) *Left*: Biconical terracotta cinerary urn with bronze helmet as lid; Tarquinia, 'Villanovan' culture of the eighth century B.C. *Florence, Museo Archeologico*

(B) *Above*: Naval battle pictured on Etruscan vase; Cerveteri, first half of sixth century B.C. *Paris, Louvre*

(A) Aged married couple portrayed on the lid of a small terracotta urn. *Volterra. Museo Guarnacci*

(B) Lid of urn from Volterra with figure of the deceased man. *British Museum*

4

Head of the Apollo of Veii: Ionic-Etruscan art of the fifth century B.C.
Rome, Villa Giulia

(A) Lid of sarcophagus from Tarquinia
British Museum

(B) Alabaster statue of woman holding a bronze gilded dove; Vulci, first quarter of the sixth century B.C.
British Museum

6

Yoked winged horses in terracotta, part of the frontal decoration of a temple;
fourth–third century B.C. *Tarquinia, Museo Nazionale*

(A) *Left*: Terracotta statuette of seated woman; from Cerveteri. *British Museum*
(B) *Above*: Archaic mask, from an antefix at Cerveteri. *British Museum*

(A) *Left: Head in terracotta, showing Hellenistic influence. Vatican*
(B) *Above: Daemon's mask in terracotta. Orvieto, Faïna Collection*

Sepulchral urn in the form of a man (life-size);
from Chianciano. *British Museum*

(A) Two antefixes mounted on cornice of roof: from Lanuvio. *British Museum*

(B) Dancing scene; low relief on an urn from Chiusi. *British Museum*

Bronze statue of Mars found at Todi; fourth century B.C. *Vatican*

Terracotta fragment of the statue of a young god (the 'Apollo' of Falerii).
Rome, Villa Giulia

(A) Wedding scene; relief on a small urn. *Chiusi, Museo Civico*

(B) Funeral scene; relief on a cippus from Chiusi.
Munich, Museum Antiker.Kleinkunst

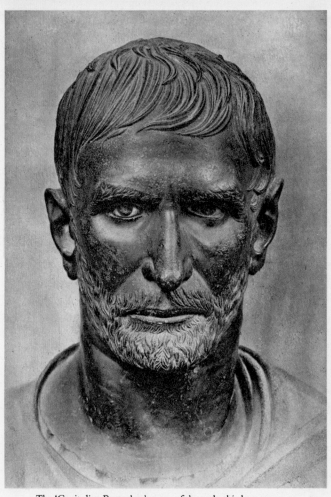

The 'Capitoline Brutus', a bronze of the early third century B.C.
Rome, Palazzo dei Conservatori

(A) The Chimaera of Arezzo. *Florence, Museo Archeologico*

(B) Reclining man; bronze of the archaic period. *British Museum*

16

Bronze statue of Aule Meteli, known as the 'Orator'.
Florence, Museo Archeologico

(A) *Left:* Warrior with cuirass; bronze statuette of the fifth century B.C. *British Museum*

(B) *Above:* Bronze statuette of haruspex. *Vatican*

(C) *Right:* Bronze statuette of a war-god. *Florence, Museo Archeologico*

18

(A) *Above: Bronze lamp. Cortona, Museo dell' Accademia Etrusca*
(B) *Right: Bronze situla from the Certosa. Bologna, Museo Civico*

Nobleman seated before the statue of a goddess; painted plaque from Cerveteri.
Paris, Louvre

Mythological scene; painted plaque from Cerveteri, sixth century B.C.
Paris, Louvre

Athletic games with spectators: detail of a mural painting in the Tomb of the Monkey at Chiusi

Jugglers and musicians: detail of a mural painting in the Tomb of the Monkey at Chiusi

(B) Piper: detail of mural painting in the Tomb of the Triclinium at Tarquinia. *Tarquinia, Museo Nazionale*

(A) The daemon Tuchulcha: detail of a mural painting in the Tomba dell'Orco at Tarquinia

24

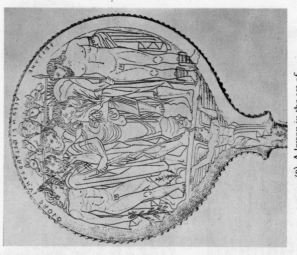

(B) A lesson in the art of divination, from a mirror found at Tuscania. *Florence, Museo Archeologico*

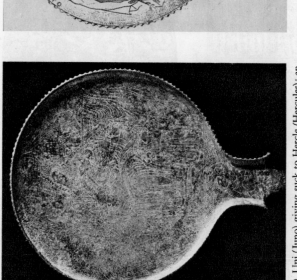

(A) Uni (Juno) giving suck to Hercle (Hercules): an Etruscan myth illustrated on a mirror found at Volterra. *Florence, Museo Archeologico*

(A) *Top:* Large gold fibula from Vulci.
British Museum
(B) *Left:* A gold bracelet from Tarquinia.
British Museum
(C) *Right:* Ornamental gold disc.
British Museum

(A), (B), (C) Portions of three gold necklaces. *British Museum*

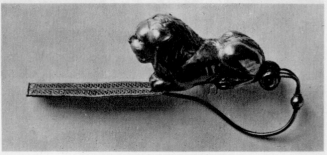

(D) Gold fibula with lion. *British Museum*

Large gold fibula of the 'orientalizing' period (seventh century B.C.), found at Cerveteri. *Vatican*

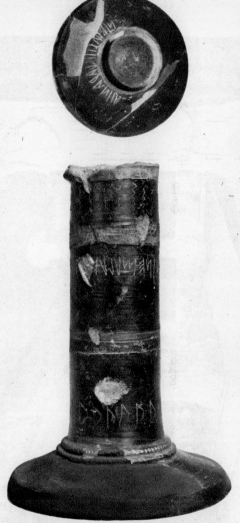

(A) Bucchero dish with Etruscan inscription found on the slopes of the
Capitoline Hill in Rome. *Rome, Musei Capitolini*
(B) Fragment of a sixth century B.C. bucchero cup found at Veii.
Rome, Villa Giulia

29

Cerveteri, Tomb of the Stucchi: interior showing alcoves and pillars

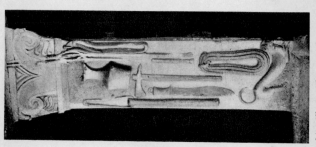

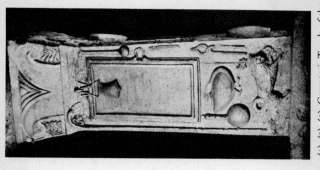

(A), (B), (C) Cerveteri, Tomb of the Stucchi: pillars with painted stucco representations of household objects, etc.

31

The Vetulonia fascis, with two-bladed axe and iron rods.
Florence, Museo Archeologico

THE POLITICAL AND SOCIAL ORGANIZATION OF ETRURIA

The Etruscan Constitution

THUS the cities of old Etruria give us the picture of a rich and interesting life, whether they show no more than a few limestone blocks above the surface of the ground, the dark mouths of their sepulchral caves well hidden in the wild Mediterranean scrub; or whether they have been unearthed and made accessible to the modern tourist. It is a picture that may reach grandiose proportions, worthy of being placed on the same level as the most famous ruins of the East, Greece, and Rome. And the question that immediately comes to the mind of the sightseer the first time he visits these monuments or of the scholar trained in the examination and investigation of ancient buildings, is the same: how can we become a little more intimately acquainted with the way of life and the civilization of the builders of these monuments and tombs?

There are ruins in the world that have come to light as if they were expected, as if carrying a passport: they are the monumental confirmation of events in the history of past civilizations already known through the songs of poets or the accounts of historians. We need only think of the grandiose buildings of Mycenae, first brought to light by Schliemann's eager pickaxe, when all around him spoke of Atreus, of Agamemnon, Clytaemnestra, and Aegisthus; even though the figures of these Homeric heroes had been relegated by official science, often unjustifiably, as we are now beginning to see, amongst the shades of small deities made human, or to the realms of poetic fantasy; even though the protagonists of the Trojan war were to be considered as no more than late and barbarized descendants of magnificent kings buried deep amongst the treasures and splendours of Cretan art in their Mycenaean tombs! When faced with such almost familiar ruins, the confident scholar does not hesitate to put forward hypotheses and utter names of places and persons. Only quite recently have the ruins of a palace with vases and tablets of inscribed terracotta been found at Koryphasion in western Peloponnesus in the area of ancient Pylos: and there was naturally no hesitation in referring to it as 'Nestor's palace', on Homer's authority.

At other times, however, as in the case of the *nuraghi* of Sardinia or the megalithic temples of prehistoric Malta, the ruins appear obscure and mysterious. Tradition, both poetical and historical, has been interrupted; it is practically useless to question stones on which no written word exists. The monuments of ancient Etruria, despite their relatively recent age and the thousand bonds that unite them to the contemporary civilizations of Greece and republican Rome, are closer to this second class of archaeological remains than to the first. This is perhaps why they exert such a strong fascination and such a desire to probe further, if only in the imagination, into the various aspects of the public and private life of their builders.

The problems concerning the political and social life of the Etruscans are many, controversial, and often still unresolved.[1] The only information we have on the subject we owe almost exclusively to indirect references in ancient writers and to the recording of events in which the Etruscans came into contact with the Romans. With the help of these data, scholars are generally agreed on a picture of Etruria in which (in historical times at least) political sovereignty coincided with the city and its surrounding territory, as it did in the Greek πόλις or in the medieval commune. It also appears that the city states were united permanently in a kind of league or federation with a common centre, and a predominantly religious and economic, perhaps even political, character, but without affecting the independence of each individual state. As for the internal political and social organization of the various cities, it is known that the aristocratic class was mainly concerned in government and that there was a gradual evolution from the monarchy of historical times to the republican oligarchy of Hellenistic times. These fundamental data are naturally accompanied by many more elements but their interpretation is a good deal less easy.

It is only quite recently that answers to some of these questions have been sought in monuments: their principal features (as for instance the characteristics of tombs), their figured decorations, their inscriptions, all help to integrate the fragmentary data provided by tradition. Naturally the inscriptions would be of decisive importance to our knowledge of Etruscan political institutions were we able to interpret them wholly and convincingly. Nevertheless the present state of our knowledge of the Etruscan language (an outline of which will be found in the latter part of this volume) allows inscriptions, and particularly funerary inscriptions, to play a most important role in the reconstruction of Etruscan political and social life.[2] It is only natural that many difficult problems arise from the study and comparison of literary evidence and monumental sources and it is to these problems that we shall devote most of the following pages, since they form the most interesting part of our subject.

The League

First and foremost, what exactly do we know of the Etruscan 'league'? The term is a modern one; ancient writers speak of the *duodecim populi*, of the *duodecim populi Etruriae*, of δώδεχα ἡγεμονίαι (Dionysius, VI, 75) or more simply of *Etruria*, or *omnis Etruria*. The fact that the great cities of Etruria proper were twelve in number (to which corresponded a like number in northern Etruria and in Campania), has in all probability a ritual significance: if we take account of the close cultural relations existing between Etruria and Asiatic Ionia during the sixth century, the possibility comes to mind that the Etruscan league had as a model the league of the twelve cities of Ionia.[3] That it was a real and political institution as well as an ideal unit may be deduced from the study of the references to the twelve Etruscan states found in ancient authors (see especially Livy, IV, 23; V, I; X, 16, etc.); reference is made, for example, to consultative meetings held by the Etruscan states and their heads (*principes*) at the *Fanum Voltumnae*. Pareti very justly pointed out that such evidence is not sufficient to prove the continuity or the strong suprastatal power of the presumed Etruscan federal union. If we admit the existence of annual pan-Etruscan festivals and games at the sanctuary of Voltumna (similar to the Pan-Hellenic games at Ephesus, Olympia, Delphi, and Corinth) it would be perfectly justifiable to suppose that only exceptional political circumstances such as the threat of Rome would have induced the representatives of the various Etruscan states to meet in consultation at the national shrine and even form a political and military coalition.[4]

There are also references that seem to point to a certain continuity in this institution and to a formal dependence on it of the various single states: e.g. a passage in Servius (*ad Aen.*, VIII, 475), which states that Etruria had twelve *lucumones*, or kings, one of whom was at the head of the others; and from Livy's references (I, 8, 2; V, I) to the election of a lictor for the *fasces*, and to the election of a *sacerdos* at the *Fanum Voltumnae* on the occasion of the meetings of the

Etruscan states. Our assessment of the Etruscan league wholly depends upon the reliability of the above statements. It is interesting to notice that in two of the passages the word king is mentioned; they must therefore refer, as far as we can tell, to a period earlier than the fifth century B.C. On the other hand the two passages in Livy mention an elected head of the alliance of Etruscan states, a personage who at the end of the fifth century (i.e. at the time of the conflict between Veii and Rome) was designated by the title of *sacerdos*, and therefore invested with eminently religious powers.

A few Latin inscriptions of the imperial age (during which ancient Etruscan institutions and titles still formally subsisted) give us the title *praetor Etruriae* accompanied at times by the name of a city in the locative case (*Tarquiniis, Pisis*). This title also appears in the form *praetor XV populorum*, i.e. of the Etruscan national community which in Roman times seems to have been increased by three cities. This is however a collegiate magistrature [5] and it is doubtful therefore whether it can be identified with the supreme head of the league. We should rather think of it as designating the representatives of each state to the federal councils, or the magistrates connected to the league itself, rather like the *principes* and the *lictores* recalled in the above-mentioned passages in Livy.

Amongst the various offices filled by Etruscan personages and recorded in Etruscan inscriptions, we know of the following:

(i) *zilaδ amce meχl rasnal* (*C.I.E.* 5360 – Tarquinii);
(ii) *zilaδ . . . rasnas* (*C.I.E.* 5472 – Tarquinii);
(iii) *meχlum rasneas clevsinsl . . . zilaχnve* (*C.I.E.* 5093 – Orvieto).

These expressions are substantially identical, as the nominal formula *zilaδ amce* 'he was "zilath"' corresponds to the

verbal one *zilaχnve* 'he filled the office of "zilath" '. Thanks
to the celebrated passage in Dionysius (1, 30, 3), where the
Etruscans are designated by their national name of *Rasenna*,
we know that *rasna* signifies 'Etruscan, Etruria'. On the
other hand, the magistrature designated by the word *zilaδ*,
apparently the highest office in the Etruscan republics, corresponds very probably with the praetorship of the Romans.
Thus there appears to be an obvious correspondence between the title *zilaδ meχl rasnal* and *praetor Etruriae;* a
correspondence that probably extends also to the name of
the city in which or on behalf of which the office was filled,
as in the case of inscription *C.I.E.* 5093, where the word
clevsinsl. may perhaps stand for Chiusi and would be the
equivalent of the expressions *Tarquiniis, Pisis* of the Latin
inscriptions mentioned above.[6]

The word *meχl, meχlum* still remains to be explained; it
has often been connected with the *meδlum* that appears in
other Etruscan texts and variously interpreted as 'league' or
'people'. In the Etruscan manuscript of the Zagreb mummy,
meδlum is found next to the word *spur*, which seems to
indicate 'city', in a passage which lists the institutions for
the benefit of which the religious ceremonies were performed, just as in the Umbrian text of the Gubbio Tablets.
We should also notice the fact that several names of offices
are accompanied by the terms *spureni, spurana* indicating
that the office was a city magistracy. It is probable therefore
that *spur* was the technical term for the single city-states
and that it is exactly rendered by the Latin *populus*; whereas
meδlum or *meχl* concerns a larger entity, perhaps the Etruscan league or nation. It should perhaps be equated with
nomen, in the Latin or Umbrian sense of this word, i.e.
the race or spiritual entity of the nation.

In conclusion, the various data in our possession are not
sufficient to allow us to form an exact notion of what the
Etruscan league was, or to outline, however briefly, its

history. If the accounts of the supremacy of one of the ancient sovereign states over the others are not wholly baseless, we may think of a close alliance of the southern Etrurian centres that flourished in archaic times under the hegemony of one or other of their number; the important role played by Tarquinii in the primitive legends of Etruria may lead us to infer a period of Tarquinian hegemony. Later, this ancient unity may have assumed the character of a religious confederation, with games and national gatherings at the sanctuary of Voltumna, near Volsinii. The election of an annual supreme magistrate is perhaps a survival of the supreme sovereignty of one head over the others. We know from Livy that in the fifth century the future king of Veii was a candidate for the election (thus implicitly confirming the importance of the national magistracy); he was however defeated. This institution may be compared – though the comparison is wholly hypothetical – to the growth of the Germanic Empire from the feudal sovereignty of the German kings during the high Middle Ages to the autonomy of the regional electorates of modern times.

The Peoples

At the time of Etruria's contacts with Rome, despite the concept of national unity and the actual existence of federal institutions, the political structure of the Etruscan nation consisted chiefly of a system of small regional states having at their head whichever city dominated them by its size and wealth. We do not know what conditions reigned during the archaic period, but the coexistence of various centres of great importance at short distances from each other (e.g. Veii, Caere, Tarquinii, Vulci), with their own sovereigns, their own characteristics and customs, remind us of the fragmentary nature that characterized the political system of the archaic Greek πόλις. As time went on the single sovereign cities must have gradually increased their territory, subjugating and incorporating rival cities perhaps, as was the case in the early history of Rome. As a result, a system of small regional states was arrived at, until the Romans came to impose their hegemony and, finally, political unity from the outside.

The Etruscan regional state was dependent in all its essentials on its central city; the latter represented something more than a mere capital: state and city were one both in name and in structure. *Populus*, the probable equivalent of the Etruscan *spur*,[7] was synonymous in some of its meanings at least with *urbs* and πόλις. The names of the *populi* were the same as those of the inhabitants of the city: thus we have Veians, Tarquinians, Caeretans, Clusians, etc. It is quite possible that in the course of the formation of regional states, certain conquered cities may have preserved an appearance of autonomy or may have contracted alliances with their conquerors: this may be the case of certain important towns like Sutrium or Nepete with respect to Veii, in whose sphere of influence they were at the time of the Roman conquest. There is also the possibility that the colonies may have retained some form of dependence on their city of origin, as in the Etruscan expansion towards Campania and the north. As far as we are aware however, the principle of autonomy and division must also have prevailed in the political constitutions of the Etruscan dominions in southern and northern Italy.

The great cities whose magnificent ruins still remain for us to see must therefore have been the centres of political and cultural life in Etruria. Tradition tells us that they were twelve in number; it is not until the days of Rome that we hear of fifteen peoples. Which were these cities? At the time of the Roman conquest the following were certainly counted amongst them: Caere (Cerveteri), Tarquinii (Tarquinia-Corneto), Vulci, Rusellae (Roselle), Vetulonia,

Populonia, Volsinii (Bolsena), Clusium (Chiusi), Arretium (Arezzo), Perusia (Perugia), Volaterrae (Volterra). To these may perhaps be added Faesulae (Fiesole), Cortona, or Salpinum. Veii had already been conquered and annexed by Rome at the beginning of the fourth century B.C. It is quite possible that a few minor centres were still autonomous during the fourth and third century B.C., as the existence of coins bearing the names of Peithesa, Echetia, and other unidentified cities seems to indicate. Centres that flourished in archaic times, as for instance Visentium (Bisenzio), Marsigliana d'Albegna (Caletra?), and Vetulonia itself, soon fell into decadence, while other cities developed only towards the end of the Etruscan civilization, when Etruria was under Roman domination: e.g. Siena, Pisa, Florence, and Luni.

There is no evidence of the stage that preceded the organization into cities, and we are thus unable to ascertain what political system originally existed in the prehistoric settlements of Etruria. Indirect references in ancient authors and the analogy of the primitive constitution of Rome lead us to the conclusion that the cities were divided into tribes, probably three in number, which in their turn were each divided into four *curiae* (Servius, *ad Aen.*, x, 202). Apart from these few surmises we are left in utter darkness as to the organization of the cities and of their dependent territories.

The Primitive Monarchy

The conditions reigning in Etruscan cities during the Roman age, on the eve of the great social upheavals that marked the political life of Italy during the first century B.C., influenced to a certain extent the judgement ancient authors had formed on Etruscan society, as recorded in their writings. The cities seem to have been governed by aristocratic oligarchies, and these were only sporadically and temporarily replaced by other classes of society. The oligarchies governed through magistrates designated at times by the name of *principes*. This tradition is for the most part confirmed by the existence of large and wealthy family tombs enclosing numerous bodies, with inscriptions referring to members of a few closely related families, in particular epitaphs listing the titles of various temporary and collegiate offices, according to a system proper to oligarchic republics.

Such a state of affairs cannot however have existed in Etruria during the earlier centuries of its history. Many sources refer to the existence of kings in Etruscan cities. The term *lucumo* (Lat. *lucumo, lucmo*; Gk. Λοχόμων, Λουχούμων; Etruscan, probably *lauχume, lauχme, luχume*) at times forms part of the name of Etruscan personages, as in the case of the King of Rome, Tarquinius Priscus; but it is generally used as a common name to designate the Etruscan chiefs. Virgil's commentator, Servius, on one occasion names lucumones the magistrates in charge of the *curiae* of the city of Mantua (*ad Aen.*, x, 202); on other occasions he identifies them explicitly with the kings of the cities (*ad Aen.*, ii, 278; viii, 65, 475). Basing himself on the aristocratic conception of the Etruscan state, K. O. Müller assumed that the lucumones must have been the eldest sons of noble families and many scholars have echoed his assumption. But there is nothing to warrant the assumption that early conditions in Etruria were mirrored in those current during the Roman era, nor is there anything to preclude that the term lucumo did refer to the Etruscan kings of the archaic period, according to the several and explicit statements made by Servius on this matter. It is thus unnecessary to seek, like S. P. Cortsen, the Etruscan word for 'king' in the root *purt* – and in the title *pursna, *purtsna, purδne*, that may have been taken for a proper name in the case of Porsenna, king of Clusium.[8] We are, on the other hand, most probably faced here with a parallel to what occurred in Greece and in Rome (for the titles βασιλεύς and *rex*), where the office filled by the ancient monarchs was not abolished when the state changed from a monarchy to an aristocratic republic; it was substantially emptied of its political content and preserved, alongside the new republican magistracies, as a religious institution. Nothing can be so misleading as the anticipation of phenomena characteristic of modern times when attempting to assess those of the ancient world. Such an error would be committed in assuming that the abolition of the monarchy must necessarily have been accompanied by the abolition of the figure of the monarch. In an inscription referring to a Tarquinian priest of the second century B.C. (*C.I.E.* 5430), we find amongst the verbs denoting the offices filled by the priest the verb *lucairce*, whose root is connected with that of the word *lucumo*. In the sacred text of the Zagreb mummy, mention is made of ceremonies celebrated *lauχumneti*, i.e. 'in the *lauχumna*', probably the residence of the *lauχume*, the lucumo (cf. the Roman *Regia*), the official residence of the *Pontifices* in Rome. Finally, the elective head of the *Fanum Voltumnae*, whom Livy designated as a priest, was originally probably no other than the king elected by the twelve peoples and the chief lucumo mentioned by Servius, even though the importance of his functions may have been substantially reduced and transformed by the passage of time and the change in political ideas.

What was the nature of the primitive Etruscan monarchy? Our knowledge is unfortunately insufficient to answer the question, and all we may do is put forward certain suppositions based on analogy with what little is known with historical certainty of the Roman monarchy. The king must have held supreme judiciary power, which he exercised, according to Macrobius (*Saturn*, 1, 15, 13) once a week in public audiences. He must have been the military and religious head of the state. We are a little better informed on certain external symbols relating to the monarchy, for these were inherited by Rome and considered by ancient writers to have had a specifically Etruscan origin. Amongst these were the golden crown, the sceptre, the *toga palmata*, the throne (*sella curulis*), the *fasces*, and other symbols of power, as well as the ceremony of the triumph where the king was identified with the supreme deity.

The problem of the origin of the lictor's *fasces* is particularly interesting. [9] Writers of the imperial age such as Silius Italicus (*Punica*, VIII, 483 ff.) and Florus (I, 1, 5) believe them to be of Etruscan origin. We have already referred to the passage in Livy in which there is a mention of the lictors sent by each Etruscan city to escort the elective head of the union. The earliest representation of the *fasces* without the axe occurs in a fifth-century Chiusi relief kept in the Palermo Museum. This destroys the hypothesis that the lictors and *fasces* in the escort of the Etruscan magistrates of the federated cities (as shown on sarcophagi from Tarquinii) were an imitation of a Roman custom.

In 1898, during the excavation of an archaic tomb in the Vetulonia necropolis, there came to light an object made up of many parts of oxidized iron. This was thought by I. Falchi to be a *fascis* consisting of small hollow rods and a double-bladed axe. The object disintegrated when it was moved, but was put together again in the Florence Archaeological Museum where it may still be seen (see plate 32). Some doubts have been expressed as to the original shape of the object and its interpretation as a *fascis*; but a careful examination of various fragments is even more conclusive than Falchi's report and interpretation. There is no doubt that the object is a *fascis*, or rather the reproduction of a *fascis*, wholly made of non-perishable materials and probably reduced in size, for funerary purposes. It is the oldest *fascis* known to us and differs from later specimens in that its axe has two blades. The use in Vetulonia of a double-edged axe for fighting or ceremonial purposes at a time roughly contemporary to that of the tomb mentioned above (seventh to sixth century B.C.) is attested by a funerary stele

Figure 4 – STELE OF AVELE FELUSKE
Sepulchral Stele of an Etruscan Warrior
armed with a two-bladed axe found at
Vetulonia (*Florence,
Museo Archeologico*)

bearing the name of Avele Feluske, where it appears in the hand of an armed warrior. But the strangest coincidence of all is the fact that Silius Italicus attributes the invention of the *fascis* to the very inhabitants of Vetulonia. Should this be true we are faced once again with a fortunate instance of the correspondence between literary traditions and archaeological discoveries.

What significance was attached to the *fascis* at the beginnings of the Etruscan civilization? The axe is well known as a political and religious symbol of the Eastern civilizations and the Mediterranean world. Ceremonial axes are quite well known in ethnology: e.g. the Polynesian axes of the Cook Islanders with carved wooden handles, connected with ancestor worship; the axes of the Basongi tribes in the Belgian Congo, etc. But it is especially in the civilization of Crete that the two- or even four-bladed axe takes on a religious character, as a symbol of divinity. The two-bladed axe of nuragic Sardinia was also probably endowed if not with religious, at least with ritual significance. Archaic Etruria, standing as it did at the confluence of various Mediterranean cultural currents, undoubtedly made use of the hatchet as a chieftain's weapon, as well as a tool and an instrument of war; this may be seen in the reliefs of the bronze *situla* of the *Certosa* at Bologna (see plate 19B) or on the figured steles of Larth Ninie or Avele Feluske found respectively at Fiesole and Vetulonia. The Vetulonia example is unusual in that it reproduces a double-edged axe, which may also in fact have been a symbol of authority. So that on the one hand there was the axe, the ceremonial weapon of the king, and on the other, the wooden rods for corporal punishment carried by the sovereign's escort when he was acting in his judicial capacity; it is quite possible that the two became united in a single object symbolizing sovereignty in its fundamental aspects: the judicial, the military, and perhaps even the religious. It is also probable that only one *fascis* was used at first and that the increase in the number of lictors was due to the extension of the sovereign's authority over a larger number of cities.

The material symbol of the *fascis* corresponded to a

political and religious authority which the Romans designated by the name of *imperium*. For further confirmation that the axe symbolized sovereign power, there is the fact that only the *imperium maius* and certain special circumstances gave the Roman magistrate the right to carry the *fascis* with the axe. The *imperium*, distinct from a more general *potestas*, represented the full judiciary and military power: it is in fact the sovereignty of the old kings of Rome passed on to the republican magistrates. The concept of *imperium*, with its religious undertones, was doubtless derived from the Etruscan monarchy.[10] A gloss of the late lexicographer Hesychius even provides us (though in a Greek form) with the Etruscan word for the Greek ἀρχή, 'power', probably corresponding to the Latin *imperium:* this is δρούνα, that probably went back to an Etruscan *truna*, *δruna*, a cognate perhaps of the pre-Hellenic root τύραννος and of the root of the Etruscan name for Venus, *Turan* (lady? mistress?).

The Republican Magistracies

When studying the transition from monarchy to republic that took place in Etruria between the sixth and the fifth century B.C., the widespread occurrence of this political phenomenon in the Mediterranean has perhaps not been sufficiently taken into account. It is found to have taken place along substantially similar lines in the constitutional histories of at least four ancient racial stocks: the Greek, the Latin, the Etruscan, and the Semitic. Analogies such as these clearly demonstrate the profound unity underlying the Mediterranean civilization, as far as certain important aspects of its public life are concerned, even before Greek and Roman times. Primitive monarchies with their religious basis gave way to oligarchic states with temporary collegiate and elective magistracies; this process is at times paralleled or followed by the seizure of power on the part of individuals (tyrannies) or by solutions of a democratic nature. In many Greek cities, this transformation was already taking place in proto-historic times, at the end of the Mycenaean age, whereas other cities, e.g. Sparta, preserve in form at least the institution of monarchy till they cease to exist as historical entities. The new solutions arrived at by the western Greek world seem to be of a precocious nature. In Rome and in Etruria the change occurs after the second half of the sixth century. The Phoenician cities of Syria and Africa too, though with outcomes that varied with time and place, tend to change their monarchies into republican oligarchies from about the eighth to the fifth century B.C.

Once this point is established, the causes of the constitutional changes in Rome and Etruria need no longer be sought only in local conditions; there was a general tendency towards the differentiation of classes in society, towards the consolidation of genealogical and religious traditions in the aristocracy and towards the ousting of primitive monarchical institutions. At the most we may ask ourselves whether archaic monarchies in Italy ever fulfilled the political needs of local tendencies: they may have merely masked a power limited originally by the authority of heads of families or of assemblies, under the influence of purely external Eastern forms. In this case the changes of government we are considering may be no more than a return to original and genuine political forms. The question ought to be discussed mainly in conjunction with the question of the primitive Roman *gentes* and their place in the monarchical state: a thorny problem indeed.[11]

The political crisis of the end of the sixth century is in any case the sign of a decisive change of direction in the development of the constitutional system of Etruria as well as that of the Italic states generally. The many theories that have been put forward to account for the passage from primitive monarchies to republican magistracies either tend to explain it as a continuous and necessary evolution, or as a sudden innovation, possibly due to the imitation of foreign (and especially Greek) institutions.[12] Whatever might be the origin of the Roman consulship, for instance, it is possible, if not probable, that the first days of the Etrusco-Roman republic saw the triumph of a strong military authority (that of the *magister populi* or of the *dictator*), replacing the archaic sovereign, perhaps as a result of the influence of Greek tyrannies (a contemporary example of which was Cumae under Aristodemus). The Etruscan figure of *Macstrna* (Mastarna) or rather of the *macstrna* (since in the François tomb of Vulci the name of the hero is not preceded by a first name and thus seems to have actually been a title), the ally of the Vulci adventurers Caile and Avle Vipina against the kings of Rome and of other cities of inner Etruria, embodies this constitutional transformation which must have originated in the large and more evolved cities of the coastal belt and gradually spread to the more secluded and backward inland regions. The title *macstrna* is no more than the Etruscan form of the Latin *magister*, with the addition of an apparently unstable suffix *-na* (cf. the case of φersu = *persona*, a mask). It reappears at a later date amongst the titles of Etruscan magistrates in the form *macstrevc* (Fabretti, *C.I.I.*. 2100). Significantly enough, Roman tradition identified Mastarna with Servius Tullius, the beneficent king who broke the dynastic series of the Tarquins and to whom the reform of the centuries was attributed; a figure therefore who does not coincide with our idea (and with that of the ancients) of the primitive monarch ruling by divine right.

But even if a period of military dictatorships occurred between the archaic monarchy and the republic of full historical times, the collegiate nature of the offices (of equal authority, as in Rome, or unequal as amongst the Oscans), their temporary nature and the authority of the aristocratic senate were soon to bring a further change in the direction of the oligarchic republic. We may reconstruct the way in which this change took place in Etruria with the help of our knowledge of the Roman republic before the great wars of conquest: a senate composed of the heads of the *gentes*; a popular assembly, most probably; a supreme, temporary, and collegiate magistracy; and other collegiate magistracies of a political and religious nature. There was in any case a general tendency to parcel out power, to decrease it and to place it under constant reciprocal control, so as to prevent the rise of a tyrant. This stiffening of oligarchic institutions was accompanied by a hatred for monarchy of which we possess few but eloquent testimonies: we need only think of the opposition of the Etruscan cities to the threatened city of Veii, owing to the fact that she was governed by a king (Livy, v, 1); Etruria seems to have carried this tendency further than Rome. Differences also appear with regard to the claims for a more active part in government made by the lower classes: for in Etruria the latter were generally bereft of any possibility of becoming included more or less peacefully in the constitution, with the result that Volsinii, Arretium, and, perhaps, Volaterrae went through short periods of popular anarchy. It was only with the crumbling of the traditional Etruscan political system and the granting of Roman citizenship (a consequence of the *lex Iulia* of the beginning of the first century B.C.) that the popular classes generally managed to assert themselves over the impoverished and archaic ruling classes.[13]

The titles of the Etruscan magistracies, in their original forms, are known to us through the *cursus honorum* of the funerary inscriptions, some of which must have been written in the form of actual poetical *elogia* to the dead man, as in the case of the Roman inscriptions of the Scipio family. It is however far from easy to establish the nature of the various offices, their inter-relations, the differences between them and their correspondence with the magistracies of the Latin and Italic worlds.

The most frequent title is one drawn from the root *zil-*, whose origin is still obscure, in the forms *zil, zili, zilc* or *zilχ, zilci* and *zilaδ*. To these nominal forms there corresponds a verb *zilχ-* or *zilaχ-* with the meaning of 'to be *zilc* or *zilaδ*'. We already know that *zilaδ* corresponds in some cases to the Roman title 'praetor'. It is quite certainly a high office, perhaps the highest in the land; but the title is often accompanied by determinants *zilaδ* or *zilχ parχis; zilaδ eterau* and *zil eteraias; zilc marunuχva; zilχ ceχaneri*) which may indicate the specialization of the office (cf. the Latin *praetor peregrinus*) or the head of a particular college (*zilc marunuχva* = head of the college of *marunuʔ*). Thus the title may well have possessed both a specific and a generic acceptation, just as in the case of the Latin *praetor*.

Another office of great importance, more important in the eyes of some scholars than that of the *zilaδ*, is designated by terms built on the root *purδ-*, which has been connected with the title πρύτανις the origin of which is probably pre-Hellenic. It appears under the forms *purδ, purδne, purtśvana, eprδne, eprδni, eprδnevc*, etc.

Yet another title frequently found in inscriptions is *maru, marniu, marunuχ*: its religious connotations are made evident by its connexion with the priestly title *cepen*, and with determinants of the type *maru paχaδuras caδsc* or *marunuχ paχanati*, which contain the names of the gods *Paχa* (Bacchus) and *Caδa*. It also appears in Umbria as the college of *marones*. It has been thought to correspond to the Latin *aedilis*. Other administrative or military offices are designated by the terms *camδi, mactrevc*, etc.

To indicate the urban character of the magistracies and to differentiate them perhaps from magistracies conneetcd with the league, the terms *spurana*, *spureni*, *spureδi*, etc. are added in inscriptions. Though cases of magistracies for life (*svalas*, *svalasi*="διὰ βίου"?) are not unknown, in most cases there is a numeral next to the title to show the number of times the office was held and to bear witness to its temporary nature.

Etruscan Society

The oligarchic state presupposes a social organization based on gentilitial lines. Only the most obvious characteristics of the latter, as revealed in inscriptions and on monuments, are known to us. The Etruscan personal name system was identical with the Latin and the Italic, and quite distinct from that of other Indo-European and non-Indo-European speaking peoples, from that of the Greeks or Semites for instance, amongst whom the simple name accompanied by a patronymic (Apollonius of Nestor, Joseph son of Jacob) does not express very clearly the idea of family continuity. The system current in ancient Italy was based essentially upon two elements, the personal name proper and the name of the family or *gens*. Thus it is the only personal name system of the ancient world to foreshadow a custom that was to become general, for social, cultural, and political reasons, in the civilization of the modern world. Next to the two principal elements, the patronymic and the matronymic were often used and even at times the names of the grandparents. A third element may be found added to the name of the *gens*, the Latin *cognomen*, which may have had a personal origin, though it was generally used to designate a particular branch of the *gens*.

The Etruscans probably created the 'gentilitial' name system at the beginning of their history, which tends to prove a keen feeling for the family unit and for its continuity. The most ancient of the two elements is certainly the personal, or individual, as its very simplicity clearly shows (*Vel, Laris, Arnð*, etc.). The gentilitial names are always derivatives and take adjectival forms: they are based on personal names (*Velna*), on the names of gods (*Velðina*), on place names (*Suðrina*), etc. The number of known *gentes* is very large indeed: an interesting fact, for it excludes the hypothesis of an original opposition between a narrow oligarchy composed of the members of the *gentes* and of a population outside the gentilitial system. Here the question becomes particularly delicate and complex especially when considered in conjunction with the gentilitial system of primitive Rome as generally reconstructed by specialists in social and constitutional history.

Indeed one has the impression that originally the whole Etruscan people was included in the framework of the gentilitial system: not in few and very large family groupings, but rather belonging to numerous separate family trees each of which was distinguished by a gentilitial name, perhaps along similar lines to those of the modern world at the end of the Middle Ages when family names began to be used and everyone, from the highest to the lowest, ended by adopting a single onomastic system. It is possible of course, although no proof has yet been given, that there existed patrician and plebeian *gentes* in archaic Etruria as in republican Rome. But the impression received is that originally there were no great differences of social levels. The only real lower class was composed of servants, acrobats, and strangers who in monuments appear distinguished by a personal name only and who are therefore outside the gentilitial system.

If a society of freemen, subdivided into numerous small family units, can be reconciled with a monarchical constitution of an archaic type (like the one dominant in Etruria up to the end of the sixth century B.C.) the same cannot be said for the later oligarchic state as it is revealed to us through passages in ancient writers referring to the public life of the Etruscans. A great many families belonging to this late period are now known to us through inscriptions in each of the cities of Etruria and are of apparent equality in social standing. But it is also possible to make out the beginnings of larger family units, with a common gentilitial name but numerous ramifications spreading at times outside the territory of the city of origin. It was the formation of the *gens* in the Roman sense of the word, and in many cases a surname (*cognomen*) was added to the name of the *gens* so as to distinguish the various branches of the family. The small archaic tombs, each of which belonged strictly to one family, were replaced by grandiose gentilitial hypogea providing for the burial of a much larger number of persons. Marriages between members of certain *gentes* became more and more frequent, those very same *gentes* whose members most often held political or priestly office. It is not easy to provide a clear explanation of these facts; certain *gentes* may have gradually predominated over others belonging to the same original social system, and formed the new oligarchy. This phenomenon was especially characteristic of some northern towns of Etruria proper: Volaterrae, for instance, where the *gens* Ceicna (Cecina) with its numerous ramifications predominated, or Arretium, where the Cilnii, the ancestors of Maecenas, seem to have ruled for a certain length of time.

Even more difficult to establish is the position of the lesser or plebeian *gentes* within the framework of the oligarchic state, and the characteristic features of the proletarian and serving classes. Funerary inscriptions belonging to personages generally designated by a single person name (i.e. outside the gentilitial system) followed by the terms *lautni*, *etera*, or *lautneteri*, occur fairly frequently, especially in northern Etruria. The word *lautni* is derived from *lautn* 'family' and literally stands for 'familiar, of the family', though its use corresponds to that of the Latin *libertus*. As for *etera*, the precise meaning of the word is unknown; some translate it as 'slave' (the interpretation of *etera* as 'of noble birth' or 'noble on the mother's side' is wholly unfounded). There were particular magistracies connected with the *etera*: the *zil eteraias*, the *ziλaδ eterav*, and the *camδi eterau*. The use of the name *leδe* or *leδi*, frequently borne by slaves, is also worthy of note: it was probably also used as a common appellative term.[14] A social and political rising of the lower classes took place in Arretium and Volsinii during the third century B.C.: as historical tradition tells us, it took the form of an actual proletarian revolution with the seizure of power and the temporary abolition of caste differentiations between the lower and the aristocratic classes (e.g. the abolition of the ban on intermarriage).[15] We still do not know however whether such a revolt should be interpreted as a clash between families of a higher and of a lower rank but still within the gentilitial system and similar to the struggle between patricians and plebeians of republican Rome, or whether it should be interpreted as a rising of those elements outside the *gentes*.

As we have been dealing with the family and the personal name system of the Etruscans, we should end by a passing reference to the so-called Etruscan 'matriarchy'. This is no more than a learned legend, born from the comparison of the customs of Etruria and of Asia Minor reported by Herodotus (I, 173), and supported by the references of ancient authors to the freedom of the Etruscan woman. The fact that Lydian children were called by their mother's name instead of their father's was compared to the Etruscan use of the matronymic as revealed by inscriptions. It is the patronymic element however that predominates in Etruscan inscriptions, even though many epitaphs bear the name of the *gens* and at times that of the mother.[16] There is no doubt that in Etruria (and later, in Rome) the woman's place in society was particularly high and quite different in any case from that of the Greek woman. The fact that both men and women took part in banquets, far from being a sign of dissolution as maliciously stated by many Greek writers astonished and scandalized at a custom quite foreign to the Greeks, is a clear indication of social equality and yet another link between the civilization of ancient Etruria and the customs of the modern Western world.

NOTES

1. Cf. especially A. Solari, *La vita pubblica e privata degli Etruschi*, 1928.

2. They have been utilized in the reconstruction of the Etruscan constitution especially in the following works: A. Rosenberg, *Der Staat der alten Italiker*, 1913; S. P. Cortsen, *Die Etruskischen Standes- und Beamtentitel, durch die Inschriften beleuchtet*, 1925; F. Leifer, *Studien zum antiken Ämterwesen*, I, *Zur Vorgeschichte des Römischen Führeramts*, 1931; S. Mazzarino, *Dalla monarchia allo stato repubblicano: ricerche di storia romana arcaica*, 1945.

3. F. Altheim, *Der Ursprung der Etrusker*, pp. 61 ff.

4. Cf. L. Pareti, *La disunione politica degli Etruschi e i suoi riflessi storici e archeologici* (in *Rendiconti Pont. Accademia di Archeologia*, VII, 1929–31, pp. 89 ff.).

5. Cf. the inscription *C.I.L.*, XI, 2115.

6. Cf. M. Pallottino, *Tarquinia*, col. 553.

7. Though *populus* itself may be of Etruscan or 'Tyrrhenian origin: see Devoto in *Studi Etruschi*, VI, 1932, pp. 243 ff.

8. S. P. Cortsen, *Die etruskischen Standes- und Beamtentitel*, 1925, p. 126.

9. See A. M. Colini, *Il fascio littorio*, 1932, pp. 5 ff.

10. For the distinction between the primitive religious concept of sovereignty (*auctoritas*) and the later and essentially military power (*imperium*), see S. Mazzarino, *Dalla monarchia allo stato repubblicano*, pp. 208 ff., 216 ff.

11. Cf. De Sanctis, *Storia dei Romani*, I, 1907, pp. 224 ff.; E. Pais, *Storia di Roma dalle origini all' inizio delle guerre puniche*, II, 1926, p. 296 ff.

12. For a critical account of these theories and of the whole question, see S. Mazzarino's *Dalla monarchia allo stato repubblicano* to which we have already referred.

13. Cf. M. Pallottino, *Gli Etruschi*, pp. 208 ff.

14. Cf. E. Vetter, in *Jahreshefte der Österr. Archäol. Inst.*, XXXVII 1948, pp. 60 ff.

15. For the sources, see K. O. Müller, W. Deecke, *Die Etrusker*, I, pp. 120, 351 ff.

16. See on the subject F. Slotty, *Zur Frage des Mutterrechtes bei den Etruskern*, in *Archiv. Orientálni*, XVIII, 1950 (*Symbolae F. Hrozný dicatae*, V), pp. 262 ff.

CHAPTER SEVEN

THE RELIGION OF THE ETRUSCANS

Problems and Documents

SINCE the aim of the present work is not so much to pile detail upon detail on the various aspects of the Etruscan civilization, but to interpret these data and to discuss certain fundamental problems as yet unsolved, there would be little point in repeating what has already been described elsewhere on the religion of the Etruscans, whether considered as a whole or in its several aspects: on the deities, the forms of worship, the interpretation of divine will, funerary customs, etc. Religion is in point of fact the best known facet of the Etruscan civilization; this is hardly surprising owing to the relative abundance of sources of a literary nature, and especially the great number of archaeological monuments that, in one way or another, throw some light upon the subject.[1] This does not mean however that everything has been said that can be said, or that the data in our possession – especially archaeological – have been so worked that no further research or results may be expected. Clemen's comparatively recent work on the subject (*Die Religion der Etrusker*, 1936) is a case in point: here, the various problems have been attacked from a most original angle, with an intelligent and modern critical approach. This book, together with the more recent and no less praiseworthy essays of Giglioli and Grenier,[2] confirms our opinion of the need for a vast future survey that would re-examine all useful sources and make use of all the various results arrived at so far to paint a single, comprehensive picture of the whole.

The reputation the Etruscans had of being a most religious race is one of those frequent literary commonplaces continually to be found in the works of ancient writers. Livy (v, 1, 6) describes them as *gens ante omnes alias eo magis dedita religionibus, quod excelleret arte colendi eas* (a people who above all others were distinguished by their devotion to religious practices, because they excelled in their knowledge and conduct of them). Arnobius (*Adv. gentes*, VII, 26) proclaimed Etruria to be *genetrix et mater superstitionum*. There is even an ingenuous folk-etymology that would derive Tusci from δυσιάζειν 'to sacrifice' (Isidore, *Etym.*, IX, 2, 86; cf. also Dionysius of Halicarnassus, I, 30, 3). Modern scholars too seem prone to give credit to this unusual reputation the Etruscans enjoyed amongst ancient peoples. In actual fact, the *quantitative* assessment of religiosity on the part of different peoples runs the risk of losing all reality unless we take into account the historical reasons prompting it. Etruscan traditions were of very great importance to the Romans of the imperial age, not only because Etruria gave the first and most important contribution to the definition of those Italic religious forms amongst which the religion of Rome developed from its very beginnings, but also because religion was that portion of the Etruscan inheritance acknowledged with the least reserve by Rome and most vigorous in its resistance to the overwhelming impact of Hellenic culture. But more important are the *qualitative* differences that existed between the religion of Etruria on the one hand and that of Greece and Rome on the other. In the former are evident a scrupulous attention to ritual, to conformity and to the will of the gods, the continual dread of dark and overwhelming forces, of time limits that could not be deferred. There was in Etruria a feeling of the nonentity of man before the divine will, unknown to the Greeks even in the anguish the latter felt before the all-powerful Fates, and which the Romans tended to resolve in a prevalently juridical conception of the relationship between man and god – both a concrete and practical solution. For both in the religion and the religious art of the Graeco-Roman world, man played in spite of all the role of the protagonist; in Etruria on the other hand, the deity appears to dominate to the exclusion of man, as if reciting an eternal monologue in which the only role left to man was that of a cautious and timorous commentator. Once this qualitative point of view is accepted, the result of the comparison becomes obvious and the statements of ancient writers on the deep and exceptional religiosity of the Etruscans are shown to be fully justified.

In attempting to reconstruct a picture of that particular combination of spiritual attitudes, tendencies, and practices that constituted the religious world of the Etruscans, the question of sources becomes all-important. These are of two kinds: direct, such as original Etruscan texts, the majority of which are still obscure: i.e. the ritual texts of the *liber linteus* (linen book) of the Zagreb mummy or those of the Capua tile; a number of inscribed objects (e.g. the famous bronze model of a liver found at Piacenza); figured monuments (paintings, sculptures, and especially scenes engraved on the back of mirrors); the ruins of temples, tombs, etc.; or indirect, such as the accounts by Latin and Greek authors of imperial and post-classical times. This second class of documents must naturally be made to undergo a thorough critical examination before being utilized towards a reconstruction of the religion of the Etruscans, for in matters as delicate as religious beliefs and ritual, there are bound to occur many alterations, misunderstandings, and contaminations of the original elements. Owing to the relative resemblance of certain spiritual attitudes of Etruria and Rome, the correspondence of certain deities and the parallelism of various ritual forms, it is hardly surprising that Etruscan traditions as transmitted by Roman writers on religious matters or as included in the treatises of Christian apologists (e.g. Arnobius) should have reached us in somewhat distorted versions. Typical in this respect is the tradition referring to the creation of the world: the Etruscans believed, according to the medieval encyclopaedist known as Suidas, that this took six millennia to accomplish – an obvious reminiscence of bibilical cosmogony. In this particular case the explanation probably lies in the contamination of Etruscan and Christian elements within the literary elaborations of the late Roman age.

To conclude, the elements that can be used towards a reconstruction of Etruscan beliefs and ritual are both limited and of uncertain interpretation. The loss of original Etruscan religious literature is irreparable: how small in fact our knowledge of the spirit, the dogmas, the rites of Christianity would be, if all we had to go by were a few sacred images and liturgical objects, and the ruins of churches. [3]

The Etruscan Conception of the Divine

But even if we did possess a greater number of documents it would not be easy to obtain a true picture of the Etruscan religion and of its original and most genuine forms. The influence exerted by the civilization of Greece upon the Etruscans was too powerful and too ancient in character, especially in mythological and artistic inspiration, not to have left a considerable mark upon Etruscan religious attitudes and manifestations. This is particularly evident in the Etruscan conception of both the individuality and the form of the divinity. Clemen has attempted to find in certain aspects of Etruscan religious conceptions the survival of fetishist forms such as the worship of weapons, trees, waters, etc. It is doubtful however whether the worship of weapons or trees was ever a genuine manifestation even amongst the earlier Mediterranean civilizations: it may have been no more than a religious symbol whereby the personality of the god, even if not conceived anthropomorphically, was represented by its chief attribute. Similarly, it is difficult to connect Etruscan animism with animism understood as the worship of ancestors.[4] There is, however, no doubt that in the most genuine aspects of the Etruscan religious expression – genuine both because they had been recorded by the ancients and because of their continued survival despite the contrast they offered with the more widespread and familiar forms belonging to the classical world – their conception of supernatural beings was permeated by a certain vagueness as to number, attributes, and appearance. This vagueness seems to point towards an original belief in some divine entity dominating the world through a number of varied manifestations which later became personified into gods, or groups of gods and spirits. This outlook is responsible for the concept of the *genius* as a vital and life-giving force which is, or may be, a single divinity or the prototype of a great number of male or female spirits (the *lasae*)[5] mingling with men and gods and inhabiting the underworld; or which may actually manifest itself in non-anthropomorphic sexual symbols. The Roman *genius*, reflecting and accompanying both human and divine beings, was originally mainly an Etruscan conception.

Thus one is naturally led to the conclusion that the great individual deities were solely due to foreign, or to be more specific, Greek influences, playing upon this vague and amorphous religiosity of the Etruscans. Such a conclusion is unlikely to be true, however, especially when it is considered that the formation of the Etruscan civilization occurred rather late in the Mediterranean world and was preceded by centuries, not to say millennia, of cultural minglings and elaborations. The concept of a supreme being, with eminently celestial attributes, manifesting his will by means of the thunderbolt, may in no way be con-

sidered to have been a late *motif* or one imitated from outside. The same may be said of the concept of the goddess of
Love, Turan (whose name probably meant originally 'the
lady'), which certainly crystallized within the compass of
the primitive religious elaborations of the Mediterranean
world. At most we may speak of a typical archaic or primitive flavour of Etruscan religious conceptions, of lingering
themes and beliefs that had already been discarded, or very
nearly, by their Mediterranean neighbours; this will
become more apparent in the light of the following considerations.

It is true on the other hand that the influence of Greece
may have assisted and favoured the individualization and
the humanization of the Etruscan deities, multiplying and
defining as a result the various aspects of the major deities,
promoting local spirits and heroes to the rank of national
gods, fusing groups of beings with analogous characteristics
into one. A typical case is that of Veltha or Veltune or
Voltumna (*Vertumnus* in its Latin form): a god with strange
and contrasting attributes, represented at times as a malefi-
cent monster, at others as a god of vegetation of uncertain
sex or as a great war god. We have here a typical example
of the process of the individualization and the transformation of a local earth spirit, pertaining to a territory of
southern Etruria, into a superior divinity, or rather into the
national god *par excellence*, the *deus Etruriae princeps* (Varro,
de ling. lat., v, 46).[6] In the same way, the protecting spirits
of war, represented as armed heroes, tend to coalesce into a
single deity, the Etrusco-Roman Mars, on the model of the
Greek god Ares.

We thus pass on to the second consequence of the Hellenic influence on the Etruscan religion: the giving of
human forms to (or anthropomorphization of) the various
deities, or, to be more precise, the external and formal
moulding of divine figures on the patterns provided by

Greek anthropomorphism. The Etruscans must have possessed from the very beginning a certain anthropomorphic image of their own for their gods, though we are unable to tell how important the early influence of the mature civilizations of the East may have been on such popular representations. This must certainly have played a part in the case of the war gods mentioned above or in that of the celestial god *Tin*, which a coarse bronze statuette represents as a young man holding a thunderbolt in his right hand.[7] But Greek literature and art soon imposed – from the first half of the sixth century at least – its own representations of the great divinities as they gradually came to be elaborated in the various cities of the Hellenic world.

As a result of this process a whole series of Etruscan deities came into being, substantially parallel, if not identical, with those of Hellas: Tin, Tinia (Jupiter) corresponding to Zeus, Uni (Juno) to Hera, Menerva (Minerva) to Athene, Sethlans to Hephaistos, Turms (Mercury) to Hermes, Turan (Venus) to Aphrodite, Maris (Mars) to Ares, etc. A number of Greek divinities were also introduced directly into Etruria: Herakles who became the Hercle of the Etruscans and the Hercules of the Romans, Apollo who in Etruria became Apulu or Aplu, Artemis, known as Artumes or Aritimi. Characteristic specializations of gods, myths, and ritual also gradually came to be modelled upon corresponding Greek forms. Original Etruscan monuments and texts give evidence of such syncretisms and contaminations: the lead tablet found at Magliano, the Capua tile or the text of the wrappings of the Zagreb mummy all mention individual deities, as also the bronze model of a sheep's liver found at Piacenza, used by the haruspices to facilitate the reading and interpretation of the liver of sacrificed sheep – its surface is in fact divided into compartments, each enclosing the name of a particular deity.

Next to the major deities whose personalities and outer

forms became fixed under the influence of the Greek Olympian gods, there were a number of indigenous supernatural beings, colleges of obscure and mysterious divinities, whose number and whose very names were unknown (Varro, in Arnobius, III, 40). Ancient writers, recalling, though often none too clearly, native traditions, speak of *Dii Superiores* or *Involuti* (i.e. enveloped in the shadows of mystery), who counselled Jupiter on when to throw his most dreaded thunderbolt (Caecina, in Seneca, *Quaest. natur.*, II, 41); the *Dii Consentes* or *Complices*, also advisers to Jupiter, pitiless and anonymous, generally thought to be twelve in number (Varro and Caecina, in the passages referred to above); the *Penates*, divided into four classes: of the heavens, the waters, the earth, and the souls of men (Nigidius Figulus in Arnobius, III, 40); the 'nine gods' (*novensiles*), casters of lightning (Pliny, II, 52, 138; Arnobius, III, 38); the *Favores Opertanei* (Martianus Capella, *de nupt. Merc. Philol.*, I, 45); the *Lares*, the *Manes*, etc. The relationships between some of these deities are far from being clear: Varro, for example, identifies the *Consentes* with the *Penates*. Indirect references appear to indicate that many should be considered as gods of fate. Etruscan texts in their frequent mentioning of the word 'gods' (*aiser*, *eiser*), most probably refer to such divine colleges, i.e. the gods considered as a collective object of worship as against individual deities (Zagreb mummy, lead tablet of Magliano, various minor inscriptions).

There is also no lack of specific determinants, as in the case of *eiser śi-c-śeu-c* (Zagreb mummy), or *aiseraś δuflδicla* or, simply, *δuflδas*, *δuplδaś*, etc. (in the genitive case):[8] in the latter word there may be correspondence with the Latin *consentes*, *complices*, on the analogy of *tuśurδir* = 'consortes, coniuges', if we accept the correspondence of the Etruscan root *δu-*, *tu-* with the numeral 'one': it would therefore also be equivalent to Latin *una*, 'together'.

Next to the colleges of twelve gods and to the enneads, the existence of triads has also been surmised on the basis of the shape of the three-cell temple and on the analogy of the religion of Rome. First and foremost, that of Jupiter, Juno, and Minerva, worshipped upon the Capitoline hill in Rome, and generally thought to be of Etruscan origin; the question however has recently been re-opened to discussion.[9] The existence of dyads is, on the other hand, more certain: each is composed of a male deity and of an accompanying goddess (e.g. the infernal pairs Aita and Phersipnai, Mantus and Mania), or of twins such as the *Dioscurides*, Castor and Pollux (*Tinas clenar*), or the δ*uluter* of a terracotta from Bolsena (*C.I.E.* 5180).

But where the religiosity of the Etruscans most clearly manifested itself was in the so-called *discipline:* i.e. that collection of rules regulating the relations between men and gods.[10] Its main basis was the scrupulous questioning of the divine will by all available means; amongst these, the most important and traditional were the reading and interpretation of animal entrails (and especially the liver: *haruspicina*) and the interpretation of lightning. The antecedents of both these sciences may be traced back to the East, and particularly to Mesopotamia;[11] in Etruria, however, they assumed specific national characteristics which were to render them in certain ways both foreign and superficial to the religious customs of the Roman world though intimately tied in other respects to the Etruscan tradition. It is interesting to note that the Romans, on the other hand, like the Umbrians before them, used the method of divination based upon the observation of the flight of birds (*auspicium*). But was this latter method really of secondary importance in the Etruscan discipline of the *ostenta* (the interpretation of divine signs and prodigies)? We know a great deal on this subject, but very much more escapes us. Amongst the other aspects of the Etruscan discipline that ought to be mentioned here are the detailed rules governing the ritual of ceremonies and sacrifices, the doctrine of fixed time-limits for both men and states (a doctrine connected with the religious chronology of the 'centuries') and the beliefs and prescriptions concerning life after death.

Among the many gaps that exist in our knowledge of the Etruscan discipline, there is one question of fundamental importance that is as yet unanswered: what is the significance of this discipline taken in its entirety, what vision of the world, human and divine, was responsible for it? Both these worlds were intimately connected, according to a principle of mystical participation and indiscrimination that calls to mind the mentality of primitive people. As far as we are able to perceive from available sources, many aspects of the Etruscan spirituality that seem obscure when appraised by means of standards belonging to Graeco-Roman thought become clear when seen from the different viewpoint provided by classification under a different system of religious conceptions.[12] Heaven and earth, supernatural and natural reality, macrocosm and microcosm appear to echo each other down open or recondite channels within a preordained unitary system in which the orientation and the division of space assume fundamental importance. In this connexion the findings of modern scholarship (susceptible of further developments) are based on the one hand upon the comparison of the names of deities written in the various compartments into which the surface of the bronze liver found at Piacenza is divided and, on the other, the partition of the sky, with its divine inhabitants, according to Pliny (*Nat. Hist.*, II, 54, 143) and Martianus Capella (*de nuptiis Mercurii et Philologiae*, I, 45 ff.).[13]

This 'sacred' space, orientated and subdivided, corresponds to a concept which in Latin finds its expression in the word *templum*. It refers to the sky or to a consecrated area on earth (such as the enclosed space within a sanctuary, city, or acropolis, etc.) or even to a much smaller surface (e.g. the liver of an animal used in divination) as long as the orientation and the partition of the area according to the celestial model are followed. Orientation is determined by the four cardinal points, joined by two intersecting straight lines of which the north-south line was called *cardo* (a word of pre-Latin origin) and the east-west one *decumanus:* both these forms belong to the Roman town-planning and surveying vocabulary which we know was closely connected with the Etrusco-Italic doctrine. If the observer places himself at the cross-point of the two lines with his shoulders to the north, he will have behind him the space to the north of the *decumanus:* this half of the total space is in fact called the 'posterior part' (*pars postica*). The other half placed before him towards the south constitutes the 'anterior part' (*pars antica*). A similar partition of space also occurs along the *cardo* line: to the left of the observer, the eastern sector, of good omen (*pars sinistra* or *familiaris*); to the right, the western sector, of ill omen (*pars dextra* or *hostilis*).

The vault of heaven, thus quartered and orientated, was further subdivided into sixteen minor parts in which were placed the habitations of many divinities. This plan appears to be reflected in the outer ring of compartments of the liver of Piacenza (which are in fact sixteen in number) and in the inner compartments corresponding, though not very clearly, to them. There are unmistakable identities between the gods of the sixteen celestial regions, quoted by Martianus Capella, and the names of the divinities inscribed upon the liver, though the correspondence is by no means absolute since the original Etruscan tradition must have reached the writer of late Roman times in a much altered state, with a number of breaks in the sequence. Nevertheless it is possible to reconstruct an approximate picture of the relative cosmic stations of the gods according to the Etruscan

PARS  POSTICA

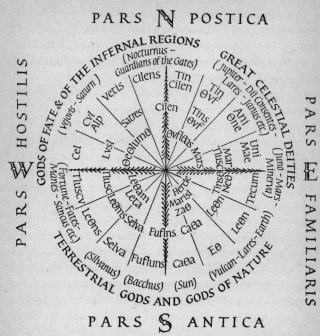

Figure 5 – THE SUBDIVISION OF THE 'SACRED' SPACE

doctrine. This shows us that the great superior deities, strongly individualized and generally favourable were placed in the eastern sectors of the sky, especially in the north-eastern; the gods of the earth and of nature were towards the south; the infernal deities and the gods of fate, inexorable and fearful, were supposed to inhabit the dread regions of the west, especially the north-west, considered to be the most inauspicious of all.

The position of signs manifested in the sky (thunderbolts, flights of birds, portents) indicates the god responsible for the message and whether it be of good or bad omen. Apart from its point of origin, a complicated casuistic body of information concerning the characteristics of the signal (e.g. the shape, colour, and effect of the lightning etc.) helps to narrow down its meaning: whether it is a friendly message, for example, or an order, an incommutable pronouncement, etc. The same exhortative or prophetic messages may be communicated through the appearance of the liver of a sacrificed animal, which the *haruspex* interprets by making its various parts correspond to the sectors of the sky. Thus the art of the *fulguriator* and of the *haruspex*, the two typical forms of Etruscan divination, appear to be closely connected and it is not surprising to find them occasionally united in the same person – as in the case of L. Cafate, whose bilingual epitaph was found at Pesaro[14] and who was both *haruspex* (in Etruscan *netśvis*) and *fulguriator* (i.e. interpreter of lightning, in Etruscan *trutnvt frontac*). Similar rules must have governed the divinatory observation of the flight of birds, as Umbrian sources (the Iguvine tablets) and Latin ones make clear. In this respect special importance was attached to the observation area on land, i.e. to the augural *templum*, with its orientation and partitions, with which are almost certainly connected the lay-out of sacred enclosures generally and of the temple itself, i.e. the sacred edifice containing the divine image. This generally faces towards the south in Etruria, with a *pars antica*, probably corresponding to the façade and colonnade, and a *pars postica* represented by the cell or cells. And, similarly, the sacred rules of orientation were observed (ideally at least) in the lay-out of cities – a concrete representation of which is given by Marzabotto in Aemilia – and in the partition of fields.

In all these practices and conceptions, as in all Etruscan ritual manifestations generally, one receives the impression of surrender, almost of abdication, of all human spiritual activities before the divine will: this is shown by the twofold obsession to know and to put into effect the will of the gods. The deity, omnipresent and vague, is generally obscure, hermetic, incomprehensible: its very name, character, form, or sex is often unknown. The whole desperate effort of life was directed towards making it speak, forcing its secret and penetrating its mysteries; recourse was taken to the strangest of means at man's disposal, generally involved and ineffectual. Once the god's will was understood, or thought to be understood, it became necessary to make good any eventual lapse, involuntary though that might be, and execute its wishes so as not to incur the tragic consequences of divine vengeance dimly foreseen in the doctrine of fatal and peremptory time limits. Such a religion, pushing as it does to extremes well-known tendencies in the spiritual life of ancient peoples, with its blind fatality and its formal and juridical aspects, does not appear to have possessed ethical values, though certain scholars[15] have found parallels with Christianity. It is however possible that at least the more rigid aspects of such a conception only took shape during the final phase of the Etruscan civilization within the orbit of the priest class and the ritual and theological elaborations that found their expression in the sacred books. This tendency was probably, perhaps unconsciously, favoured by the desire of the priests to become the sole interpreters of the divine will and thus gather into their hands the reins controlling the spiritual life of the nation. What is certain is that, with the exception of mystery cults (which appear to have been somewhat widespread in Etruria), Greek religion, with gods made human and intelligible in all their aspects through myth, appears diametrically opposed to the Etruscan. And perhaps it is this clash that underlies the variety, confusion, and even contrasts to be observed from time to time within the complex of Etruscan religious phenomena and, in the realm of figurative art, the decorative superficiality given to the illustration of Greek myths – modified occasionally with local elements – and the few existing Etruscan myths.

Another aspect of this 'primitive' mentality of the Etruscans is illustrated by the illogical and mystical interpretation of natural phenomena which, persisting as it did till a fairly late period, contrasts strikingly with the scientific rationalism of the Greeks. Particularly significant and revealing in this respect is the following passage from Seneca (*Quaest. nat.*, II, 32, 2) on the subject of lightning: *Hoc inter nos et Tuscos . . . interest: nos putamus, quia nubes collisae sunt, fulmina emitti; ipsi existimant nubes collidi, ut fulmina emittantur (nam cum omnia ad deum referant, in ea opinione sunt, tamquam non, quia facta sunt, significent, sed quia significatura sunt, fiant)* . . . 'The difference between us [i.e. the Graeco-Roman world] and the Etruscans . . . is the following: that whereas we believe lightning to be released as a result of the collision of clouds, they believe that clouds collide so as to release lightning (for as they attribute all to the deity, they are led to believe not that things have a meaning in so far as they occur, but rather that they occur because they must have a meaning) . . . '

Life After Death

The mystic unity between the celestial and the terrestrial world extended in all likelihood to the underworld as well, which, according to later Etruscan doctrines, was the abode of the dead.

Much of our knowledge of the civilization of ancient Etruria comes, as we know, from tombs: the very great majority of inscriptions are funerary in character and we owe our fundamental data on the development of artistic forms and on various aspects of everyday life to funerary paintings, sculptures, and furnishings. And it is natural that tombs should offer us, more or less directly, indications of the beliefs concerning the future destiny of man and the customs and rites connected with these beliefs. Nevertheless, we are still a long way from possessing a clear picture of Etruscan eschatology. Complex and contrasting themes point to different levels of religious attitudes and to heterogeneous influences: a source of many problems as yet unsolved but particularly alluring to the research worker.[16]

The very character of the tombs and of their furnishings, especially during the earliest phases, is an unmistakable pointer to the persistence of those primitive beliefs common to the whole Mediterranean world according to which the individuality of the dead man, in whichever way it was conceived, survived in some way linked to its mortal spoils, wherever the latter were laid. Hence the necessity on the part of the living to guarantee, protect, and prolong in a concrete way this survival not only as the sentimental tribute of loving piety, but also as a religious obligation where the element of fear played in all likelihood an important part. To this type of belief was owed the tendency in Etruria and elsewhere, especially in ancient Egypt, to give the tomb the shape and layout of a house, to provide it with furniture and household objects, to ornament it with decorations that must, originally at least, have carried a magical meaning; to surround the corpse with its clothes, jewels, or arms, to provide it with food and drink and an entourage of statuettes to represent the servants; and, finally, to reproduce the features of the dead man himself so as to provide an incorruptible 'seat' for the soul menaced by the decomposition of the body: whence the development of the funerary portrait in Etruria, reflecting what had earlier taken place in Egypt.

But what may have been the true and deeper nature of the religious ideas that break to the surface in such customs and how they might have been able to subsist and evolve by the side of other and contrasting beliefs are both matters that remain on the whole very obscure. At the beginning of the history of the Etruscan cities we see in fact the almost exclusive dominance of the funerary rite of cremation which, wherever it appears and in whichever way it spreads, cannot help reflecting beliefs incompatible to that of a material link between the body and the soul of the dead man. Indeed, cremation appears at times to carry the idea of a 'liberation' of the soul from the shackles of matter towards a celestial sphere.[17] It is all the more odd, therefore, that in Etruscan tombs of the 'Villanovan' and 'orientalizing' period, the ashes and bones of the cremated dead are sometimes contained in urns in the shape of houses or in vases attempting to reproduce the features of the dead person (the so-called *canopics* of Chiusi). This reveals, from the very earliest formative period of the Etruscan nation, a mingling of beliefs including perhaps the re-establishment of Mediterranean funerary traditions over crematory customs.

Nor is it possible categorically to state that belief in man's survival in the tomb excludes all belief in the transmigration of souls to a realm beyond the grave. It is certain, however, that in Etruria the latter belief became progressively more established and definite under the influence of Greek religion and mythology, with a consequent weakening of the original beliefs. This realm beyond the grave was conceived according to the Homeric Avernus and peopled with local divinities, the spirits of ancient heroes and the shades of the dead. Monuments as early as those of the fifth and fourth century, but especially those belonging to the Hellenistic period, represent death as a journey to the kingdom of the dead, the future subterranean abode of the soul: a sad, hopeless sojourn dominated at times by the fear inspired by the presence of monster demons or even by tortures inflicted upon the souls of the dead. It is, basically, the materialization of the fear of death in an atmosphere of true pessimism. And two infernal figures are the most symbolic of death: Vanth, the goddess with the great wings, representing, like her Greek counterpart Moira, implacable fate; and Charun the demon, a semibestial figure armed with a heavy hammer, who may be considered as a frightening deformation of the Greek Charon, whose name he assumes.[18] The Etruscan infernal demonology is both rich and picturesque: it includes a number of other personages partly inspired by Greek mythology (e.g. the Erinyes) as well as completely original ones such as the horrific Tuchulcha with the face of a vulture, the ears of a donkey, and armed with serpents (see plate 24A).

Even for this later period monumental sources are insufficient in their fragmentary and external aspects to provide a reliable or complete picture of contemporary beliefs concerning the underworld. If we are to go by funerary paintings and reliefs, the fate of the dead would appear to be inexorably mournful and equalitarian: the merciless law spared not even the most illustrious dignitary – his superiority is expressed only in the sumptuous clothing, the attributes of office and the retinue that accompanied him on his journey to the underworld. However, a number of references to consoling doctrines of salvation, more or less explicit in nature, exist in literary tradition (Arnobius, II, 62; Servius, *ad Aen.*, III, 168; Martianus Capella, II, 142): these mention the possibility of attaining a state of beatitude or even of deification, by means of certain rituals supposed to have been described by the Etruscans in their *Libri Acherontici*. A precious original document of such a ceremony of suffrage, with prescriptions as to offerings and sacrifices to deities (especially infernal deities), has been preserved in the Etruscan text of the Capua tile, that dates back to at least the fourth century B.C.[19] We do not know how much the development of these new eschatological beliefs owe to the diffusion in Etruria of Orphic or, still more, of Dionysiac doctrines (the cult of Bacchus is in fact widely attested in Etruria, even in connexion with the funerary world).[20] Nevertheless hopes of salvation appear to be tied mostly to the concept of magico-religious rituals proper to a primitive type of spiritual development, rather than to a superior ethical principle of recompense for the good done during life on earth.

Forms of Worship

Monumental sources and documents written in Etruscan (as far as we are able to understand them) together with references in classical literature provide us with numerous data towards the reconstruction of the religious life and the forms of worship of the Etruscans. Traditional customs in this respect, at least as far as their material aspects are concerned (i.e. sacred places and temples, organization of priestly bodies, sacrifices, prayers, offerings of votive gifts, etc.) do not differ substantially from their counterparts in the Greek, Italic, and especially Roman worlds. This may be explained by taking into account on the one hand the common spiritual orientation of the Graeco-Italic civilization beginning with the archaic age; on the other, the very strong influence exerted by Etruria on Rome in matters of religion. A study of Etruscan religious antiquities should not therefore be considered apart from the much more detailed and complex picture given to us by Greece and Rome on the chapter of ritual, and, as a result, it becomes all the more difficult to estimate how much the development of rituals of worship owed to the religious mentality of Etruria.

In the first place we should attribute to the Etruscans that concrete and almost materialistic adherence to rules established *ab antiquo*, that scrupulous formalism of ritual and frequent demand for expiatory sacrifices that may be detected within the body of Roman religious traditions as elements foreign, as it were, to the simple and rustic religiosity of the earliest Latins and indicating the presence of a collateral factor that it is impossible not to identify with the ceremonial of an ancient and mature civilization such as, in fact, the civilization of Etruria. This *ars colendi religiones*, to quote the expression used by Livy in a passage to which we have already referred,[21] fully agrees with the feeling of subordination of man to the deity, which, as we have seen, was a predominating factor in the Etruscan religion, and presupposes faith in the magical virtue of ritual, a faith frequently met in more primitive mentalities.

This concrete quality is shown by precise determinations as to place, temple, persons, and formalities in which or by means of which the acts of invoking or placating the deity take place: proceedings which the Romans designated by the term *res divina* and the Etruscans (probably) *aisna* (i.e. 'divine' service, from *ais* 'god').

These proceedings take place within consecrated ground (the *templum*) of which mention has already been made: an enclosure with altars and sacred buildings containing images of the gods. Such buildings were often made to face the south.[22] The concept of consecration for worship of a particular piece of ground or building was perhaps expressed in Etruscan by the word *sacni* (whence the verb *sacniśa*): this status could be extended, as in Greece and Rome, to a complex assemblage of enclosures and temples as on the acropolis of many cities (e.g. Marzabotto). Characteristics in some ways similar were shown by funerary enclosures, near which or within which sacrifices were offered and gifts deposited.

The regulations pertaining to the timing of feasts and ceremonies must also have been of especial importance in Etruria; these, together with the ceremonial surrounding acts of worship, constituted the subject-matter of the *Libri Rituales* mentioned by tradition. The longest ritual text in Etruscan in our possession, the manuscript on cloth preserved in the bindings of the Zagreb mummy, contains an actual liturgical calendar with indications as to the month and day on which the ceremonies described were to take place. It is probable that other documents were also drawn up, similar to the sacred calendars of the Romans: i.e. consecutive lists of days countermarked solely by the name of the feast or of the deity to be honoured. The Etruscan calendar was probably similar to the pre-Julian Roman calendar: we know the names of some of its months,[23] and it appears as if the 'ides' had, at least in name, an Etruscan origin; the numbering of the days of the month is, however, consecutive. Each sanctuary and each city must have had, as is to be expected, its own particular feasts: as in the case of the *sacni cilδ* – the sanctuary of a city which remains unidentifiable – referred to in the Zagreb ritual. On the other hand, the yearly celebrations at the sanctuary of Voltumna, near Volsinii, were national in character.

Even when we come to try and understand the nature and organization of the priestly bodies we are forced to have recourse to comparisons with the Italic and Roman worlds. There are at any rate grounds for believing that they were many and had specialized functions, closely connected with public magistracies and often grouped into colleges. The priestly title *cepen* (with variant *cipen* found in Campania), particularly frequent in Etruscan texts, is, for example, often followed by an attribute that determines its sphere of action or its specific functions; e.g. *cepen δaurχ*, a name that almost certainly indicates a funerary priest (from *δaura* 'tomb'). Other words connected with priestly offices, both general and specific in character, include *eisnevc* (connected with *aisna*, the sacrificial action), *celu*, *ceχasie*, and, perhaps, *tamera*, *santi*, etc.

There are moreover the priests with divinatory functions: the haruspices (*netśvis*), represented on Etruscan monuments in characteristic dress consisting of a pointed cap and a fringed mantle (see plate 18B), and the interpreters of lightning (*trutnvt frontac*). The title *maru*, *marum* was connected, as we know, with sacred functions as, for example, in the cult of Bacchus (*marunuχ paχanati, maru paχaδuras*). The double *cepen marunuχva* is worthy of note, combining as it probably did a priestly title with the functions pertaining to the *maru*; and also *zilχ ceχaneri* which must probably be understood as something approaching the Roman *curator sacris faciundis*. The collective *paχaδuras, alumnaδuras*, etc., probably refer to confraternities and should be compared as to their formal structure with such formations as *velδinaδuras*, i.e. members of the *Velδina* family. At Tarquinii there existed in Roman times an *ordo LX haruspicum* (*C.I.L.*, XI, 3382), of probable ancient origin. An attribute particular to the priest was the *lituus*, a stick curved at one end.

Worship could be directed either towards interrogating the will of the gods, according to the rules of divination, or invoking their help or pardon by means of an offering. It is probable that both these operations were closely connected one with the other, though literary sources distinguish between victims sacrificed for the consultation of entrails (*hostiae consultatoriae*) and victims destined to act as actual offerings in place of human beings (*hostiae animales*). The offerings of liquids and food appear to be similarly mixed in complex ceremonials with the blood-offerings of animals. These liturgies are minutely described in prescriptive tones by the great ritual of Zagreb and the funerary ritual of the Capua tile; unfortunately our knowledge of Etruscan is not sufficient to allow us to establish accurately the meaning of the terms used in the description of the rites and, consequently, prevents us from reconstructing the ceremonies. Prayer, music, and dance must all have played a large part in such ceremonials.

Votive gifts offered in sanctuaries for favours requested or received mainly consist of statuettes in bronze, stone, or terracotta, reproducing the features of the divinity or of the giver or even of animals, in substitution for victims and parts of the human body. These objects, kept together in coffers or deposits, often carry dedicatory inscriptions. They vary greatly in value, artistic and otherwise, but, for the greater part, consist of modest moulded terracotta figurines: a sign that deep and widespread popular religious feelings existed round the great centres of worship.

NOTES

1. Here are the names of some of the scholars who have studied the problem: C. Thulin, G. Herbig, R. Pettazzoni, C. Clemen, G. Furlani, C. C. van Essen, H. M. R. Leopold, B. Nogara, G. Q. Giglioli, and A. Grenier.

2. G. Q. Giglioli, *La religione degli Etruschi*, in *Storia delle Religioni*, 4th ed., 1949, I, pp. 635 ff.; A. Grenier, *Les religions étrusque et romaine*, in '*Mana*', *Les religions de l'Europe ancienne*, 1948. Both works are easy to consult and contain all the preceding bibliography.

3. Cf. H. J. Rose, *On the relations between Etruscan and Roman religion*, in *Studi e materiali di Storia delle Religioni*, IV, 1928, pp. 161 ff.

4. The attempt to connect certain aspects of the Etruscan religion (divination, ecstasy, belief in the journey to the underworld, asexuality or bisexuality, bells, etc.) with Shamanistic ideas and practices (cf. W. Muster, *Der Schamanismus bei den Etruskern*, in *Frühgeschichte und Sprachwissenschaft*, herausg. von W. Brandenstein, 1948, pp. 60 ff.) rests upon very slender arguments when it is considered that such *motifs* are very widely spread throughout the world, and that it is doubtful whether some of these aspects were native to Etruria.

5. A mistaken attempt has recently been made to deny the existence of the *lasae* as minor deities and to substitute for them a single great goddess *Lasa* (cf. R. Enking, *Lasa*, in *Mitteilungen des Deutschen Arch. Int. Rom.*, LVII, 1942, pp. 1 ff.).

6. See R. Pettazzoni, *La divinità suprema della religione etrusca*, in *Studi e materiali di Storia delle Religioni*, IV, 1928, pp. 207 ff., where the hypothesis is advanced that the god was a local gentilitial form of the uranic god Tin (Jupiter). On the origin of the names *Vertumnus-Voltumnus*, see G. Devoto, in *Studi Etruschi*, XIV, 1490, pp. 275 ff.

7. At the *Museo di Villa Giulia*, in Rome: see G. Q. Giglioli, in *Archeologia Classica*, IV, 1952, pp. 189 ff.

8. See *Studi Etruschi*, XX, 1948–9, pp. 253 ff.

9. See L. Banti, *Il culto del cosidetto tempio 'dell'Apollo' a Veio e il problema delle triadi etrusco-italiche*, in *Studi Etruschi*, XVII, 1943, pp. 187 ff.

10. C. O. Thulin, *Die etruskische Disciplin*, in *Göteborgs Högskolas Årsskrift*, 1905, 1906, 1909.

11. R. Pettazzoni, in *Studi Etruschi*, I, 1927, pp. 195 ff.; G. Furlani, in *Studi e materiali di Storia delle Religioni*, IV, 1928, pp. 243 ff.; VI, 1930, pp. 9 ff.; *Studi Etruschi*, V, 1931, p. 203 ff.

12. See in this respect M. Pallottino, 'Partecipazione' e senso drammatico nel mondo figurato degli Etruschi, in *Arti Figurative*, 1946, pp. 149 ff., and R. Enking, *Etruskische Geistigkeit*, 1947 (to be consulted with a certain amount of care).

13. C. Thulin, *Die Götter des Martianus Capella und der Bronzeleber von Piacenza*, in *Religionsgeschichtliche Versuche und Vorarbeiten*, III, 1, 1906, pp. 60 ff.; S. Weinstock, *Martianus Capella and the Cosmic System of the Etruscans*, in *Journal of Roman Studies*, XXXVI, 1946, pp. 101 ff.; A. Grenier, *Les religions étrusque et romaine*, op. cit., pp. 18 ff., 34 ff.

14. A. Fabretti, *Corpus Inscriptionum Italicarum*, 69.

15. E.g. T. Zielinski, *Studi e materiali di Storia delle Religioni*, IV, 1928, pp. 179 ff.

16. See F. Cumont, *Lux perpetua*, 1949.

17. Cf. A. Brelich, *Aspetti della morte nelle iscrizioni sepolcrali dell'Impero Romano* (*Dissertationes Pannonicae*, I, 7), 1937, pp. 80 ff.; F. Cumont, *Lux perpetua*, p. 390.

18. F. de Ruyt, *Charun, démon étrusque de la mort*, 1934.

19. See pp. 271 ff.

20. See A. Bruhl, *Liber Pater*, 1953, to which should be added the not inconsiderable direct epigraphic documentation (Capua tile, C.I.E., 5430, 5472, C.I.I. 2250, etc.).

21. See p. 155.

22. For the shape of the temples, see pp. 188 ff.

23. See pp. 279 ff.

CHAPTER EIGHT

LITERATURE AND THE ARTS

Literature

WE have already noted the particular character of Etruscan monuments, that though they belong to full historical times, in some aspects they are regarded and studied almost as if they were prehistoric documents. There is not, in fact, the direct light thrown by a great literary tradition to allow us to penetrate deep into the thought, the feelings, and the ways of life of their creators as is possible with the other great peoples of the classical world. We owe much to the indirect information, whether contemporary or not, which Greek and Roman authors have left us, as also to actual documents written in Etruscan (consisting mostly of short inscriptions often of difficult interpretation): we have seen this when dealing with the political and social organization and the religion of Etruria. But neither can in any way make up for the lack of a national literature with poetical, historical, and scientific works.

Doubts may arise on whether a true literature ever existed among the Etruscans.[1] Its total loss, however, is no valid argument against its existence. We possess Greek and Latin literature almost entirely because it was passed down to us uninterruptedly from scribe to scribe, right through the centuries of the Middle Ages. Ancient texts on papyrus and epigraphic documents restored to light by archaeology are relatively insignificant in importance. But if the works of classical writers were copied and handed down to modern times, it was because they were written in a living language and constituted an essential foundation of European civilization. On the other hand, the original texts of ancient Italic peoples, including the Etruscans, had lost all interest right from imperial times: they were couched in languages no longer spoken and presumably incomprehensible to all, with the exception, perhaps, of a few isolated scholars. It is obvious that it would occur to no one to transcribe and preserve them for future generations.

A certain type of Etruscan literary activity, it is true, has been positively, though indirectly, attested by the notice it has received in Greek and Roman sources, consisting of fragmentary references chiefly to the existence of books with religious content known in translation or in compendia amongst priestly or scholarly circles in Rome. We know that they were classified into three fundamental groups under the names of *Libri Haruspicini*, *Libri Fulgurales*, and *Libri Rituales*.[2] The first dealt with divination by the examination of animal entrails and the second with divination from objects struck by lightning. As for the *Libri Rituales*, they seem to have dealt with a field much vaster and more complex: the rules of worship, the formalities governing the consecration of sanctuaries, the foundation of cities, the division of fields, civil and military organization, etc. Moreover they contained special texts on the division of time and the limits of the life of men and peoples (*Libri Fatales*), on life beyond the grave and the rituals of salvation (*Libri Acherontici*) and, finally, on the interpretation of miracles (*Ostentaria*).

Etruscan and Roman tradition tends to attribute to these works an extremely ancient and venerable origin, to the extent that a number of them were actually believed to go back to the teachings of the genius Tages (*Libri Tagetici*, corresponding, as far as we can tell, to the *Libri Haruspicini* and *Acherontici* – see plate 25B) or the nymph Vegoia or Begoë (*lasa Vecui*) to whom were assigned the *Libri Fulgurales* and the passages on mensuration contained in the *Libri*

Rituales. They were, in fact, believed to have been divinely inspired and to have originated in a kind of primordial 'revelation' identified with the very origins of the Etruscan civilization. And it is quite possible that the collection of sacred books as known during the last centuries of the Etruscan nation and as translated (in part at least) into Latin, did contain elements of great antiquity. But on the whole the essentially normative aspect of the texts appears rather to reflect an evolved and, perhaps, final phase in the spiritual and religious development of Etruscan society. It is quite possible that their final, and as it were, 'canonical' elaboration, may have taken place within narrow priestly circles such as the Order of the Sixty Haruspices which still flourished at Tarquinii in Roman times (see p. 175), a world to which doubtless belonged a certain Tarquitius Priscus (or Tuscus?) to whom Roman tradition attributed the composition, vulgarization, and translation into Latin of a number of sacred books.[3]

Let us now consider the nature of this religious literature. It was probably varied and heterogeneous, with sections in verse or at least metrically composed (*carmina*) and others minutely ritual and descriptive. We are able to form an idea of the latter by considering surviving original texts in Etruscan such as the manuscript of the Zagreb mummy or the Capua tile. Some scholars have in fact already pointed to an eventual connexion between the funerary ritual of the tile and the *Libri Acherontici*. Altogether, the corpus of sacred books must have possessed a fundamentally religious inspiration but, at the same time, a genuinely juridical character. It was a treatise of sacral doctrines and, at the same time, a constitution, a collection of laws, including profane ones. This is where its originality lies when compared to the body of Greek literary works and, perhaps, its analogy to the religious, juridical, and sapiential contents of certain eastern literatures and particularly that of the Hebrews.

There remains the question whether the Etruscans did pursue other forms of literary activity and up to what point these manifestations developed independently of sacred literature. The existence of annals or historical documents seems confirmed by the mention of *Tuscae Historiae* quoted by Varro (Censorinus, *de die nat.*, 17, 6). There is on the other hand a complete lack of references to epic or mythological narrative; and though we should not exclude the possibility that this *genre* may have been cultivated in Etruria, we should point out that the Etruscan mentality does not appear to have possessed to any great extent that mythographic inventiveness that flowed with such distinctive and productive force among the Greeks. With only a few exceptions, figured art imitates and re-elaborates only the sagas of gods and heroes received from the Greek world.

That convivial poems and Fescennine satires (whose origins used to be traced back to the Faliscan town of Fescennia) had their parallels in Etruria is quite possible, but cannot be definitely proved. There are on the other hand a number of funerary inscriptions longer than average and with, perhaps, a metric or rhythmic structure that may point to the existence of *elogia*, or praises, sung in honour of important deceased personages. Dramatic poetry, as evidenced by the mention of a certain Volnius, author of tragedies in Etruscan (Varro, *de ling. lat.*, v, 55), was probably only a late phenomenon modelled upon Greek drama.

The presence has often been pointed out in Etruscan texts of regular groupings of words and syllables, repetitions, alliterations, rhymes, etc., that point to a marked disposition for the rhythmic form. But we have no reliable data on the existence of a quantitative metre comparable to that of Greek or Latin verse.[4] It is highly probable at any rate that votive inscriptions, particularly those belonging to the archaic period, and certain funerary inscriptions were in verse form, as was frequently the case among the Greeks

and Romans. Sacred hymns and prayers, and perhaps profane songs as well, must also have possessed a metric form.

Music and Dancing

Music, whether accompanied by song or not (and especially the latter) must have played a very important role in
the ceremonies and the public and private life of the
Etruscans if we are to judge from the evidence of both
literary and monumental sources.[5] The instruments (and,
consequently, the rhythms, harmonies, and melodic
arrangements) are manifestly the same in Etruria as those
met in the musical world of the Greeks; this identity cannot
fail to surprise us, even if we take into account the many
debts Etruscan cities owed to the civilization of Greece.
Among the string instruments we should mention the
zither, the lyre, and the *barbiton;* among the wind instruments, the double pipes (*tybiae pares*) and the straight
trumpet (*salpinx, tuba*) or curved trumpet (*cornu*); among
the percussion instruments, the castanets played by dancing
women. As in Greece, duets consisting of a zither player
(or a lyre or *barbiton* player) and a double pipe player were
a common combination, as can be deduced from the frequency with which they are represented in tomb paintings.

And yet Etruria must have had its own individual tendencies and traditions of style and practice against this
common musical background. We should not disregard the
insistence with which ancient writers speak of the popularity of the double pipes amongst the Etruscans, almost as
if it were a national instrument (see Athenaeus, IV, 154a)
brought over from Lydia and transmitted by the Etruscans
to the Romans: the pipe player was called *subulo* in Rome,
a name derived from the Etruscan. Indeed the art of pipe
playing was widely diffused in Greece, but it was attributed
originally to the Phrygians and the Lydians: it reflects a

taste for the pathetic and the orgiastic in music. In this case too, as with other manifestations of their artistic culture, the Etruscans appear to have adopted those elements of the complex artistic experience of the Greeks that were closest to their own sensibilities,[6] especially in the direction of those forms elaborated in the Graeco-Oriental cities of Asia Minor. We must logically suppose that Etruscan music preferred those modes defined by Greek theorists as Lydian, Hypo-Lydian, Phrygian, and Hypo-Phrygian, with their respective tonal systems, as against the grave and solemn Dorian music. On the other hand, Greek tradition agrees in attributing the trumpet or *salpinx* to the Etruscans (Aeschylus, *Eumen.*, 567 ff.; Sophocles, *Ajax* 17; Euripides, *Phoen.*, 1377 ff.; etc.). Though we need not take this to mean that the trumpet was actually invented in Etruria, nevertheless this ancient instrument must have played a characteristic part in Etruscan military and, perhaps, religious ceremonials and must eventually have been made and exported by Etruscan bronze manufacturers. Figured monuments, however, more commonly show a curved trumpet, or horn, or a straight trumpet curved at one end, like the *lituus*.

At any rate the great popularity of wind instruments corresponds to a notable development in the practice of music away from song. Music not only formed with dancing and mime part of the religious celebrations and stage performances of Etruria, but it also frequently accompanied, as an exciting rhythmic and melodic commentary, various moments of the ritual and of the public and private life of the Etruscans, i.e. games, hunting, the preparation of banquets, and even the scourging of slaves. This connexion of music with gesture rather than the spoken word finds its parallel in forms of stage performances peculiar to Etruria; these, our sources tell us (Livy, VII, 2, 4 ff.), were mimed by masked actor-dancers (*histriones* or *ludiones*), reminiscent at times of both farce and satire. This does not exclude the actual possibility of dialogued dramatic actions, which after the fourth century must certainly have been affected by the influence of Greek dramatic forms, as borne out by the many statuettes in Etruscan tombs representing masked comedy types.

Etruscan dancing is chiefly known to us through the funerary paintings of the sixth and fifth centuries. It generally appears to be performed by professional dancers: single dancing girls accompanied by a double pipe player or dancing pairs and especially troops of men and women. The latter advance separately with individual movements and are guided by musicians who perhaps filled the role of dance leaders, for they join in the steps of the dance. Occasionally – as for example in the paintings of the Tomb of the Inscriptions at Tarquinii – members of the gentilitial class to which the family of the dead man belonged may also be seen dancing. The jerky movements of the legs and the emphatic and presumably rapid gestures of the arms and head reveal a type of dance that must have been markedly rhythmical and animated if not actually orgiastic, probably inspired by the Greek *sikinnis* of Dionysiac origin. But the documents we possess, limited in time and range by funerary art, are not sufficient to prove that this was the only type of dance practised in Etruria, though it was attuned to the musical 'modes' we have assumed to be dominant in the Etruscan world (see plates 11B, 23, and 24B).

Architectural Monuments

Of quite a different order is the wealth of direct evidence we possess on the architecture and figurative arts of ancient Etruria, for these are the very monuments and materials brought to light by archaeological discovery. In spite of the destruction of so many ancient works of art, whether buildings or objects, by the slow inexorable agency of time or the superimposing of new civilizations, these documents are sufficient to allow us a broad enough vision of the artistic activity of ancient Etruria both in its tendencies and in its developments.[7]

The buildings of Etruria cannot of course be evaluated on the same basis as those of Greece and Rome. Only in fortifications and tombs was stone employed to the exclusion of all other materials; in other constructions, such as temples or civic buildings, it was only used for the foundations: the remainder of the building was composed of lighter materials such as wood, rubble, baked or unbaked clay. This means that all that remains of such edifices is their layout and a few fragments of the decorations. Nevertheless it is possible to reconstruct their original aspect by using as a model the rock tombs and urns or small votive reproductions made to imitate them.[8]

Walled structures offer much variety in materials and techniques according to the time, place, and type of building. The commonest materials were limestone, travertine, sandstone, and tufo, all locally quarried; the absence of marble (so important in Greek architecture) is due to the fact that the exploitation of the Carrara quarries only began in Roman times. The style of masonry varies from large irregular roughly hewn blocks (as shown, for example, in the city walls of Vetulonia), to the fine revetments of small square blocks met with in the walls of southern Etruscan cities and other, though especially funerary, constructions. Generally speaking no evolution from a rougher and more primitive type of structure to more refined and elaborate styles may be detected: the square and regular type was known and employed from the earliest stages of the Etruscan civilization and differences in technique seem to be due to particular conditions such as materials at hand, available craftsmanship, urgency, etc. Contrary to opinion current among many archaeologists, the true polygonal style must be considered foreign to the building customs of the Etruscans and a late introduction on the part of the first Roman colonists in the case of the fortresses of Pyrgi, Cosa, and Saturnia.[9] The exceptional use of bricks in the late city walls of Arezzo constitutes, as far as we can tell, a local departure, even if it did derive from the brick constructions of Greek military architecture (though in the latter case the bricks were unbaked). Also widely diffused in Etruria was the system of pseudo-vault and pseudo-cupola revetments, formed by the gradual convergence of blocks laid in horizontal courses: a system widely spread throughout the Mediterranean.[10] Later, the technique of the perfect arch became established, evidenced by city gates (e.g. at Volterra, Perugia) and sepulchral monuments, a prelude to the dominant structures of the architecture of Rome. In this predilection for vault lining, Etruscan architecture carries over and perfects (though without innovations) ancient eastern forms which Greek classical architecture rejected as foreign to the rigorous rectilinear motif of its conceptions, based upon the architrave.

Among the more notable examples of military architecture we should mention the city walls of Tarquinii (and surviving sections of similar constructions at Veii, Caere, Vulci, Sutrium, etc.), of Volsinii (Bolsena), Vetulonia, Clusium (Chiusi), Cortona, Perusia (Perugia), Faesulae (Fiesole), Arretium (Arezzo). These works are generally attributed to between the sixth and the fourth centuries, with later additions and rebuilding, since they generally remained serviceable in Roman times and, in one or two cases, even later. In spite of the variety of styles, they are all continuous walls, originally uninterrupted by towers: projections and indentations only occur in connexion with gates. The latter may at first have been spanned by lintels; but the grandiose monuments of the *Porta dell'Arco* at Volterra and the *Porta Marzia* and *Porta 'di Augusto'* at Perugia feature the true arch together with architectural and figured decorations (though the *Porta 'di Augusto'* probably does not date further back than the third century B.C.; see also plate 1B). The ancient nature of city walls with battlements and arched gateways is also evidenced by figured urns and sarcophagi.

Funerary architecture is somewhat heterogeneous in character owing to the fact that it represents the occasional complement or development of sepulchral styles of varied origin and inspiration. The great majority of tombs, even those of a monumental type, were in fact hewn out of the living rock, whether they consist of underground chambers (ranging from the modest *pozzetti* and primitive pits to the grandiose and complex hypogea of a later age) or of external adaptations in the shape of circular tumuli and quadrilateral constructions covered over with earth or of façades sculptured on the cliff face. These works, though not architectural in character, are closely connected with architecture in so far as they often faithfully imitate down to the minutest detail the shapes of real buildings both in their exterior and their interior aspects. Walled structures, however, are frequently found, whether they are simply additions to the rock walls and ceilings or whether they make up the whole of the monument. Sepulchral chambers built during the earliest phase feature revetments with false vaults or, but exceptionally (as in the tomb of Casal Marittimo near Volterra), with false cupola structures. In later years, finely constructed barrel-vaulted chambers were built, e.g. the tomb of the Grand Duke at Chiusi, and the San Manno hypogeum near Perugia. The round tumulus type of monument (with drum hewn out of the rock as at Cerveteri – see plate 1A, or built upon it as at Populonia) became far less frequent after the fifth century B.C., but it evolved, owing perhaps to contacts with Hellenistic funerary architecture, towards the type of the great circular Roman mausoleum of imperial times such as those of Augustus or of Hadrian in Rome. There is also no lack of quadrilateral tombs shaped like small temples (e.g. at Populonia). Finally, mention should be made of a type of tomb built on a plinth and surmounted by large cippi, in the shape of truncated cones, or by obelisks: a type known chiefly through the reliefs of sepulchral urns, but directly attested, though outside Etruria, in the so-called Tomb of the Horatii and Curiatii near Albano in Latium. A fine monument of this type, with several obelisks adorned with bells, is mentioned by ancient sources as having existed at Chiusi and identified as the Tomb of King Porsenna.[11]

Domestic and religious architecture have common origins and characteristics. Mention will later be made of the various forms of Etruscan house (see p. 210). The temple, at first identified as in the palaeo-Hellenic world with the rectangular house with inclined roof but without portico (as evidenced by votive models and the remains of an edifice discovered on the Veii acropolis -- see, for example, plate 2A) later assumed more complex forms, parallel in certain aspects to those of the Greek temple. The type attributed by Vitruvius to the Etruscans (*de archit.*, IV, 7) is characterized by a layout where the width is slightly less than the length, with the first half occupied by a colonnaded portico and the back consisting of three cells, each dedicated to a different deity, or by a single cell flanked by two *alae* or open ambulacra. Monumental remains at Veii, Orvieto, Bolsena, and Marzabotto show that this layout was in effect widely and lastingly used in Etruria from the archaic to the Hellenistic period: it is the one used for the Temple of Capitoline Jove in Rome, first built in the days of the Etruscan dynasty of the Tarquins.[12] It seems certain, however, that sacred edifices were also built with a layout more similar to that of the Greek temple: i.e. with a lengthened rectangular base and a columned façade (prostyle) or even with a continuous colonnade on all four sides (*peripteros*) as in the great temple of the 'Ara della Regina' at Tarquinia. The originality of Etruscan temples does not therefore reside so much in their layout as in the materials used for their construction, in the proportions and forms given to the rest of the building and in the types of decoration. We have already referred to the fact that, apart from the foundations, they were generally built entirely of light materials with wood for the framework of the building. This meant limited development as to height (as in effect was the case in the measurements of the 'Tuscanian' temple, according to Vitruvius), wide intercolumnar spaces and a broad roof with marked lateral projection of the eaves. Wooden beams require the protection of compact but light materials, whence the universal use of polychromic terracotta coverings;[13] these developed colourful geometric and figurative decorative patterns, with longitudinal or terminal facings for the beams and cornices, adorned with antefixes and acroteria (see plate 11A). Later (but not before the fifth or fourth century B.C.) was added the decoration of the pediment, which originally was left open so that the roof timbers could be seen from the front of the building.

All these characteristics of the Etruscan temple have undoubted counterparts in the primitive architecture of Greece and, as has been said, partial parallels with the archaic and classical Greek temple. The difference resides in the fact that the Greek temple tends to transform itself as early as the seventh century B.C. into an edifice almost entirely built of stone and evolving its own unmistakable architectonic forms, whereas in the Etruscan temple there is no departure from the tradition of using wood as a building material until full Hellenistic times; if anything, the decorative exuberance of the terracotta facings became more accentuated. These show (especially during the sixth and fifth centuries) many variations in conception and development: the longitudinal facings of the beams for example may form a continuous frieze figured in relief, of Graeco-Oriental inspiration (the so-called 'first' or 'Ionic' phase) or they may simply feature painted ornamentations accompanied by the stressing of the overlying and projecting cornice, as in the fictile decorative systems of Greece proper and its colonies in southern Italy and Sicily. This latter type of decoration became established after the end of the sixth century and coincided with the period of greatest wealth of the Etruscan temple, characterized by shell-shaped antefixes and by large figured acroteria as shown by the typical decorations of the temple at Veii ('second' or 'archaic' phase). This state of affairs was to remain substantially unchanged during the centuries that followed. The only innovation worthy of note was the introduction of a decorated pediment with figured compositions in high relief, though still in terracotta: an imitation of the decoration of Greek pediments. Remnants of this 'third' or 'Hellenistic' phase have been found at Tarquinii, Telamon, and Luna.[14] When treating of the forms and coverings of the Etruscan temple we should not neglect to mention the historically fundamental fact that these same characteristics and developments are also met in the temples belonging to Faliscan territory, Latium and also, though with a number of differences, to Campania. Thus we may speak of an architectural cultural link uniting all Tyrrhenian Italy north of the area directly affected by Greek colonization. On the other hand the establishment of the stone temple during the Hellenistic age, under Greek influence but with original characteristics, in place of the traditional wooden temple, occurred earlier in Latium and only affected Etruria as the result of its romanization.

The predominance even in works belonging to a comparatively recent period of elements of archaic inspiration may moreover be observed in all motifs of Etruscan architectural decoration (whether in stone or in wood and terracotta buildings) as also in their innumerable reproductions and imitations for funerary or votive purposes. Vitruvius speaks of a 'Tuscanian' order, distinct from the Doric, Ionic, and Corinthian orders of Greek architecture. It is characterized by a type of column that is in fact found employed in Roman monuments and represents a variant of the Doric column, with smooth shaft and footings. Its Etruscan origin is proved by testimonies that go back as far as the archaic age; it was, presumably, the shape of the majority of the wooden columns in sacred and civic buildings. In reality, it is a survival and an elaboration of the so-called 'proto-Doric' type, with moulded plinth, a noticeably swollen shaft devoid of channellings and capital with curved cushion. In primitive Greece, it was very soon replaced by the true Doric column. Together with it, there was also in Etruria another widespread type of column and pilaster with capitals adorned with flowered volutes, both simple and composite, which owe their inspiration to eastern capitals from Syria and Cyprus and to the so-called 'Aeolian' capitals of eastern Greece that also disappeared from the Greek world after the establishment of the Ionic capital.

Figured Works of Art

The documents we possess on the figurative arts of Etruria come to us almost exclusively from sanctuaries and tombs. This is not merely due to the circumstances surrounding their preservation and discovery. In Etruria more than elsewhere the religious and funerary inspiration of works of art does in fact seem to prevail over the profane. There is at any rate an almost complete lack of evidence of a monumental art aimed at exalting or commemorating historical events or civic occasions such as are met in the Greek and

Roman worlds: in this respect, a parallel may be drawn with Etruscan literature. On the other hand, the solid ties binding art with religion and the generally concrete – we could almost say utilitarian – bent of the Etruscan mind must have obstructed the process that can be detected more or less clearly in the Greek world and which led to an autonomous conception of the artistic phenomenon as an activity that was not merely practical and ethical, but aesthetic as well. This incapacity of arriving at a conception of art for its own sake, an incapacity shared by all pre-classical civilizations, explains why the Etruscan figured arts generally present the characteristics of applied art and never reach, or very exceptionally, the level of what is usually termed 'great' art, i.e. the personal work of an artist aware of his creative capacity and socially appreciated because of it. In fact we have notice of only one Etruscan craftsman through ancient tradition (Varro, in Pliny, XXXV, 157): Vulca the modeller, of Veian origin but who also worked in Rome during the sixth century B.C.

A short review of the categories of surviving monuments according to their techniques may help to clarify these preliminary considerations. The plastic arts[15] are found represented by bronzes (other metals are less frequent), terracottas, and sculptures in stone: marble is absent for it was not available locally and only very rarely imported. Indirect sources allow us to presume that wood was also very widely used; moreover, small objects feature intaglioes in ivory, bone, and amber. Statuary belonging to holy places may be classified as follows: divines images as objects of worship, often mentioned in ancient authors (e.g. the famous painted terracotta statue of the Capitoline Jove in Rome, attributed to Vulca) but now generally lost; statues and votive groups representing deities or worshippers of which we possess copious examples, in particular small bronzes and terracottas from sanctuary deposits; parts of the architectural decoration of temples, such as the great acroteria to which the famous Apollo of Veii belonged. Within the funerary sphere should be mentioned the statuettes found in tombs, the Chiusi 'canopics', the great portrait-statues and the figures sculptured upon the lids of sarcophagi: it is especially with this latter genre that the development of the personal portrait or likeness is connected (see plate 4A). Apart from these sacral or funerary manifestations there may have been a type of statuary of an honorary character such as the statues erected to celebrate illustrious men, as was the custom in the Rome of republican times (Pliny, *Nat. Hist.*, XXXIV, 26). We should however be especially careful in attempting to identify this type of monument: until recently, for example, it was thought that the famous statue of the Orator in the Florence Archaeological Museum was an honorary statue; but since K. Olzscha interpreted the Etruscan word *flere* as 'god', the inscription accompanying the statue appears to be of a votive character and would therefore point to some religious purpose for this work of art (see plate 17).[16]

Among the architectural terracottas, figures in relief often alternate with figures in the round.[17] In the archaic acroteria and antefixes of southern Etruria and Faliscan territory, figures and groups are met standing free in space though modelled as if they were reliefs. Conversely, in pediments belonging to a late period, figures in high relief tend to detach themselves from the background as if they were statues. Both characteristics have their counterparts in the great ornamental sculpture decorating the Greek temple. True low relief is met in friezes found on beam facings. The mythological repertoire usually provided the craftsmen with their subjects. But reliefs appear to have become especially common in funerary art, as witnessed by the Tarquinii slabs ornamented with chequered patterns and friezes belonging traditionally to the 'orientalizing' repertoire; by the sepulchral steles of Volterra, Fiesole, and Bologna belonging to a period dating from the sixth to the beginning of the fourth century and picturing the dead person or his surroundings or his journey to the nether world; by the scenes on the *cippi* and archaic urns from Chiusi, with realistic subjects such as funerals, banquets, dances, and athletic games; by the mythological compositions sculptured on the walls of tombs but especially on the sides of stone sarcophagi (southern Etruria, Chiusi)[18] and of alabaster (Volterra), terracotta (Chiusi), or travertine (Perugia) cinerary urns produced between the fourth and first centuries B.C. Of especial importance is the working of laminated bronze with embossed decorations for the ornamentation of furniture, shields, chariots, vases, and candelabra; this was initiated during the orientalizing period and flourished in the course of the sixth century: an especially productive centre may be identified with Perugia, and we should not forget to mention in this respect the famous situla of the Bologna *Certosa* (see plate 19B). A similar technique, but for objects of smaller proportions, is met in precious metal vases and in goldwork. Mention should also be made of intaglios on ivory, bone, etc., and of the very rich collection of seals carved in hard stones. In all these more strictly decorative or 'applied' productions, figures and compositions derived from Greek mythology prevail.

Painting is represented by monuments of conspicuous importance, an exceptional state of affairs for the classical world before late Hellenistic times.[19] These Etruscan documents are of especial importance to us owing to the total or almost total loss of the original works of the great painters of Greece. The custom of painting the walls of subterranean tombs (generally with frescoes) was especially prevalent at Tarquinii, but it also occurs, though less intensely or sporadically, at Chiusi, Orvieto, Caere, Vulci, Veii, and elsewhere. Of those paintings that have come to light in the last few centuries, many have been lost or are irreparably damaged, others have kept in good condition; in certain cases they have been detached so as to preserve them from further deterioration.[20] Besides wall paintings we also possess a number of paintings on terracotta slabs which were originally fitted together to line and decorate the inner walls of sacred buildings (as is almost certainly the case with those found in the Portonaccio sanctuary at Veii) or even of tombs (such as the Caere groups – see plates 20 and 21). Finally, in a few isolated cases, the sides of sarcophagi and urns feature painted decorations instead of reliefs. The subject-matter was originally purely decorative (like those of orientalizing inspiration) or taken from Greek mythological themes. But the great funerary paintings of the archaic period and of the fifth century at Tarquinii and Chiusi reproduce funeral scenes with banquets, dancing, and circus games (see plates 22, 23, and 24B), or, more generally, scenes from everyday life (hunting, fishing, etc.). Later (i.e. after the fifth century), the prevailing subjects include journeys to the nether regions, infernal banquets, etc., together with mythological compositions (Orvieto, Tarquinii, Vulci); particular attention was given to the portrayal of the dead person's features.

Etruscan painted ceramics appear more or less faithfully to imitate Greek ceramics which were in any case very popular in Etruria, especially during the archaic period. But we should speak of designs rather than paintings, for only exceptionally were polychromous patterns employed.[21] Greek and Oriental craftsmen probably worked in the cities of Etruria during the sixth century and formed local schools: this occurred in the case of the production of the Caere *hydriae*, decorated with lively mythological themes. The activity of the ceramic workshops of the fourth century is also important. Draughtsmanship appears to be even more directly inspired by Greek models: it is manifested in engravings on the backs of mirrors and on bronze cists, and often exhibits a high degree of workmanship (see plate 25). Owing to their prevailingly antiquarian interest, bronzes, ceramics and jewellery will be found more fully treated in the chapter dealing with aspects of Etruscan life (see pp. 212 ff.).

The Problem of Etruscan Art

Having considered the various categories of artistic monuments we are now faced with the greater problem, the problem *par excellence* in fact: that of their aesthetic meaning. Many of the works in our possession cannot obviously be considered as original creations: they belong to the products of traditional craftsmanship and only distantly reflect the main trends in the history of art. There are however a number of monuments or groups of monuments where both subjective impressions and objective considerations allow us to detect more or less distinctly the hall-mark of a certain artistic personality. The problem consists in attempting to establish up to what point this possibility corresponds to reality, i.e. whether we are really faced in such cases with original creations, great or small as the case may be, or whether we are still dealing with simple imitations of objects now lost; and, if this be the case, where could we expect to find the originals.

The fact that immediately springs to our attention is that the very great majority of themes, types, and patterns of the artistic production of Etruria find their antecedents and their inspiration in Greek models. This dependence extended also, broadly speaking, to stylistic forms. As a result, the development of Etruscan art, from the beginnings of the archaic period down to late Hellenistic times, mainly re-echoed the various phases of development undergone by Greek art. But a number of differences occur: Etruria ignored certain Hellenic motifs while developing others which in Greece met with little popularity or which belonged to styles that had already been discarded. There are also indications of certain attitudes foreign, or even opposed, to the figurative conceptions of the Greek world.

We should ask ourselves up to what point Etruscan artists meant to react and did react with original solutions against the dominant formulae from Greece. We should then seek to establish whether in the realization of a personal artistic vision, conditions were laid for the formation of local traditions distinct from those of Greece, and how widely and for how long these traditions were able to impose themselves. On the other hand, if we accept the growth of autonomous trends in Etruscan art, it becomes necessary to decide on whether such trends were ephemeral and unrelated or whether a connexion existed between them; and also whether a hypothetical 'constant' in the tendencies of Etruscan taste down the centuries should be attributed to historical continuity or whether it corresponded rather to a deep-seated predisposition in the Etruscan mind for ways of expression different from those of the Greeks. All these questions may, all things considered, be gathered into the single one: how far and in what sense may we speak of 'Etruscan art'?[22]

Nineteenth-century critics, largely dominated by classicist or naturalistic preconceptions, tended on the whole to answer this question in the negative. For them, Etruscan art productions were to be considered as provincial manifestations of Greek art, composed of rough and artistically valueless works: all finds made in Etruria possessing a certain value were straightway attributed to Greek artists. But the new directions taken by art historians in the matter of aesthetic criticism at the beginning of the twentieth century, particularly as a result of studies made by A. Riegl, allowed full validity of expression to artistic experiences outside the classical orbit and opened the way to the comprehension of stylistic phenomena of the ancient world that hitherto had been misjudged, as did in fact occur with the artistic production of Etruria. From the analysis of recently discovered single works of art (such as the Apollo of Veii – see plate 5), or of works rediscovered in the light of a new aesthetic sensibility (such as the 'Capitoline Brutus' – see plate 15), there was put forward the more or less cautious affirmation of the originality and independence of Etruscan art with respect to that of Greece, based upon a different, unmistakable vision of form, evident even in imitations of Hellenic types and patterns. Mention was even made of a peculiar disposition of the Italic peoples (including therefore not only the Etruscans but also, though later, the Romans) to conceive reality according to an 'illusionistic', 'inorganic', immediate and strongly individualized picture as against the 'naturalistic', 'organic', 'typal' vision of Greek art; a disposition whose definition was attempted by G. Kaschnitz Weinberg in his concept of 'structure'. A number of justified criticisms have been made to these points of view. More recently, in fact, the statement was even made that there do not exist in Etruria true works of art except under the direct influence of Greek forms, and that the Etrusco-Italic 'originality' was no more than the occasional and ephemeral manifestation of a colourful popular craftsmanship incapable of quickening a truly artistic tradition (R. Bianchi Bandinelli).

The problem, therefore, remains for the most part unsolved. This is perhaps due to an unsatisfactory formulation of it by both sides. Etruscan art is in fact generally considered as a whole, ignoring the fact that it embraces many types of manifestations over a period of seven centuries at least, and that the transformations that took place in the course of such a long span of time (from protohistory to the beginnings of the Roman Empire) do not merely concern

Etruria and Greece but have decisive bearings over the whole development of ancient art. It is obvious that perspectives vary according to the times: it would therefore seem more logical, and closer to the concrete reality of history, to examine the problem of 'Etruscan art' by referring to the situation of each period rather than abstractly seeking a hypothetical and unitary solution.

Thus it may be that at first, between the eighth and the beginning of the seventh century, artistic activity in the cities of Etruria developed parallel to that of other Mediterranean countries, including Greece, in a complex interplay of themes of prehistoric origin (particularly evident in the lively realism displayed by the smaller products of the plastic arts) and of oriental influences which characterize that phase in the history of Etruscan decoration which we in fact call 'orientalizing'. It is obvious that for this period it would not be correct to speak of subordination to Greek art. It would be better to say that Etruria participated, in a western peripheral position, in one of the last elaborations of an ancient 'pre-Hellenic' Mediterranean artistic experience. But with the exception of a few traces of originality in the plastic funerary arts (as in the expressive heads of the Chiusi canopics) there is no sign of the burgeoning of local, or national, artistic traditions. This is in fact where the difference with Greece lies, a difference that was to have far-reaching repercussions, for at this crucial age, Greece with its vigorous creative spirit was to leave the formulas of the old world far behind and open a new chapter in the history of world art.

Unsupported by a tradition of its own, Etruria was fatally destined to be absorbed into the orbit of Greek artistic experience. For the latter's power of attraction did not only consist in the intrinsic superiority of its aesthetic values: it owed much to its very widespread implantations in the Greek colonies of Sicily and the Italian mainland. This took place effectively from the beginning of the sixth century, and it is most likely that the artistic influence of Greek archaism on Etruria (together with parallel influences in the fields of religion, institutions, music, dress, etc.) did not exert itself merely through the importation of objects and models, but also through the direct activity of Greek artificers in Etruscan cities. But it is just during this period (from the sixth to the first decades of the fifth century) that the artistic production of Etruria burst into a wonderful, and even, in certain aspects, unsurpassed, flowering, specially in temple architecture, in the plastic arts, in painting and in 'minor' decorated objects: a large number of works appear refined in technique, of high stylistic value and not without a certain peculiar 'character' that makes them often recognizable as Etruscan or of Etruscan inspiration. The original dilemma of dependence or independence now acquires overtones that render it all the more delicate as the facts seem to lead towards contradictory judgements (thus explaining the hesitancies of modern critics): these works of art, though 'Etruscan', do not in fact cease to be 'Greek' – a statement that may at first seem paradoxical, but which clearly is not, once we have freed ourselves of the notion of 'national art', inapplicable in this particular case.

We should also keep in mind the fact that Greek archaic art does not represent a rigidly unitarian or stylistically logical phenomenon; it is rather the result of the local elaborations of many and varied scattered centres with changing, lively, and multiform currents crossing and re-crossing each other in all directions. Within this essentially regional framework, partly Greek and even non-Greek territories found their place under the influence of the civilization of Hellas: e.g. Cyprus, Lycia, Caria, Lydia, and Phrygia in the east, Macedonia and Thrace in the north, Etruria in the west. These countries were not merely recep-tive 'provinces' in the elaboration of archaic art, passively submitting to the stamp of the Greek creative genius; they themselves participate as the 'regions' of a vast civilized community according to their own particular circumstances, requirements, and capabilities and, therefore, featuring characteristics of their own within the greater compass of a peri-Hellenic unity. In the case of Etruria, an outline of the 'regional artistic peculiarities of the archaic period may be traced in the following principal traits: (1) the existence of religious and funerary requirements predisposing the figurative arts towards a concrete, immediate, and actual representation of reality;[23] (2) a notable persistence of formal patterns, techniques, and traditions belonging to the earlier 'Mediterranean' and orientalizing phase; (3) direct and very close relations with the artistic experiences of the eastern Greek world, i.e. of the coastal and island centres of Aeolis and Ionia in western Asia Minor; these relations were close enough for many decades (from the middle of the sixth to the beginning of the fifth century) for the figurative arts of Etruria to follow much the same patterns as those of the eastern Greek world, so as to create what in fact has come to be known as Ionic-Etruscan art; (4) the local appearance of considerable schools and artistic personalities with a high standard of achievement (bronze-casters at Perugia, painters like the decorator of the Tomb of the Baron at Tarquinii, modellers in terracotta at Veii such as the creator of the 'Apollo' or his followers, etc.); it would be difficult to deny these artists an authentic, original and, at times, powerful creative genius.

A radical change occurred during the first half of the fifth century. Greece passed from archaic to classical art in a process of fundamental importance to the history of human civilization. But the activity of the great Greek masters tended to become more closely knit from a stylistic point of view and to acquire a more 'national' character, concentrating more and more around Athens and the Peloponnesian cities. At the same time, the peripheral regions declined for reasons of a political and economic order. Etruria was left isolated. The classical spirit, the result of an unrepeatable and inimitable moment, found no echo in Etruria, where, amongst other things, the historically favourable conditions that encouraged the artistic flowering of archaic times came to an end, bringing in their wake a long period of depression and decadence. Thus we witness for the whole of the fifth and well into the fourth century, the persistence of patterns and formulas belonging to the archaic tradition or inspired by Greek art of the 'severe' style, i.e. of that transient stage between archaism and classicism. The phenomenon of delayed action proper to marginal countries (as, for example, in the contemporary 'sub-archaic' art of Cyprus)[24] is most clearly manifested. The penetration of classical influences was slow and sporadic. In this atmosphere, deprived of a unitarian and respected tradition such as existed previously, artistic vitality only broke out in small, ephemeral bursts of expressive originality. The activity of bronze craftsmen continued, however, unabated.

Contact was re-established between the artistic worlds of Greece and Etruria after the fourth century B.C. and continued throughout the Hellenistic age, merging finally into the triumphal victory of Hellenism in Roman Italy at the end of the republic and the beginning of the empire. But the attitude of Etruscan artists towards the products of Greece does not this time appear to be the same as in archaic times: we can no longer speak of the elaboration, with original elements, of a common inheritance: it is rather the imitation of 'foreign' models, more or less faithfully and successfully reproduced. Not only are forms and single typological patterns taken over, but whole compositions for the decoration of buildings and objects, especially in the case of paintings. In this last phase, and in this type of

Hellenizing decorative production the concept expressed by certain modern critics, namely that of Etruria as a 'province' of the Greek world – i.e. the denial of all artistic originality – appears particularly justified.

Account however should be taken of another aspect, of quite different order and importance, of the figurative activity of the Etruscans during the Hellenistic age. In a number of isolated cases or in groups of monuments, especially funerary monuments, there appeared stylistic patterns and solutions that presented a clear contrast with classical taste: compact structures with geometric tendencies, 'unfinished' forms, disproportions, exasperation in the treatment of certain expressive details, etc. We may well ask how far these manifestations were to be explained as the handing down by craftsmen of remote archaic formulas, survivals favoured by the static quality of the Etruscan ritual, or as popular improvisations of no consequence or even as the effect of a falling-off in quality of manual techniques. But it is possible that they may have been the reflections, however indirect, of the activity of artists who by adopting age-old local conventions and reacting against Greek models according to their temperament, may have sought new forms of expression.

This hypothesis becomes transformed into certainty as far as the art of portraiture is concerned: for it offers us many authentic and original works of art (large bronzes, paintings, etc.) and innumerable secondary products (sarcophagus lids, terracottas) which witness in their turn the crystallization of a solid and lasting local tradition centred around the activity of the greatest masters of the craft. In contrast with the Greek portrait (its original inspiration in the fourth century), the Etruscan portrait tends to seek a maximum of expressive concreteness for the features and, in certain ways, for individual 'character', neglecting the organic coherence of natural forms but stressing essential elements by means of the simple, rough, discontinuous and, at times, violent use of lines and masses. We may well say that a new style was born, a new artistic tradition independent of the Greek world: a tradition which may be 'Etruscan' but which was also more generically 'Italic', for its seeds were carried on beyond the decline of Etruria as a nation, by the art of Roman Italy and of the Western world under the empire. Such an 'expressionistic' view of reality – particularly manifest in the portrait but also present in other art forms – was to live in popular art currents of the first centuries of the empire, spread to the provincial art of Europe, and break out impetuously as the great courtly art of the end of the second and the third century A.D.: it was destined to form one of the most significant contributions to the artistic inheritance of late imperial and medieval times.[25]

NOTES

1. B. Nogara, *Gli Etruschi e la loro civiltà*, 1934, pp. 405 ff.

2. For a complete account and an interpretation of classical sources on the sacred literature of the Etruscans, see especially C. O. Thulin, *Die etruskische Disciplin*, in *Göteborgs Högskolas Årsskrift*, 1905, 1906, 1909.

3. See E. Bormann, in *Jahreshefte der österr. Archäol. Inst.*, II, 1899, pp. 219 ff.; M. Pallottino, *Tarquinia* (*Monumenti Antichi dell'Accademia dei Lincei*), XXXVI, 1937, col. 561 and in *Studi Etruschi*, XXI, 1950–1, pp. 167 ff.; J. Heurgon, in *Latomus*, XII, 1953, pp. 462 ff.

4. See in this connexion, B. Nogara, *Gli Etruschi e la loro civiltà*, 1934, pp. 425 ff.

5. No up-to-date or detailed analyses exist on this question, which has only been touched on in general works such as K. O. Müller and W. Deecke, *Die Etrusker*, 1877, II, pp. 200 ff.; P. Ducati, *Etruria antica*, 1927, pp. 167 ff. For a recent work on the music of the Greeks, see M. Wegner, *Das Musikleben der Griechen*, 1949.

6. For a connexion between pipe-playing and the 'primitive' spirituality of the Etruscans, see R. Enking, *Etruskische Geistigkeit*, 1947.

7. On the subject of Etruscan art, the following general works may be consulted: P. Ducati, *Storia dell'arte etrusca*, 1927; G. Q. Giglioli, *L'arte etrusca*, 1935; P. J. Rijs, *An Introduction to Etruscan Art*, 1953.

8. On the subject of Etruscan architecture, besides the works quoted above, see especially A. Andren, *Architectural Terracottas from Etrusco-Italic Temples* (*Acta Inst. Rom. Sueciae*, VI), 1939–40; G. Patroni, *Architettura preistorica generale ed italica. Architettura etrusca*, 1946; L. Polacco, *Tuscanicae dispositiones*, 1952 (to be consulted with care).

9. See F. E. Brown, in *Memoirs of the Amer. Acad. in Rome*, XX, 1951, pp. 102 ff.

10. A. Minto, *Pseudocupole e pseudovolte nell' architettura etrusca delle origini*, in *Palladio*, III, 1939, pp. 1 ff.

11. F. Messerschmidt, *Das Grabmal des Porsenna*, in *Das neue Bild der Antike*, pp. 53 ff.

12. An attempt to throw doubt upon the Etruscan origin of the three-celled temple and to attribute it to the Romans will be found in L. Polacco, *Tuscanicae dispositiones*, 1952. See also *Studi Etruschi*, XXII, 1952–3, pp. 458 ff.

13. Metal coverings (Vitruvius, III, 3, 5) must be considered to have been exceptional and limited to small and unusually rich buildings.

14. The chronological classification of Etruscan temple decorations into 'phases' is due to A. della Seta, *Museo di Villa Giulia*, 1918, pp. 120 ff. Further details will be found in A. Andrén, *op. cit.*, pp. CXXX ff., and M. Pallottino, in *Bullettino Archeol. Comunale*, LXVIII, 1940, p. 253.

15. Apart from the general works on Etruscan art already quoted, see also: P. Ducati, *La scultura etrusca*, 1935; G. Hanfmann, *Altetruskische Plastik*, 1936; L. Goldscheider, *Etruscan sculpture*, 1941 (Phaidon); P. J. Rijs, *Tyrrhenika. An Archaeological Study of Etruscan Sculpture in the Archaic and Classical Periods*, 1941.

16. See K. Olzscha, *Interpretation der Agramer Mumienbinde*, 1939, pp. 20 ff.

17. See A. Andrén, *op. cit.*, p. 241, note 1.

18. R. Herbig, *Die jüngeretruskischen Steinsarkophage*, 1952.

19. On the subject of Etruscan painting, see F. Weege, *Etruskische Malerei*, 1921; F. Poulsen, *Etruscan Tomb Paintings*, 1922; F. Messerschmidt, *Beiträge zur Chronologie der etruskischen Wandmalerei*, I, 1923; M. Pallottino, *La peinture étrusque* (*Etruscan painting*), 1952.

20. The friezes of the François Tomb at Vulci, the property of the

Torlonia family, had been detached as early as the last century; more recently, the removal and restoration took place of frescoes at Tarquinii (Tombs of the Chariots, of the Triclinium and of the Funerary Couch) and at Orvieto (see *Bollett. dell'Ist. Centr. del Restauro*, 2, 1950; 3-4, 1951; 5-6, 1951).

21. See J. D. Beazley, *Etruscan Vase Painting*, 1947.

22. For a comprehensive view of the problem, see J. Martha, *L'art étrusque*, 1889, p. 614; A. della Seta, *Antica arte etrusca*, in *Dedalo*, I, 1920-1, pp. 559 ff.; C. Anti, *Il problema dell'arte italica*, in *Studi Etruschi*, IV, 1930, pp. 151 ff.; G. Kaschnitz-Weinberg, *Bemerkungen zur Struktur der altitalischen Plastik*, in *Studi Etruschi*, VII, 1933, p. 135 ff.; R. Bianchi Bandinelli, *Storicità dell' arte classica*, 2nd ed., 1950, pp. 77 ff., pp. 93 ff.; pp. 115 ff. (see also the 1st ed., pp. 257 ff.); M. Pallottino, *Sul problema delle correlazioni artistiche fra Grecia ed Etruria*, in *La parola del passato*, fasc. XIII, 1950, pp. 5 ff.

23. See M. Pallottino, '*Partecipazione' e senso drammatico nel mondo figurato degli Etruschi*, in *Arti Figurative*, II, 1946, pp. 149 ff.

24. See *The Swedish Cyprus Expedition*, IV, 2; E. Gjerstad, *The Cypro-Geometric, Cypro-Archaic and Cypro-Classical Periods*, 1949, pp. 93 ff., 117 ff., 364 ff.

25. See G. Rodenwaldt, *Über den Stilwandel in der Antoninischen Kunst*, in *Abhandl. der Preuss. Akademie der Wissensch., Phil.-Hist. Klasse*, 1935, and *Römische Reliefs-Vorstufen zur Spätantike*, in *Jahrbuch des deutsch. archäol. Instituts*, LV, 1940, p. 12 ff.; M. Pallottino, *Civiltà romana, arte figurativa e ornamentale*, 1940, p. 81 ff.; R. Bianchi Bandinelli, *Tradizione ellenistica e gusto romano nella pittura pompeiana*, in *La critica d'arte*, IV, 1941, p. 3 ff.

CHAPTER NINE

LIFE AND CUSTOMS

Monuments as a Source of Information

HOWEVER important our knowledge of the cultural life of a people as revealed by the manifestations of its religious feelings, of its thought, of its organizing abilities and artistic aptitudes, we shall never come fully close to it nor understand its most intimate psychology unless we are able to visualize and understand the various aspects and habits of its everyday life, to penetrate its homes, to catch it in its familiar surroundings and become fully conversant with its traditions and customs.[1]

There is no doubt that literature, especially in such forms as comedy, satire, letters, etc., is irreplaceable as a source of information on the private life and habits of ancient peoples. The complete loss of Etruscan literature (if we admit that there ever existed a literature with *bourgeois* or private themes, such as the Roman satire or epistle) deprives us of a means precious in the reconstruction of family life and customs of ancient Etruria.

But besides literary sources there also exist monumental, or archaeological, sources: on the one hand these consist of objects actually preserved in the interior of tombs, as well as the character, the peculiarities, the very arrangement of such tombs together with the very few remains we have from inhabited sites; on the other of figured works of art reproducing actual scenes taken from contemporary life. As far as this type of monument is concerned, Etruria finds itself in an exceptionally privileged position. We have already referred to the deep-rooted tradition of recreating life-like surroundings for the entombed dead, surroundings as authentic and as sumptuous as possible, with jewels, weapons, instruments, household articles. To it we owe that our excavations of Etruscan cemeteries have provided us with such ample and direct sources of information on the personal clothing, the weapons, the articles of everyday life, and the shape of objects that furnished the home. Our only limitation in this field, unfortunately a limitation of fundamental importance, is the almost total disappearance of objects made of perishable materials such as cloth, leather, wicker, or wood. The climate of Italy, as against the hot dry North African climate, has not allowed in the great majority of cases the preservation of such objects: hence the gaps present in the 'ethnography' of ancient Etruria. Only exceptionally, as in the case of the tombs of Visentium and Vulci, have we been able to recover fragments of perishable materials: a wooden tray, the handle of an axe, a razor sheath, wicker baskets, pieces of leather ornaments, etc. We have also been able to find a few small pieces of cloth or traces of cloth on oxidized bronze.[2]

The Home and its Furnishings

Figured monuments allow us to see what objects have survived as they were actually used in everyday life; they also complete the picture of the furnished house by including those that have perished. Such monuments, funerary paintings in particular, have a documentary value surpassing that normally offered by artistic representations left to us by the classical world, with the exception of a few 'popular' Roman frescoes and reliefs, which however derive their naïve realism and directness of expression from the tradition of Etrusco-Italic art. In the Greek world, as far back as the archaic period, man played a preponderant or even exclusive role, with a background reduced to a few necessary elements strictly dependent on the human form and not infrequently rendered symbolically or by simple allusive touches. With the Etruscans however, as with Oriental peoples, artistic composition has a descriptive and narrative character and indulges in background detail. Thus funerary paintings and sculptures introduce us, plunge us so to speak, into the very heart of a past reality. And though to us these reproductions appear naïve and stylized both in form and technique, they are nevertheless faithful in the highest degree, almost photographically faithful, to the chosen subject. He who can read through the difficulties of formal language, and knows how to translate it (there is often no need for a translation) may, thanks to these monuments, witness the unfolding of banquet scenes, dances, games, etc., as if he were living two thousand five hundred years ago. Added to this general scenic faithfulness there is a close faithfulness to detail in furniture and dress. So that even though Etruria lacks literary sources, we possess the highly valuable evidence of figured monuments: it can even be stated that from a certain point of view the latter are more important still in the study of life and customs: narrative always requires a reconstructive effort of the imagination where subjective elements often intrude; whereas the visual arts are direct, immediate, and impose themselves with peremptory force.

The archaeological evidence on Etruscan life covers the whole development of its history, from its beginnings to the threshold of imperial Rome. In the case of figured monuments, the richest crop of documents was yielded by the golden age of the Etruscan civilization, that is by the sixth and fifth centuries B.C., to which period the greatest number of painted tombs belong. We shall therefore principally refer to this period, the period during which the Etruscan way of life was formed and defined; but we shall also take into account the variations that took place through the centuries, especially where customs are concerned. It should also be understood that the data supplied by monuments concern principally the higher or well-to-do strata of society: i.e. those classes whose financial means and requirements of prestige or of aristocratic pride allowed or imposed the building, decoration, and furnishing of grandiose and lasting funerary monuments.

Let us in the first place try to picture to ourselves the home, the centre of family life, its main features, and the activities of which it is the stage. There have been long discussions on the shape and layout of the Etruscan house: all too often it has been considered as an abstract architectural entity, as a type, reproducing substantially a single original plan, as in the case of the so-called 'Pompeian' house.[3] In actual fact the numerous documents that may be used in the reconstruction of Etruscan private dwellings offer considerable variations, variations that do not merely occur in an evolutionary direction, i.e. in the successive phases of the Etruscan civilization. Direct evidence is provided by the foundations of houses found in many parts of Etruria, but especially at Marzabotto near Bologna (where an entire residential centre may be seen), and at Vetulonia, Tarquinii, and Veii. From the very beginnings of the Etruscan civilization the house with rectilinear walls has everywhere replaced the ancient rectangular or ovoidal dwellings of Italian prehistory: a relic of the earliest phase of this movement is the 'cottage-shaped' cinerary urn of the Villanovan culture. It is likely that on the actual borders of Etruscan territory, as for example in Latium or at Bologna, this phase lasted right up to historical times. The belief that the dead man's life continued in the grave is chiefly responsible for the fact that tombs and urns were made to look like houses; and these were at times imitated down to the smallest detail of architecture and furniture. The rock-hewn tombs discovered in the Caere (Cerveteri) necropolis provide us with precious documentary evidence of the various types of interior by giving us the layout and general arrangement of the rooms, the decoration of doors, windows, and ceilings, and even the furniture (round tables, hampers, chests, beds). Details as to the external architecture of the house may be obtained from the rocky façades of tombs in the inner zones of Blera, Norchia, Castel d'Asso. As for the house as a whole, especially in its later phase, useful information may be gathered from a number of cinerary urns found at Chiusi.

The house originally consisted of a rectangular building comprising a single room, protected by a double-sloped roof set at a low gradient. In its simplest form, this is the type of house that spread from the East via the land route and which forms the basis of the Mycenean *megaron* and of the Greek temple. At a very early stage, however, it grows richer and more complex in form by the addition of external elements with porticoes, or by an increase in the number of rooms. The sixth century tombs at Cerveteri present in their most usual form a plan that may to some extent be considered the ancestor of the Italic or 'Pompeian' house: an unroofed entrance hall (corresponding to the corridor in the tomb), a central room, possibly a small courtyard (the future atrium?) on to which open two lateral rooms, and, at the back, the main body of the house; this consists of a transverse passage shaped like a transept with a coffered ceiling or a double-sloped roof, which in its turn gives access to one, two, or three rooms similarly protected by a double-sloped roof. The three-roomed type became the most usual and its resemblance to the Etruscan three-cell temple is significant. The transverse passage would correspond on the one hand to the porticoed forecourt of the temple, on the other to the *alae* of the Pompeian house; whilst the back rooms are thought to be preserved in the three rooms of the typical Pompeian house. It is worth noting that the transverse vestibule assumed in a few cases the form of a portico supported by pilasters and columns; there is no lack of variants, which may take the form of circular or semicircular rooms, or of vestibules roofed with radially set beams.

Ancient sources appear to agree in attributing the invention of the atrium to the Etruscans: the very word *atrium* is said to be of Etruscan origin, and in fact the form *aδre* does occur in an Etruscan text. The atrium does not however appear in its typical form of a half-covered room with an *impluvium* at the centre in models of tombs belonging to the archaic period; it only becomes recognizable in later monuments such as in a rock-hewn tomb at Tarquinii whose ceiling is shaped like the roof of an atrium, or in a small urn from Chiusi kept in the Berlin Museum. From amongst the many examples that attest the variety and complexity of the various types of dwellings we may mention an urn in the Florence Archaeological Museum modelled in the shape of a small palace with arched doorway and two floors, and an urn from Chiusi featuring on its first floor a veranda supported by columns.

We have referred to the furniture, which must have been rather limited, as with all civilizations of the ancient world.[4] Funerary paintings depict beds with ornamental legs, cushions, and covers painted or embroidered in lively colours and geometrical patterns, rectangular or circular tables, chairs shaped like thrones, stools, foot-rests, etc. A typical piece is the wicker or wooden chair with a round seat and a wide splayed back found sculptured in a few Cerveteri tombs or, reproduced in bronze, amongst objects belonging to funerary *trousseaux* from Chiusi and Palestrina; it also survives in marble in that curious and late archaistic monument known as the 'Corsini chair':[5] its shape lives on to reappear in provincial figured monuments belonging to Roman Imperial times.

Bronze candelabra too may be included amongst the

furniture; many of these have come down to us as actual specimens or reproduced in paintings. Some are rather elongated in form, surmounted by a statuette and tips in the shape of a bird's beak on which candles or torches were fixed. We also possess many oil candelabra with a small dish at the top that were meant to hang from the ceiling, such as the famous carved candelabrum of Cortona (see plate 19A).

We ought to mention too the whole series of metal and clay containers, ranging from large archaic *lebetes* (cauldrons) supported on tripods or on circular pedestals, to vases imported from Greece or their Etruscan imitations such as *amphorae*, kraters (for wine), *hydriae* (with three handles, for water), jugs, pails, pans, plates, goblets, chalices, glasses, balsam containers in the shape of various animals, etc. Vases made of precious metals – gold, silver, or electrum (an alloy of silver and gold) – must naturally have been rare, though they occasionally appear reproduced in painting. Specimens in our possession are limited to silver and electrum and have mostly been found within graves belonging to the orientalizing period.

The oldest fictile vases (eighth to sixth century) were made with an unpurified and roughly mixed clay (the *impasto*) and have a slat-smoothed surface: they vary in colour (black, brown, red, or yellow) and in shape (occasionally imitating embossed types), and are ornamented with graffiti or paintings. Greek influence from the seventh century onwards helped to spread the use of potter's clay, decorated with figured and geometrical patterns: 'proto-Corinthian', Corinthian, Ionic, Rhodian, Laconian, Chalcidian and, lastly, Attic vases were imported and imitated locally. During the second half of the sixth century and throughout the whole of the fifth, Attic pottery alone was imported, black-figured vases preceding in time the ones with red figures. A type of native pottery, probably derived from the *impasto*, the *bucchero*, dominates in Etruria from the end of the seventh to the beginning of the fifth century with many varied forms; *bucchero* pottery is characterized by the use of surface-polished black or grey clay. The fourth century witnesses the spread of pottery decorated with red figures in imitation of the vases of Attica and of the Greek cities of southern Italy: the most important local school belongs to the Faliscan territory, but others are known at Vulci, Perugia, Volterra, etc. At a later period there is a predominance of clay vases gilded or varnished in black and red, with decorative elements stamped or in relief. From this late type of pottery was developed the great vase industry of Arezzo that was to flourish at the beginning of the imperial age to give rise to the characteristic pottery of the Roman world, the so-called *terra sigillata*. Besides these metal and clay vessels, we should also make a passing reference to vases made of ivory, alabaster, or wood, though it is only exceptionally that specimens made of the last-mentioned material have survived.

One monument which may be considered unique in the ancient world has provided us with an exceptional picture of all the objects that go to furnish a home: furniture, instruments, everyday objects, etc. This is the 'Tomb of the Stuccoes' or of 'the Reliefs' at Cerveteri (see plates 30 and 31). It consists of a large room shaped to resemble the inside of a house along the walls of which the dead were arranged in cells rather like niches with beds, whilst the actual surface of the walls and pillars is decorated with painted stucco reliefs representing objects that are supposed to be hanging there. Amongst these we can recognize weapons (helmets, shields, swords, thigh-pieces), vases, small flower wreaths, a fan, a double bag, a complete knapsack, kitchen knives, spits, tools (axe, tongs, knife), a round table, ropes, wooden trays, sticks, etc. These reproductions are remarkably impressive because of relief and colour and an extraordinary faithfulness to the chosen subject. We are filled with wonder at the resemblance, or rather the identity of some of these objects belonging to the third and second centuries B.C. with objects in use to-day: as for example the rectangular wooden kitchen trays or the knapsack. This picture of everyday life outlined by the tomb of the Reliefs is completed with materials found in funeral *trousseaux* of the various Etruscan cemeteries, both in the case of weapons and of instruments. Bronze fans, similar to the one found reproduced in stucco at the Tomb of the Reliefs or pictured on other Etruscan monuments (such as in the paintings of the Bruschi Tomb or of the Tomb of the Shields at Tarquinii) have been discovered in the 'Tumulus of the Fans' at Populonia. Objects belonging to the *mundus*, that is to the requirements of feminine toilet, must also be considered as household articles: *cistae*, bronze mirrors, small wooden boxes in the shape of animals for cosmetics, etc.

Aspects of Etruscan Life

The reconstruction of the life led in the houses of the rich does not present excessive difficulties. We have already referred to the place of the woman in the home: how she participated in banquets and feasts on a footing of perfect equality with men. During the archaic period men and women banquet stretched out on the same couch: Aristotle is probably referring to this custom when he states in *Ath. Pol.*, 1, 23, d: 'The Etruscans take their food in the company of their women lying under the same mantle.' This statement has also been supposed to refer to a false interpretation of some sarcophagi on which husband and wife appear lying under a mantle, a symbol of marriage. The Etruscan marriage ceremony included in fact the rite – also found in present-day Jewish custom – of covering the bride and bridegroom with a veil: this is borne out by the relief, whose interpretation cannot be mistaken, on a little urn from Chiusi (see plate 14A). But it is also possible that the veil may have actually been used for the convivial couch. It is certain nevertheless that the Greeks tended to misunderstand the Etruscans, undoubtedly because of ancient political rivalries that made them find cause for scandal in the formal liberty of Etruscan women so unlike, at least up to the Hellenistic period, the segregation which was the lot of the Greek woman. It was easy and almost natural therefore to attribute to Etruscan women the character and behaviour of the *hetaerae*, the only women in Greece who took part in banquets with men. And thus, with that ease with which the classical world accepted and transmitted information, though unchecked, to be used as literary topics, were born and spread those libellous statements on Etruscan licentiousness insisted upon by Athenaeus (IV, 153, d; XII, 517 ff.) and re-echoed even by Plautus (*Cistellaria*, II, 3, 20 ff.). After the fourth century women no longer take part in banquets lying down on beds like the men, but seated, thus following the custom which was to remain firmly established throughout the Roman world. Paintings of banquets with several beds (generally three: hence the Roman *triclinium*) such as those found in the Tombs of the Leopards and of the *Triclinium*, both at Tarquinii, are full of natural and joyful simplicity. There are also a number of banquets in the Greek style, men only being present, culminating at times in abandoned orgies accompanied by dances and abundant libations (Tomb of the Inscriptions, Tarquinii). Banquets, like most other festivities and solemn occasions (e.g. games, funerals, etc.), were regularly accompanied by music and dancing.

A noteworthy series of paintings deals with games and entertainments (Tombs of the Augurs, the *Bigae*, and Francesca Giustiniani at Tarquinii, and the painted and relief tombs of Chiusi). It is evidently the Hellenic influence that dominates this aspect of Etruscan life; but the agonistic and professional character of Greek games and matches tends to give way in the Etruscan world to the spectacular. There is nothing more interesting or more suggestive in this respect than the Tomb of the *Bigae* at Tarquinii, where the artist has pictured a large sports field or circus bisected along its two axes, the long and the short, showing its arena and the wooden stands on which the spectators sit. In the arena we see charioteers on *bigae*, horsemen, wrestlers and boxers, vaulters with and without pole, an armed runner (hoplitodrome), umpires, and various other characters (see plate 22). On the stands, spectators belonging to both sexes take the liveliest interest in the result of the games, as the impassioned expressions on their faces clearly indicate. Quite possibly members of the most illustrious families took part in these sports. The Etruscan game of the Truia (*ludus Troiae*) is worth mentioning in this respect: it consisted of a horse race along an intricate course shaped like a maze: this is borne out by a graffito on an archaic Etruscan vase, and we know that it was still performed as an exercise for Roman youths at the beginning of the Empire.[6] Of a more popular character, the various activities of the showman (acrobatics, trick riding, clowning) are expressively portrayed in paintings at the Tomb of the Monkey in Chiusi (see plate 23). Lastly we must mention a bloodier kind of sport in which it is possible to recognize a forerunner of the Roman gladiatorial combats; these were in any case believed by ancient tradition to be of Etruscan origin (Athenaeus, IV, 153 f.): they certainly reached Rome by way of Campania which had come early under the influence of Etruria. They probably owe their origin to a funeral rite, an attenuation of the human sacrifices that accompany in many primitive civilizations the death of princes or of the illustrious. For in blood fights the stronger or the abler of the contestants has a chance of survival. A match of this kind is reproduced in the Tomb of the Augurs at Tarquinii: a masked figure, designated by the name of φersu (corresponding to the Latin *persona*, 'a masked figure'), with a hood and a ferocious dog on the leash, fights another figure armed with a cudgel and with head enveloped in a sack. Obviously if the latter manages to hit his opponent's dog with the cudgel victory will be his, and his adversary will be at his mercy; should the opposite come about, he will be torn to pieces by the dog.

Economic and Technical Achievements

Outside the home, we have public life and the life of commerce, navigation, agriculture, and industry. We obviously cannot dwell on all the aspects of Etruscan production and economy especially as in the majority of cases we only possess documents that are of little worth, and as it is chiefly by comparison with the Graeco-Roman world that we derive the knowledge we have: we are thus unable to point out any specifically Etruscan characteristics. It is better therefore to stress those technical aspects which have, quite early, transformed certain districts of Etruscan territory into areas whose economy was mainly industrial, although the greater portion of the country remained faithful to a predominantly pastoral and agricultural life.

A sufficiently accurate picture of Etruscan production during the later phase of the nation's history is given by that well-known passage in Livy (XXVIII, 45) listing the contributions given by the principal annexed or federated Etruscan cities to Scipio Africanus' oversea expedition. Here is the list of the loans drawn up according to each district's resources:

Caere (Cerveteri):   corn and other foodstuffs;
Tarquinii (Tarquinia): sail-cloth;
Rusellae (Roselle):   corn and timber for ship building;
Populonia (id.):   iron;

Clusium (Chiusi):   corn and timber;
Perusia (Perugia):   corn and timber;
Arretium (Arezzo):   corn, weapons, and wrought tools;
Volaterrae (Volterra): corn and pitch.

We can see in this list, clearly defined within the Central and Southern zones, the agricultural districts (Caere, Rusellae, Clusium, Perusia, Arretium, Volaterrae) some of which were also given to exploiting the last remnants of the large forests that once covered the area; Populonia on the other hand appears as an iron-working centre, and Arretium as an important industrial city. The mining area in Etruria is mainly situated within the territories of Vetulonia (with its metalliferous hills) and of Populonia (which included the island of Elba). The extraction of metals, practised from the earliest times, is an activity whose importance has not perhaps been sufficiently stressed so far, for the bearing it has on the history and life of the Etruscans and, more generally, on the Mediterranean world: we need only consider that the Etruscan mines were the only ones of any importance to be exploited in the Central Mediterranean. The continuous pressure and menace of Greek colonists on the northern coasts of Etruria is a certain sign of the importance attached to the possession of the mining areas, to being able to influence them, or even merely to bring in their neighbourhood. We have no knowledge of the technical aspects concerning the extraction and the first working of the ores, unless we include a certain amount of archaeological evidence (shafts driven in certain parts of the metal-bearing hills, tools that have been found in them, slag produced during the smelting of iron around Populonia); a few ancient sources also tell us that Populonia was the first centre for the smelting of crude metal extracted from the Elba mines, and for its sorting and distribution, though no further treatment took place there.[7]

The whole of Etruscan production is determined by this abundance of mineral ores: the quantities of weapons, tools, and domestic objects in bronze and iron found in graves prove this. Archaeological data have allowed us to establish that, as regards the manufacture of bronze and iron articles, the most important cities were Perugia (for tripods and other objects in wrought iron) whence its products spread towards Umbria (the famous bronze chariot found at Monteleone di Spoleto, now at the New York Metropolitan Museum, was probably made at Perugia); Visentium (Bisenzio) with its manufactured articles, especially during the archaic period; Vulci with its tripods, candelabra, weapons, etc.; Arezzo too, as mentioned by Livy in the passage quoted above. Etruscan iron and bronze were also worked in Campania, and it is probably from here that both the crude metal and the finished products reached the Greek world (Diodorus Siculus, v, 13). Etruscan bronze trumpets and statuettes were also well known in Greece: a fragment of a tripod of the Vulci type was found on the Acropolis of Athens.[8] Nor must other aspects of Etruscan industrial production be overlooked, such as the textile industry, the leather industry, with especial reference to footwear renowned throughout the Mediterranean world (Pollux, VII, 22, 86).

The progress of Etruscan technical achievements is also manifested by the search, exploitation, and transport of water. The search for water was entrusted to the *aquilices*, or water-diviners. Pliny (*Nat. Hist.*, III, 20, 120) mentions the canals dug by the Etruscans in the lower Po valley; and only an advanced hydraulic technique, such as is attested by rock-cuttings at the *Ponte Sodo* in Veii (spanning one of the branches of the Cremera), can explain the conquest of the marshy lands of the lower Po valley wrested inch by inch from the river and its stagnant pools, and where cities such as Ravenna had still to be built on piles. Nor could such intensely active life on the marshy areas of the Maremma or of the lower Po be explained had malarial infection already been common during the golden age of Etruscan civilization; malaria must in fact have contributed, during the late Hellenistic period, towards hastening the decadence of many Etruscan coastal towns.[9]

Weapons and Dress

A large bronze *situla* (a kind of pail) found in the vault of the *Certosa* of Bologna is an interesting witness of Etruscan provincial life during the first half of the fifth century B.C. (see plate 19B). It portrays military scenes, a procession, and episodes with domestic, hunting, and agricultural themes. Round the decorated top band of the situla a remarkable military parade unwinds itself: there are horsemen armed with battle-axes, three infantry platoons belonging to different services as shown by their armament, and a group of pioneers with axes. As to the Etruscan art of war, tradition tells us but little; we know however that the primitive military organization of the Romans owes much to the Etruscans. At first, battles were fought in chariots; after the sixth century, only cavalry was used. The three infantry services of the *Certosa* situla correspond perhaps to the three Roman orders of the *velites*, the *principes*, and the *triarii*.

As offensive weapons, the Etruscans had the heavy lance whose point and *saurocter* were made of iron or bronze; the light lance or javelin; the long sword, the use of which already seems to have ceased at an archaic period, and which was merely a relic of the armament of the late bronze age; the short sword or glaive; the curved sabre in use between the sixth and fourth centuries B.C.; the dagger; the battle-axe, which in oldest times possessed two blades, and, as already stated, probably belonged to the armament of chiefs. Their defensive weapons were the bronze helmet, the shield, the cuirass, and greaves. Primitive helmets have a crest or a crown with cheek-pieces; but the use of Corinthian and Attic helmets spread quite early from Greece. The classic Etruscan bronze helmet has roughly the shape of a morion surmounted at times with a crest of plumes; many specimens of these have been found in tombs: one has appeared as a votive offering in the Hellenic sanctuary of Olympia, bearing an inscription to Zeus which tells how it was dedicated by the Syracusan tyrant Hiero, as war-booty after the naval battle waged by the Greeks against the Etruscans in the vicinity of Cumae in 474 B.C. Cuirasses were originally made of cloth with attached discs or squares of laminated metal: later they were made entirely in bronze with detachable parts, or all of a piece, moulding the muscles of the male torso. Round bronze shields appear both in archaic and in more recent periods; the *Certosa* situla however also shows elliptical and almost square shields probably made of wood or leather. A mention should be made of offensive and defensive cudgels in which may perhaps be recognized a relic of the ancient clubs used by primitive men; archaic monuments give one or two examples of such cudgels, whilst a type of stick with curved end, the *lituus*, tended to become more and more a mark of priestly office and as such was passed on to the Roman world.

Let us now examine the ordinary clothes worn by Etruscan men and women through the centuries. Though we have no direct evidence (unless we except jewellery and a few items made of time-resisting materials) we are very amply documented in this respect thanks to figured monuments. It is only natural that climate should influence the nature of clothes; but the force of tradition must also be taken into account, for it exerts in many cases a tyrannical influence on the development of fashion. Thus, masculine semi-nudity, a typically Mediterranean custom, was still very common in archaic Etruria. This custom, deriving as it did from the Eastern civilizations of Egypt and the Aegean, evolved in Greece into a complete athletic and 'heroic' nudity (though remaining foreign to everyday life). In Etruria and in Rome, however, it was limited to covering the lower part of the body by means of a short skirt or bordered loin-cloth. Even in the full civilization of the sixth and fifth centuries men went naked to the waist (especially in the intimacy of the home), though at the same time wearing expensive footwear and pointed caps on their heads. This traditional usage is reflected in the 'epic' dress worn by the banqueting dead, as shown by the carved lids of sarcophagi belonging to later periods. Only slaves and athletes went completely naked. A tight-fitting jacket that covered the whole trunk, derived from the bordered loin-cloth, was in vogue during the last years of the sixth century. It was then superseded by the tunic, an imitation of the Greek *khiton*.

The second most typical item of masculine attire was the mantle made of a thicker, coloured cloth, which protected the upper part of the body from the cold; its use was already quite widespread during the archaic period. As the items of masculine dress increased in number – and as the tradition of Mediterranean semi-nudity became progressively weaker – the mantle acquired an ever-growing importance until, enlarged and enriched with painted or embroidered decorations, it became the Etruscan national dress, the *tèbennos*, the direct ancestor of the Roman toga. Women and old people wore without any substantial variations, from archaic down to more recent times, a tunic shaped like a shirt that reached down to the feet, of light material pleated or decorated at the edges; over this was placed a painted mantle of heavier cloth. From about the end of the seventh to the beginning of the fifth century net-work patterned materials were used that are thought to have been embroidered: these may be seen made into tunics (on a Caere statuette at the Capitoline Museum in Rome, and on a canopic vase from Chiusi made in the shape of a standing female figure) or into mantles (on the *Certosa* situla).

Right from the earliest times one is struck by the very special care and interest which Etruscans devoted to their footwear. The archaic tombs at Visentium have yielded sandals in the shape of jointed wooden clogs with bronze reinforcements. Shoes could be of leather or of embroidered cloth. During the sixth century, the most typical form of shoe was raised behind the calf and curved upwards to a point at the front: these are the so-called *calcei repandi* of Ionic-Oriental origin, some characteristics of which still survive to-day in the *ciocie* of the mountainous regions of Central Italy; at a later period high ankle-boots were still in use, together with low sandals. All these various forms were passed, almost without change, to the Roman world.

For the head, a kind of dome-shaped cap in embroidered cloth was used during the sixth century; this was worn by both men and women and many variants of it were common. It is the *tutulus* of Oriental and Ionic origin, and it became the typical Etruscan head-dress. Other current forms are a pointed or hooded cap worn by certain personages such as priests and deities (as instanced by the above-mentioned φersu at the tomb of the Augurs); a woollen or leather cap with a wide base and cylindrical crown, as worn by haruspices and attested in various monuments;[10] finally, a wide-brimmed hat in the Greek style (*pètasos*) that seems to have been particularly popular amongst the lower classes (cf. the piper in the Tomb of the Monkey at Chiusi) and in the colder North (*Certosa* situla). Usually however both men and women went bare-headed, a custom that after the fifth century became quite general.

At first men wore beards and their hair long, well over the shoulders; but towards the latter years of the sixth century, young men already went clean-shaven and had their hair cut short, thus following the Greek fashion. The beard disappeared altogether after the third century B.C. and did not become fashionable again in Italy till four hundred years later under the emperor Hadrian. In earliest times (eighth to sixth century) women wore their hair long and knotted or plaited behind their backs; afterwards they allowed it to fall in ringlets over their shoulders, until finally (sixth to fifth century) it was knotted into a crown over the head or gathered in a net or cap. The bleaching of hair was a probable practice, for it seems attested by paintings in the tomb of the Leopards at Tarquinia. During the fourth century, the prevalent hair-style allowed the hair to fall in ringlets over the cheeks; later, when the Hellenistic period was in full swing, women preferred to wear their hair tied in a knot at the back of the head in the Greek style.

Jewellery played an important role in the attire of the Etruscans. Towards the end of the bronze age, the use of safety-pins or *fibulae* spread widely throughout the Mediterranean world: they are amongst the most characteristic objects found in tombs belonging to the iron age. Those worn by men differ from those worn by women in that the bow is broken and serpentine in shape. Fibulae were generally made of bronze though precious metals were also used; they were often richly adorned with paste jewellery or amber. Some specimens belonging to the orientalizing period, such as the disc-shaped fibula of the Regolini-Galassi tomb (see plate 28), are huge and lavishly decorated. The use of the fibula becomes less popular during the sixth century and practically ceases after the fifth: they are only preserved by traditional costumes such as those worn by haruspices. Other types of jewellery included diadems, ear-pendants, necklaces, bracelets, and rings. During the orientalizing period, the lavishness with which they were used was almost barbaric; and the same may be said of the Hellenistic age. The only time jewellery was worn in elegant measure by Etruscan men and, especially, women, was the golden age of the sixth and fifth centuries; and it is to this period that we attribute those magnificent necklaces hung with *bullae* and acorns, and ear-rings wrought by means of the exquisite technique of granulation (see plates 26 and 27).

NOTES

1. A general treatment of the subject-matter of this chapter will be found in A. Solari, *La vita pubblica e privata degli Etruschi*, 1928.

2. We are dealing here with unpublished material kept in the Museum of Villa Giulia in Rome. Objects found at Vulci are mentioned in *Studi Etruschi*, III, 1929, pp. 109 ff. For the wooden objects, see *Studi Etruschi*, IX, 1935, pp. 267 ff.; X, 1936, pp. 361 ff.; XII, 1938, pp. 237 ff.; XIV, 1940, pp. 305 ff.; XV, 1941, pp. 267 ff.

3. G. Patroni, *L'origine della domus*, in *Rendic. Accad. Lincei*, V, XI, 1902, pp. 467 ff.; A. Gargana, *La casa etrusca*, in *Historia*, 1934, pp. 204 ff.; G. Patroni, *Architettura preistorica generale e italica. Architettura etrusca*, 1941, pp. 294 ff.

4. See G. M. A. Richter, *Ancient Furniture: Greek, Etruscan and Roman*, 1926.

5. P. Ducati, in *Monumenti antichi dei Lincei*, XXIV, 1916, col. 401 ff.

6. G. Q. Giglioli, *L'oinochoe di Tragliatella* (in *Studi Etruschi*, III, 1929, p. 111 ff.).

7. G. d'Acchiardi, in *Studi Etruschi*, I, 1927, pp. 411 ff.; III, 1929, p. 397; cf. also XI, 1937, pp. 305 ff.; XV, 1940, pp. 315 ff.

8. See note 3, p. 83.

9. Cf. P. Fraccaro, *La malaria e la storia degli antichi popoli classici*, in *Atene e Roma*, XXII, 1919, pp. 57 ff.; N. Toscanelli, *La malaria nell' antichità e la fine degli Etruschi*, 1927.

10. Cf. M. Pallottino, *Uno specchio di Tuscania e la leggenda etrusca di Tarchon*, in *Rendiconti Accademia dei Lincei*, 1930, pp. 47 ff., and *Studi Etruschi*, X, 1936, p. 463, plate L.

PART THREE

The Problem of the Language

CHAPTER TEN

THE NATURE OF THE PROBLEM

The Interpretation of Etruscan

IN 1936, in the Introduction to my *Elements of Etruscan* (*Elementi di lingua etrusca*), I wrote the following words: 'Unless we are biassed in our opinions, we feel the need, more than ever to-day, for a publication conceived along the lines of the present work; for the quick succession of ephemeral discoveries on the part of amateurs has brought in its wake the very natural disorientation of all those interested in the Etruscan language. At the other end of the scale, there is the obstinate scepticism of those who, sweeping aside the good with the bad, prefer to look upon the problem of Etruscan as the favourite playground of cranks or the "comic" section of linguistic science. We should be both greatly pleased and proud if the perusal of these pages were in some way to provide a better understanding of the difficulties involved and the direction to be followed. Our aim is to narrow the problem down to its real limits and to contain it within prudent, methodical, but also accurate and real statements, equally removed from the intransigent certainty of those who claim to have found the "key" as from the uninformed scepticism of Pyrrhonian critics.'

The situation has changed very little during the many years that have passed since the above passage was written. The slow and painful advance towards a solution of the language problem together with the doubts and prejudices of the majority on what may be considered as the 'Etruscan mystery' *par excellence* continue as before. It is thus most fitting that a work that has as its main task the examination of the most important problems concerning the Etruscans, should deal fairly fully with the language problem by giving an idea of its nature, an outline of its history, methods, and processes, and of the results that have so far been obtained; i.e. the complex achievements of linguists working in particularly unfavourable conditions, in a field bristling with dangers and difficulties, with only the prospect of gathering a meagre harvest or no harvest at all or, worst of all, of complacently following a mirage that will later reveal itself for what it is. And though we should deplore the activities of those – and they are not few – who, without adequate preparation, believed they had solved the problem as a whole, we should not fail to render praise to the patient painstaking labour of scholars to whom we owe the slow but real advances achieved by our discipline within the last two hundred years.[1]

The first and fundamental query: Have Etruscan inscriptions been interpreted, or do they still remain undeciphered (this is the form in which the question is usually put) only very roughly corresponds to a correct formulation of the problem. A categorical answer, whether in the affirmative or in the negative, would only be possible if the interpretation of Etruscan depended essentially upon external factors, i.e. the possession of a mechanical 'key' or 'translator': a known language, for example, so close to Etruscan that the meaning of Etruscan words would be intelligible to us, or a bi-lingual inscription written in Etruscan and in a second language known to us (e.g. Latin or Greek), or again a vocabulary or glossary of Etruscan words translated or explained in a known tongue. It is well known that the interpretation of ancient languages and alphabets whose meaning was lost to us (i.e. Egyptian, Assyro-Babylonian, Sumerian, Hittite (both hieroglyphic and cuneiform), Lydian, etc.) was at first almost wholly founded upon such a 'key'.

Despite the few and brief key-documents available for Etruscan and the frequent attempts made to establish connexions between Etruscan and other known languages and language families, we can definitely state that so far no key has been discovered. The history of the numerous attempts that have been made since the eighteenth century shows clearly that the knowledge gained and universally accepted as the most reliable has had to be wrested slowly, by degrees, never abruptly, from the very first elementary observations (such as the recognition of personal names) down to the present complex morphological and lexical notions. Everything points to the fact that, unless something unforeseen occurs, such as the finding of a lengthy bi-lingual text, discovery will proceed in slow gradual stages before reaching the final goal set by the limits of material possibility.

The problem, therefore, is more quantitative than qualitative in nature. What we ought to ask ourselves is not so much whether Etruscan has been deciphered, but how far has it been deciphered. The general meaning of a context is often acquired as the result of hard work in the slow circumscription of dark, obscure areas. Even in languages that are by now generally known, such as Egyptian, Hebrew, or even Greek, there still more or less obstinately persist, in spite of the advances of modern linguistic science, small dark corners of morphology and vocabulary, i.e. ἅπαξ λεγόμενα, isolated words scattered in the texts, reflections of individual or dialect 'languages' introduced in the literary language. Why should we be surprised then if Etruscan, linguistically isolated (at least so far as the possibility of useful comparisons is concerned), documented in brief and not very numerous texts unsupported by bilingual passages or glossaries of any importance, should offer so many deep uncertainties? In theory, Etruscan words that are still obscure can be considered as so many ἅπαξ λεγόμενα; with the difference that in known languages they do not affect the comprehensibility of the text, whereas in Etruscan their very considerable number is inevitably reflected in the general obscurity of the context.

In order to convey more concretely the nature and limitations of the problem a simile may be drawn from contemporary life: were an Englishman faced with a newspaper written in a language not directly related to his own (e.g. Hungarian or Polish), as long as he possessed average culture and intelligence, his general knowledge of the events and news presumably contained in it, the names of persons and places known to him, technical terms and words belonging to the 'universal' vocabulary, and, perhaps, the illustrations, would all help him to reconstruct and to understand the general meaning of the headlines, the shorter pieces of news, and sections of the longer articles. Such is the position of modern interpreters confronted by Etruscan inscriptions: and thus it is that difficulties grow in proportion to the length of the texts, and hence the vague and approximative character of the majority of the translations that have been put forward.

The Development of the Chief Methods of Research

Until the last quarter of the nineteenth century, attempts to decipher Etruscan were mainly based upon etymological comparison with other languages and language families. The criteria employed in this process belong to the amateurish researches of seventeenth-century or even Renaissance enthusiasts (e.g. Annius of Viterbo or Pier Francesco Giambullari), the only difference being that attempts at deriving Etruscan words from the Hebrew (it was thought at the time that all languages derived from Hebrew) were slowly replaced, owing to the advance of general linguistic knowledge, by theories seeking to establish a relationship between Etruscan and the Italic dialects (Lanzi, Fabretti, Corssen, and Lattes) or hypotheses of a presumed affinity with Greek, Armenian (Bugge), Basque and Caucasian (V. Thomsen), Ugro-Finnish (Martha) or even Dravidian (S. Konow). Such attempts did not exclude the examination of various intrinsic features of the text, whether epigraphic, phonetic, morphological, or lexical (this is, in fact, the beginning of the 'combinatory' method), but the chief criterion in research consisted in deducing semantic and grammatical values from the outside, from languages of those linguistic groups to which it was thought Etruscan belonged. And in spite of much diversity of opinion, the system was founded upon a common axiom: the conviction that there existed one or more languages so close to Etruscan as to allow without great difficulty, by means of straightforward comparisons, the working out of its principal characteristics and the interpretation of the texts.

The almost wholly negative results of these various attempts – which by their very nature had to be accepted or rejected as a whole – and the progress of scientific criticism led inevitably to a reaction. This was prepared by the slow, conscientious, often unrecognized labours of collectors and epigraphists, notably Italian (e.g. Lanzi, Vermiglioli, Migliarini, G. C. Conestabile, and Fabretti), whose attention was mainly directed towards the isolation and direct examination of monuments. This work culminated in the publication of Fabretti's monumental *Corpus Inscriptionum Italicarum*, completed later by Gamurrini's *Appendix* (1880). It is to these first steps in critical research that we owe some of the fundamental discoveries in the interpretation of Etruscan: e.g. the conjunctive value of the enclitic particle *-c* (corresponding to Latin *-que*), the genitive or adjectival endings in *-s*, *-sa*, *-al*, the feminine endings in *-i*, *-ei*, the pronoun *mi*, the meaning of a number of words

such as *ril* 'annos', *clan* 'son', *turce* 'has given', etc., especially
in connexion with the very frequent onomastic formulas
found on funerary inscriptions. Such victories were won
without any recourse having to be made to other languages,
by submitting the texts to an acute critical analysis and comparing one with another in order to wrest out, as in a puzzle,
their original meaning.

But the insufficiency of the method of etymological comparisons with other languages only became generally established after the publication of a work by the famous latinist
Corssen *Über die Sprache der Etrusker* (1874), stating that
Etruscan belonged to the Indo-European family of languages and, in particular, to its Italic branch, and following
this premise (with apparent methodological rigour) with a
general attempt towards a morphological analysis and an
interpretation of the texts. The thirty-nine pages of Deecke's
Corssen und die Sprache der Etrusker. Eine Kritik (1875) were
sufficient to bring down, like a house of cards, the imposing
construction erected by Corssen.

This significant episode resulted in a change of direction
in research. The uncertainty that still persisted as to the true
linguistic relationship of Etruscan together with the incon-
sistencies proper to the etymological method led Deecke
and other scholars such as Pauli, Herbig, and Torp to
abandon external comparisons with other languages and
take up the internal study of Etruscan texts and their
reciprocal relations on the basis of facts previously ascer-
tained by the straightforward epigraphic examination of
monuments. The internal, or 'combinatory' method was
thus born. New discoveries, such as the Capua tile and the
manuscript wrappings of the mummy in the Zagreb
museum, together with more up-to-date means of research
such as the *Corpus Inscriptionum Etruscarum* begun in 1893 by
Pauli and still in course of publication,[2] as well as the lexical
indices drawn up by Lattes,[3] gave a vigorous momentum

to research in this new direction. Much progress, mainly due to the work of Torp (*Etruskische Beiträge*, 1903–6), was made both in our knowledge of Etruscan grammar and in the interpretation of the texts, especially of the shorter ones. More recently, the activity of other etruscologists has done much to extend still further our knowledge of the subject. It is true that the etymological method, though superseded, has occasionally been used by scholars belonging to the 'combinatory' school (Deecke, Pauli, and even Torp) and obstinately followed for some time by Lattes and E. Goldmann; nevertheless it was by now mainly relegated to those amateurish improvisations that grew with tenacious persistence on the borders of Etruscan studies and which vainly sought to explain Etruscan by means of Greek, the Semitic languages, Egyptian, etc.

Meanwhile research on the linguistic relationships of Etruscan was progressing independently of the actual work of decipherment. Such research was much assisted by the more reliable and broader criteria furnished by modern general linguistics. The obvious, though not very close, similarities between Etruscan and certain Indo-European, Caucasian, and Asianic languages were explained in a number of ways: by postulating the existence of pre-Indo-European linguistic groups as understood by Trombetti, by recognizing in these similarities traces of a proto-Indo-European stratum, i.e. of an archaic Indo-European layer not yet differentiated in its various elements (Kretschmer),[4] or, finally, as suggested most recently by Devoto, as remnants of a peri-Indo-European structure, the result of the dissolution and transformation of the archaic Mediterranean substratum under the action of subsequent and repeated Indo-European infiltrations.[5] In each case it was a question of recognizing in the Etruscan of the historical period direct or indirect echoes of those pre-Indo-European Mediterranean languages that had already been largely extinguished in the course of the last stages of prehistory and which only sporadically remained unsubmerged. Toponymy, the science of place-names, was mainly responsible for providing a concrete basis for these theories: for even in present times there survive in many place-names fossil elements of very ancient languages that reveal a certain primitive Mediterranean linguistic unity and point to affinities uniting Etruscan with the Eastern group of pre-Hellenic languages and those of Asia Minor and even with the pre-Indo-European linguistic layer of the Italian peninsula and islands and with 'Ligurian'. Only the language spoken in the Aegean island of Lemnos before the Athenian conquest was recognized, not without a certain amount of discussion, to be linked more closely to Etruscan (see p. 59).

The possibility of classifying Etruscan with a fair degree of precision among the linguistic groups surrounding the Mediterranean was destined to re-open, but upon new bases, the problem of etymological comparisons. Alfredo Trombetti, who had already contributed so much to the genealogical classification of Etruscan and who, by the great breadth of his erudition, was singularly well placed to attempt the arduous task of comparing badly known languages or linguistic remains, cautiously re-introduced the use of the 'etymological' in conjunction with the 'combinatory' method in his *La Lingua etrusca* (1928). He succeeded in achieving some results before his untimely death, especially in the morphological analysis of the language and in integrating the interpretations of texts made by his predecessors, especially by Torp; these results, however, did not fulfil the hopes that had been nourished. After his death, the methodological principles which he had expounded were misinterpreted, for they were too intimately linked with his personal capacities and scientific preparation: this prompted a fresh outbreak of those amateurish attempts at finding an etymological and deductive explanation for Etruscan words, while at the same time official science adopted a policy of 'wait and see' for a few years.

Attempts at analysing phonetic, morphological, and epigraphical data and at reaching a satisfactory interpretation of the texts have been started again with renewed vigour, but only in recent years. In the meantime, prospects have changed in a truly decisive way: with very few exceptions, previous research had all been conceived and conducted at the purely technical level of linguistic analysis, not taking into account that a language, and especially its written documents, form a living part of the history of the people and times to which it belongs. To neglect such historical factors is equivalent to depriving oneself of an essential tool in the study of a language and the understanding of its texts. Only recently has this fact really been understood, but already a rich crop of results is being gathered as the result of the study of Etruscan with that of classical data, of cultural aspects as revealed by monuments, and of the contents and formulas of those literary and epigraphic texts belonging to the Greek, Latin, and Italic worlds with probable affinities with Etruscan documents (the 'bi-lingual' method). This is particularly true in the case of the interpretation of the longer texts such as those of the Zagreb mummy and of the Capua tile: here, the 'combinatory' method had, on the whole, produced only inconclusive results. Among those chiefly responsible for this new direction in research, mention ought to be made of Ribezzo, K. Olzscha, and the author of the present work.[6]

NOTES

1. The following three chapters contain a fuller treatment of the matter contained in my article *Gli studi sulla lingua etrusca nelle loro condizioni attuali* (in *Archivio Glottologico Italiano*, XXXII, 1940).

2. The first volume (1893–1902) contains inscriptions found at

Fiesole, Volterra, Siena, Arezzo, Cortona, Chiusi, and Perugia. Of the second volume, four fascicules have been published: Section I, fasc. 1, 1907 (Orvieto and Bolsena); fasc. 2, 1923 (Coastal Etruria from Populonia to Vulci); fasc. 3, 1923 (Tarquinii); Section II, fasc. 1, 1912 (Faliscan territory). A supplement (1919–21) was also published containing the text of the Zagreb mummy. In preparation, a fascicule on the inscriptions of Campania and of Lower Etruria. The parts dealing with Northern Etruria, the *instrumentum*, additions and indexes are as yet in a state of project.

3. E. Lattes, *Saggio di un indice lessicale etrusco*, in *Memorie dell'Accademia d'Archeologia e Lettere di Napoli*, I, 1908; II, 1911; III, 1918; *Rendiconti del R. Istituto Lombardo*, XLV, 1912, pp. 303 ff., 351 ff., 412 ff.; *Memorie del R. Istituto Lombardo*, XXIII, 1914. This invaluable work is unfortunately incomplete and difficult to consult, buried as it is in various academic publications. The work is now being completely revised and brought up-to-date in a great scientific lexicon of the Etruscan language by the *Istituto di Studi Etruschi* in conjunction with the Universities of Florence and Rome.

4. For the most recent developments of P. Kretschmer's theory attributing Etruscan to a 'Tyrrheno-Pelasgic' linguistic stratum of Balkan-Danubian origin, see *Glotta*, XXVIII, 1940, pp. 260 ff.; see also *Glotta*, XXX, 1943, pp. 213 ff., where the author prefers to speak of a 'Raeto-Tyrrhenian' group. See also p. 31.

5. G. Devoto, *Pelasgo e peri-indoeuropeo*, in *Studi Etruschi*, XVII, 1943, pp. 359 ff.; *Etrusco e peri-indoeuropeo*, in *Studi Etruschi*, XVIII, 1944, pp. 187 ff.

6. On the subject of the history and methods of research on the Etruscan language the following studies will prove useful: E. Fiesel, *Etruskisch*, 1931, with reviews by S. P. Cortsen and E. Vetter, in *Glotta*, XXIII, pp. 144 ff.; XXVIII, pp. 117 ff.; M. Pallottino, in *Doxa*, III, 1950, pp. 29 ff.; F. Ribezzo, in *Studi Etruschi*, XXII, 1952–3, pp. 105 ff.

CHAPTER ELEVEN

THE SOURCES AND THE METHOD

Present Means and Future Possibilities

NEXT to the uncertainties due to the relative isolation of Etruscan and the lack of key-documents such as bi-lingual texts and glossaries, the major obstacles encountered in obtaining a full and accurate knowledge of the language are the scarcity, brevity, and limited contents of the texts. Present knowledge leads us to the conclusion that unlike the Greeks, the Etruscans were late and parsimonious in their use of writing, at least as far as monuments are concerned. With the exception of a very few texts of importance, our material is limited exclusively to brief, monotonous funerary or votive inscriptions amounting to little more than a few oft-repeated formulas containing a vocabulary pertaining to limited aspects of the religious life of the people. Etruscan literature is completely lost to us and, with it, that great variety of linguistic facets reflecting family, social, and economic life, abstract notions, and the structure of direct speech. Thus we can say that even if possessed the technical ability to translate precisely and completely all the texts in our possession, an important part of the vocabulary of Etruscan and many of its grammatical features would still remain unknown to us.

What possibilities have we of adding to our stock of Etruscan inscriptions? Every year, as a result of chance discoveries and regular excavations in the territory of ancient Etruria, a number of funerary and votive inscriptions are brought to light; they are usually short, however, and add little to our knowledge of the language. These are gathered and published in the epigraphic section of the review *Studi*

Etruschi. In spite of the apparent poverty of such material, it is occasionally of considerable value to us, especially in connexion with the analysis and discussion of known texts of greater importance: often, a single word, a single grammatical form may be sufficient to resolve doubts and problems of many years standing. Sometimes the epigraphic harvest is quite considerable, as in the case of the votive inscriptions on fragments of bucchero vases found on two separate occasions in the course of excavations on the site of the Apollo sanctuary at Veii.

But the hope that some day we may stumble upon an unforeseen discovery of real importance is still alive. We have already seen that the great majority of excavations in Etruria have been concentrated on the exploration of tombs: a type of search that is by far the easiest, most profitable, and economical. The excavation of sites of cities where the continuity of life down to present times has been interrupted has only been conducted in a sporadic and unsystematic manner or merely exists in a state of project: such is the case with Veii, Caere, Tarquinii, Vulci, and Rusellae, to mention just a few of the major centres. Now it is obvious that long inscriptions of a non-funerary character could only be found within ancient inhabited centres. Thus if we call for the excavation of Etruscan cities, it is also in order to increase our stock of epigraphic texts in the hope of furthering our knowledge of Etruscan.

What could we expect from the exploration of a city, should fortune be good enough to present us with a lucky find despite the passage of time and the inevitable upheavals suffered by an urban site? Above all, the much longed-for bi-lingual text: not merely meagre Etrusco-Latin epitaphs such as we already possess, but a full and complete text comparable to the Graeco-Egyptian inscription of the Rosetta Stone or the tri-lingual texts of Persepolis or the inscriptions in Phoenician and hieroglyphic Hittite recently come to light at Karatepe, in Cilicia: all documents that have led to the decipherment and interpretation of the writing and language of great Oriental peoples. Now since the Etruscans, from the fourth to the first century B.C., inhabited states federated to or included in Roman territory with other members of the Italic community, and since many Latin funerary inscriptions have been found in Etruscan cities, we are justified in believing that either public or juridical inscriptions may occasionally have been couched in both Etruscan and Latin. The discovery of one such inscription would revolutionize the whole development of research in Etruscan by providing external data fundamental to the interpretation of the texts and would, in all probability, solve once and for all most aspects of this centuries-old problem.

But even without the discovery of a bi-lingual text, a new long religious text comparable to the Umbrian tablets found at Gubbio, or a juridical text similar to the Latin laws of the Twelve Tables would greatly widen the scope of research. At the present stage of Etruscan studies, one single new source may be sufficient to lead scholars to a final and successful solution of the problem. But the gap presented by the absence of texts of a literary nature would almost certainly always remain open, a gap that removes all possibilities of our knowing Etruscan as well as the other languages of the classical world. In this respect our only hope, however fantastic and illusory, rests on the discovery of papyri in Egypt or at Herculaneum: such a miraculous find would re-echo the extraordinary discovery of an Etruscan text written on the linen wrappings of an Egyptian mummy.

Direct and Indirect Sources

Let us now put aside future hopes and possibilities and examine the actual sources of our knowledge of Etruscan.[1]

These may be divided into direct and indirect sources. The first consist of those texts that have come down to us preserved on architectural monuments or through archaeological discoveries: in only one case can we speak of a manuscript; the rest of the material is epigraphic.

The manuscript is of exceptional interest not only to Etruscan studies but also as a unique document on the writing habits of the ancients: for it is the only preserved example of a *liber linteus*, or manuscript book on linen cloth. It was originally in the form of a roll or *volumen*, but was later cut into strips and used to wrap the mummy of an Egyptian woman in Ptolemaic or Roman times; the mummy was probably discovered in Middle Egypt, though we do not know the exact place. Important fragments of the original roll were lost in this process; we are also ignorant of the circumstances that determined the presence of an Etruscan religious book in Egypt. The mummy was brought to Europe by a Croatian traveller and later donated to the Zagreb National Museum; here, J. Krall identified the writing on the wrappings as Etruscan. When the separate strips were fitted together, it was possible to reconstruct the text within at least twelve vertical columns: it comprises 1185 words more or less clearly and completely legible, to which may be added about a hundred more words that can be accurately reconstructed with the help of the context. Since repetitions and parallel formulas are frequent, the number of distinct and original words becomes reduced to about 530. The Zagreb text is by far the most important, both for size and content, of the Etruscan texts in our possession.

Epigraphic texts – found almost exclusively in Etruria and Campania (small numbers have also been found in Latium, Umbria, Liguria, and in North Africa) – consist of carved or painted inscriptions on architectural monuments, cippi, urns, tablets, tiles, statues, bronzes, vases, etc. Including the most recent discoveries, their total reaches the figure of 10,000, but only a very few are worthy of special notice. First of all, an inscribed tile found in the neighbourhood of Capua and now preserved in the Berlin Museum: it comprises 10 chapters (separated by horizontal lines), 62 preserved lines and more than 300 legible words; the second part of the text is very damaged. The writing runs from right to left and from left to right on alternate lines. A stone cippus kept in the Perugia Museum (*C.I.E.* 4538) features on two of its faces an important inscription of 46 lines and 130 words. A round thin lead plaque found at Magliano and kept in the Florence Archaeological Museum (*C.I.E.* 5237) contains an inscription carved spirally on both sides and reading towards the centre, consisting of at least 70 words (it is difficult sometimes to decide whether a group of letters contains 1 or 2 words). On a sarcophagus kept in the Tarquinii Museum, the reclining figure sculptured on the lid holds an open scroll in his hand containing an inscription of 9 lines and 59 words (*C.I.E.* 5430).

Other inscriptions in our possession include a number (funerary for the most part) that contain a few lines of text with a certain variety in the words used; in the great majority of cases, however, they merely consist of a few words composed according to a few fixed formulas. The most numerous group is represented by funerary inscriptions (carved on the walls of tombs and on sarcophagi, urns, ossuaries, and tiles) consisting of the *praenomen*, the name of the *gens*, the patronymic and, occasionally, the matronymic of the dead person together with indications as to his age and, in a few exceptional cases, *curriculum vitae*. Votive inscriptions may be subdivided into an archaic group, with special formulas and the name of the dedicator, and a later group where it is the name of the divinity that is most prominent; they too, however, are generally very brief and stereotyped, with the exception of those found on a number of archaic vases. The few Etrusco-Latin inscriptions that we possess all belong to the funerary class and consist almost entirely of proper names. They provide nothing but the most meagre of morphological and lexicological clues: the title *netśvis trutnvt frontac* is, for example, translated *haruspex fulguriator* in the bi-lingual inscription of Pesaro (Fabretti, *C.I.I.* 69); the form *Cahatial*, the oblique case of the gentilitial name *Cahati*, is translated *Cafatia natus* in inscription *C.I.E.* 3763, etc.

Among the indirect sources in our study of Etruscan, we may distinguish the following:

(a) the glosses and other information provided by classical and post-classical writers;

(b) Etruscan elements that have passed into Latin and common Etrusco-Italic elements;

(c) Etruscan elements surviving in place-names;

(d) the supposed fragments of Latin versions of original Etruscan texts.

The *glosses* are Etruscan words with a Latin or Greek translation: they may be either found inserted haphazardly in texts by classical authors or gathered together to form actual glossaries. We possess about sixty such glosses, but their value in the interpretation of Etruscan texts is somewhat limited, just as in the case of Etrusco-Latin bilingual texts. Glosses of a varied nature appear in Varro (*de lingua latina*), in Verrius Flaccus (*de verborum significatione*, in the compendia of Festus and Paul the Deacon), in Isidore of Seville (*Etymologicum*) and especially in Hesychius' Lexicon. E.g.: *atrium* (Varro); *arse verse* = *arce ignem* (Verrius Flaccus); *cassis* = helmet (*galea*) (Isidore); ἄνδας, ἄντας = north wind, eagle (Hesychius). In exceptional cases Etruscan words are found quoted in the works of other authors such as Livy, Strabo, Plutarch, Dion Cassius, Macrobius, Servius, and John Lydus: e.g. ἄριμος = monkey (Strabo, XIII, 626), *capys* =

falcon (Servius, *ad Aen.*, x, 145). The original form may be preserved intact or may be modified by a Greek or Latin ending: e.g. αἰσαρ =god (in Dion Cassius), αἰσοί =gods (in Hesychius). The reliability of such glosses may be checked by means of the Etruscan texts themselves (*aiser*, 'gods'; *versum*, cf. *verse*, 'fire'?) or by a study of their form (e.g. *fala(n)do*=sky, according to Verrius Flaccus in Paul the Deacon: cf., for the root, such Etruscan words as *falaś*, *falzaδi*, and for the termination, *aranδ*). In a few cases the authenticity of the Etruscan gloss appears to be belied by the Latin character of the word: e.g. δέα, κάπρα (Hesychius). Specialized vocabularies are represented by glosses of medicinal plant names (Dioscorides, though here too some of the names are Latin), and of names of the months (Papias, in the *Liber Glossarum* of Leyden) which also seem to appear in Etruscan texts: e.g. *Aclus*=June, and, in the Zagreb text, *acale*. Phonetic and grammatical remarks of very little value may be found in Varro, in Agrecius' *Ars de orthographia*, and in Martianus Capella.[2]

A special study has been made by A. Ernout of those Etruscan elements that have passed into Latin.[3] They are thought to be characterized by their endings in *-na* (*atena*, *persona*: cf. Etr. φersu), in *-rna* (*santerna*), in *-mna* (*antemna*), in *-sa* (*favisa*: cf. Etr. *faviti*), in *-nt*, *-nd* (*fleкuntes*, *mundus*: cf. Etr. *munδ*, *munδuχ*), in *-on* (*subulo*: Etr. *suplu*?; *fullo*: cf. Etr. *fulum-*), in *-it* (*veles*, *poples*), etc. The Etruscan derivation of certain words is explicitly stated by classical authors (*mantissa*, *histrio*, *lucumo*, *atrium*, etc.); in other cases it is hypothetical and may possibly be due to analogical formations, i.e. Latin words with endings imitating Etruscan derivatives; or again they may be remnants of the general pre-Indo-European substratum of Italy rather than actual borrowings from the Etruscan of the historical period. On the other hand, an Etruscan origin may be more correctly attributed to Latin words with obscure etymologies and an

Etruscan-looking ending related to the technical languages
of religion, the army, the navy, or agriculture: such borrowings would be explained by the very strong cultural
influence exerted by Etruria upon primitive Rome. There
are also abundant examples where Etruscan acted as an
intermediary between Greek and Latin: e.g. *groma* (an
instrument used in direction finding and field measurement)
from γνώμων, by way of a hypothetical Etruscan **cruma*.
It is also quite possible that Etruscan may have had a
limited influence on the phonetics and morphology of
Latin. The whole question deserves more careful examination, if only for the help it may bring to the deciphering of
Etruscan. Equally if not more obscure is the question of the
possibility of Etruscan words surviving in the vocabulary
of central Italian dialects; on the other hand, the hypothesis
attributing an Etruscan origin to the aspiration of certain
consonants in Tuscan dialects (the well-known *gorgia
toscana*) appears to be acquiring more and more supporters. [4]

Despite the fundamental difference between Etruscan and
the Indo-European languages of Italy, there are a number
of words and roots common to both: e.g. Etr. *sac-, sacrn:*
Lat. *sacer;* Etr. *eiser* 'gods, deities': Umbrian *esono-,*
Volscian *esari-* 'sacred ceremonies, sacrifices'; Etr. *nefts*
'nephew': Lat. *nepos;* Etr. *prumts* 'great-nephew': Lat.
pronepos; Etr. *vinum:* Lat. *vinum,* Umbrian *vinu;* Etr.
cletram: Umbrian *kletra* 'trolley for sacred offerings'. These
correspondences may be due to contacts established during the prehistoric period (as derivations from the 'Tyrrhenian' linguistic substratum, or as the result of very
ancient Indo-European 'infiltrations' as understood by
Devoto) or perhaps to reciprocal borrowings during the
historical period. At any rate they throw light upon the
Etruscan forms. The same phenomenon can be recognized
in connexion with names of persons and gods. In the first
group (masterfully treated by W. Schulze in *Zur Geschichte*

der lateinischen Eigennamen, 1904) the resemblance first appears in the fact that the formula is composed of two or three members (the *praenomen*, the name of the *gens* and, eventually, the *cognomen*: Etr. *Larece Zuχu Mutu*, Lat. *Marcus Tullius Cicero*); this formula is common and limited to those peoples inhabiting the Italian peninsula (Etruscans, Latins, and Umbro-Sabellians), as we have already seen in considering the common social features of the most ancient Italian civilization (see p. 148). But in addition we note that a certain number of *praenomina* and a large number of gentilitial names are identical in Etruscan and Latin (e.g. Etr. *Aule:* Lat. *Aulus;* Etr. *Marce:* Lat. *Marcus,* amongst the *praenomina;* Etr. *Fapi:* Lat. *Fabius;* Etr. *Petruni:* Lat. *Petronius;* Etr. *Vete:* Lat. *Vettius,* amongst the gentilitial names). Forms of proper names belonging to the common Etrusco-Italic stock spring from Etruscan, Latin, and Umbro-Sabellian roots, with a certain preponderance of Etruscan roots.

In the case of names of gods and goddesses a number of common elements are also observed: Etr. *Menerva:* Lat. *Minerva;* Etr. *Selvans:* Lat. *Silvanus.* Such correspondences should be compared with such clearly marked divergences as Etr. *Tin, Tinia:* Lat. *Iuppiter;* Etr. *Fufluns:* Lat. *Liber.* Very ancient linguistic contacts are also revealed by correspondences of the type Lat. *Lar* (name of male genius) and Etr. *Lasa* (name of female genius): here the phenomenon of rhotacism should be taken into account, i.e. the passage of *s* to *r* in certain given positions. Many names of gods, both Etruscan and Latin, derive from the Greek; such names, together with a number of cultural terms (e.g. names of vases) also deriving from Greek, represent an important additional source to our knowledge of Etruscan, since the various changes which they have undergone provide us with a clue to the phonetic tendencies and morphological **exigencies** of the language. E.g.: Greek Ἀλέξανδρος: Etr.

Alcsentre, Ελαχśantre, Ελαχśntre, Ελχsntre, Αlεχsantre, Elcste,
etc.; Gk. *Κλυταιμήστρα*: Etr. *Cluδumusδa, Clutmsta;* Gk.
῾Ελένη: Etr. *Elina, Elinai, Elinei.*[5]

Despite the rich collections made by S. Pieri and the
studies, limited to single questions, of P. Aebischer, V.
Bertoldi, G. Bottiglioni, and C. Battisti,[6] the problems
relating to the Etruscan toponymy of central and northern
Italy are still a long way from being solved. The fundamental difficulty resides in distinguishing the various layers and
the various areas of diffusion of pre-Indo-European place-
names, such as, for example, place-names of the 'Ligurian'
type (found as far south as central Italy, as in the case of the
derivatives of the roots *carra-, pala-, gava-,* etc.), from place-
names belonging to the Etruscan of historical times.
Wherever the latter can be identified with absolute certainty, it is even possible to use them to assess the semantic
value of certain Etruscan words as attempted by Bertoldi
with place-names of the *falar-* type. Account should also
be taken of the close relationship existing between place-
names and personal names, as indicated by Schulze. Names
of Etruscan cities are particularly important in this respect,
for their ancient forms are known to us through the writings
of classical authors and from inscriptions: they are often
closely related to the name of a god or hero: e.g.**Tarχuna,*
Tarquinii, with the hero *Tarχun-,* Tarchon; *Puplona,* Populonia, with the god *Fuflun,* Bacchus; *Manδua-,* Mantua,
with the god *Mantus;* etc.[7]

Finally, we should consider the hypothetical fragments of
Latin versions of original Etruscan texts. We already know
that the main body of Etruscan sacred books was translated
or abridged into Latin. In the congeries of indirect references, shortened or re-written versions of Etruscan texts
(some echoes of which have come down to us), there are
passages of especial interest to the study of Etruscan literature, but also, in certain aspects, to our knowledge of the

structure of the language: as in the passage taken from the Vegonic books and quoted by the *Gromatici* (Lachmann ed., I, pp. 350 ff.) enclosing the teachings of the Lasa Vegonia on the division of fields. [8]

Methods of Research

Having examined the sources of our knowledge of Etruscan, let us now pass to the question of method. All attempts to make use of factual data without adequate linguistic preparation, a critical approach, and a good measure of prudence and common sense are bound to fail. Above all, it is important to keep in mind the basic axiom that a possible or even very likely solution need not necessarily be the correct one. The history of Etruscan hermeneutics is littered with failures due to the fact that scholars remained satisfied with more or less sensible and likely results, accepting them as final and correct. Often, in support of a given method or system, the fact that the translation made sense was adduced as an unanswerable argument. This, however, is by no means sufficient to prove the correctness of a given translation: it is quite easy to show that an Etruscan text can adapt itself to as many likely and reasonable translations as there are methods or presumed 'keys' with which to tackle it. Another requirement to which it is worth calling attention while still on this subject of method and common sense, is the humility and diffidence of the scholar before his own results. For though boldness and imagination are essential for fruitful research, it is impossible to dispense with rigorous self-criticism, methodical doubt, and cold detachment in evaluating the results obtained. The whole painful history of the failures with which the path of etruscology is strewn is little more than the story of men who became overfond of their own hypotheses and lacked the mental agility to abandon them as soon as unfavourable evidence began to accumulate. It is in the impartial estimation of one's own and one's colleagues' reconstructions – however brilliant and satisfying – that lies the prime condition for a steady, if slow, progress towards ultimate success.

To this general 'method', made up essentially of elementary preparation and common sense, should be added more specific methods, i.e. those tactical criteria to be adopted as we advance step by step over the difficult terrain presented by the uncertainty of linguistic phenomena and the obscurity of inscriptions. From the character of the documents in our possession and the retrospective examination of the attempts made during the past decades, we may exclude the possibility of a complete deciphering of Etruscan by means of an external agency, whether in the nature of one or more known languages with which it could be compared, or of a 'translator', be it a glossary or a bilingual text. The fundamental basis of research can only reside, therefore, in the direct examination of the texts in our possession, taking into account their purpose, the objects to which they refer, the figures that may accompany them and the onomastic formulas which they contain. Hence, it is naturally most important that an accurate archaeological estimate be made of the character, meaning, and chronology of the objects or monuments connected with the inscriptions. Lexical and grammatical values thus inductively obtained should then be checked by combining texts and passages with one another, i.e. by testing the reliability of the first hypothesis by means of new proofs. This is the classical procedure of the 'combinatory' method. Even when not rigidly adhered to, it remains irreplaceable as a means of control even in the case of information obtained from external sources.

Naturally the information obtained by the internal inductive method is, by its very nature, a good deal less precise than what might have been obtained from external sources.

In many cases, the function of a case ending is known only approximately or in part, as in the word *Menervas* found written upon a vase where final -*s*, added to the name of the goddess Menerva, may just as easily be a genitive of possession or a dative of advantage. The same may be said of lexical values as their differentiation is often generic, according to category, within the limits of the *genus proximum* rather than those of the *differentia specifica:* such is the case with terms referring to sacred ceremonies or political institutions and offices. We know quite well, for example, that the word *śacni* stands for a sacred place or institution, but are unable to tell exactly to what term it corresponded in Latin or any other language. Naturally, in the interpretation of words, the determination of meaning falls gradually from a maximum of accuracy and probability to vague and generic working hypotheses on which it would be rash to build further hypotheses. The uncertainty characterizing certain complex hermeneutic constructions built up entirely by means of combinatory processes is in fact due to this piling of hypothesis upon hypothesis till the whole structure appears to be devoid of all reality.

The weightier role played by the inductive or 'combinatory' method does not exclude the use of deductive processes based upon external data. Glosses and bi-lingual texts provide us, or, rather, have provided us, with certain lexical determinations, not, however, always absolutely reliable: e.g. *ais*=god, *arim*=monkey, *netśvis*=haruspex, etc. Other data could be obtained from an intelligent sifting of the Latin lexical material of supposed Etruscan derivation, so long as it is carefully checked by means of the combinatory method. Should we, for example, admit that Latin *mundus* is connected with Etruscan *munδ*, then the interpretation of the latter word as 'ornament', as proposed by Cortsen and accepted by Trombetti, would seem evident. But the meaning proposed is unintelligible in the context of the funerary inscription in which the word is found (*C.I.E.* 5470): it would lead to the odd translation 'he placed within the tomb twenty sarcophagi, ornament of the dead'! On the other hand, several other inscriptions include words derived from the same root *mun-*: it appears as if the meaning was rather that of 'repository for the dead, *locus* (in the funerary meaning of the Latin word)'. The connexion with *mundus* might then be established, if at all, in the way indicated by F. Leifer,[9] by way of the special funerary and religious meaning of the Latin word which, besides signifying 'world' and 'ornament', also stood for 'pit of communication with the underworld'. This example will suffice to show the importance of broadening our knowledge of Etruscan life and customs in order to gain a better understanding of the language.

From examples of etymological analysis of single Etruscan words, prudently carried out by M. Hammarström (for *natis*, *netśvis*)[10] and Devoto (for *ais*, *culsu*, etc.),[11] we are inclined to believe that the old etymological method, as long as it is not considered as an instrument capable of interpreting the whole of Etruscan by means of a known language or group of languages (which, as we have already stated, has shown itself to be critically impossible), but cautiously applied to single words or forms, is destined to furnish useful confirmations or even new contributions in the deciphering of Etruscan. In this connexion we should not forget the possibility of a tentative application of the methods of linguistic geography to the study of Etruscan, not only as a help in determining more accurately the position of Etruscan among the Mediterranean languages, but also in confirming, if only indirectly, some of its lexical and morphological values.

But next to the two traditional methods of Etruscan hermeneutics (etymological and combinatory), a new deductive principle has become established during the last twenty years as a major tool of research: the bilingual method. It operates in a completely different field from that of linguistic affinities and comparisons, tending instead to explain the meaning of words and phrases by using the same principle as the 'translators', i.e. bilingual texts or glossaries. Assuming that the Etruscan civilization was closely bound to the Greek and the Italic (as the comparative study of religion, art, customs, etc. clearly shows) and that such cultural affinities are reflected in analogies in modes of expression, in sacrificial, votive, and funerary formulas, we are justified in concluding that in many cases an Etruscan text may be compared with a Greek, Latin, or Italic text with presumably similar contents, and may be interpreted on the basis of such a comparison almost as if dealing with a bilingual inscription. Such a process was first applied by the writer in establishing the meaning of the Etruscan pronoun *mi* (=I, me), by comparing two formulas inscribed on two vases found on Faliscan territory: one in Etruscan: *mi qutun Lemausnas . . .*, the other in Faliscan (i.e., for practical purposes, in archaic Latin): *eco quto . . . enotenosio . . .* 'I (am) the pitcher of . . . Enotenus (name of the possessor) . . .' – identical expressions couched in two different languages. Practically at the same time, Olzscha recognized the great importance of Roman and Umbrian sacrificial formulas in the interpretation of Etruscan ritual texts, especially in the case of the longest and most important, that of the Zagreb mummy, to the interpretation of which he devoted studies of fundamental importance. Naturally, the bilingual method rests substantially upon the reciprocal translatability of words and expressions in Etruscan on the one hand and in Latin or Italic on the other, i.e. upon the existence of those 'translated loan-words' which inevitably follow the close cohabitation of peoples of different tongues within a common cultural orbit (as, for example, is the case with Romance and Germanic speakers in the modern world). Such a correspondence existed between the Etruscan title *zilaδ meχl rasnal* and the Latin *praetor Etruriae*, as we have already seen when dealing with the political organization in Chapter Six. This new method, used in the spirit of the new 'historical' directions taken by Etruscan hermeneutics and applied cautiously and intelligently with the assistance of the older, well-tried methods, opens up unhoped-for vistas of new conquests in this field.[12]

Variations in Time and Space

It is chiefly owing to the work of Miss Fiesel that the attention of scholars has been drawn to the problem of the internal evolution of the language during the seven centuries of development for which we have material.[13] So evident a phenomenon is the rapid evolution of epigraphic Latin from archaic to imperial times that we may *a priori* suppose some similar development in Etruscan. Hence the need always to keep in mind the date, be it only approximate, of each inscription; this may be determined from the characteristics of the monument concerned and of its accompanying objects, the shape of the letters, etc. This attitude contrasts with the previous habit of studying and combining texts without taking their relative ages into account. Both from the palaeographic and phonetic points of view notable differences can be found between archaic inscriptions (seventh to fifth centuries B.C.) and later inscriptions. As an example, we may quote the fall of unstressed vowels and the reduction of diphthongs in the later texts: e.g. *lautn* (archaic Etr. *lautun*), *zusleve* (arch. Etr. *zuslevai*). In morphology too a number of differences are now beginning to be observed: the genitive ending *-al* corresponds, in archaic inscriptions, to *-a*. It would be advisable, therefore, to indicate the relative age of every lexical, morphological, or phonetic form quoted, by placing before it the abbreviations *a.Etr.* (archaic Etruscan) or *n.Etr.* (later or neo-Etruscan).

Much the same remarks could be made with respect to problems concerning topographical variations in Etruscan. The study of such phenomena is still less advanced than that of chronological variations. Only the completion of that great collection of Etruscan inscriptions, the *Corpus Inscriptionum Etruscarum*, which is to include the Etruscan regions of Campania and the Po valley, can provide sufficiently broad and reliable foundations for an attempt to disentangle regional – we may even say dialectal – peculiarities in vocabulary, phonetics, and grammar. Up to the present such research has proved extremely arduous owing to the rarity of preserved texts, especially in certain regions such as northern Italy. Nor is it always possible to establish up to what point the peculiarities of certain inscriptions are the result of local differentiations or reflect a given stage in the development of the language; such is the case with the archaisms found in the Capua tile or those (palaeographic and orthographic in particular) of the Po valley inscriptions. It is probable, moreover, that the outlying districts of Etruria, conquered and flourishing in archaic times, were slower to evolve linguistically compared with the central regions. Here, the language rapidly developed towards a neo-Etruscan which, without doubt, formed the basis of the literary κοινή of the Etrusco-Roman era. But neo-Etruscan too features a number of variants (e.g. in the treatment of sibilants) according to whether it was spoken in southern or in central and northern Etruria; it is such variants that allow us, for example, to establish that the text of the Zagreb mummy was written in the idiom of one of the central or northern cities.[14]

NOTES

1. Cf. M. Pallottino, *Testimonia linguae etruscae*, 1954, a collection of the more notable texts and of the glosses.

2. Cf. G. Buonamici, *Fonti di storia etrusca tratte da gli autori classici*, 1939, pp. 354 ff.

3. *Les éléments étrusques du vocabulaire latin*, in *Bulletin de la Société linguistique*, XXX, 1930, pp. 82 ff.

4. See C. Merlo, in *Studi Etruschi*, I, 1927, pp. 303 ff.

5. Cf. G. Devoto, in *Studi Etruschi*, I, 1927, pp. 255 ff.; E. Fiesel, *Namen des griechischen Mythos im Etruskischen*, 1928.

6. *Studi Etruschi*, vols. I ff.

7. M. Pallottino, in *Scritti in onore di B. Nogara*, 1937, pp. 341 ff.

8. Cf. B. Nogara, *Gli Etruschi e la loro civiltà*, p. 420.

9. *Studien zum antiken Ämterwesen*, quoted on p. 152, note 2.

10. *Glotta*, XI, 1921, pp. 213 ff.

11. *Studi Etruschi*, V, 1931; VII, 1933, etc.

12. On the bi-lingual method and its applications, see M. Pallottino, in *Studi Etruschi*, VII, 1933, p. 241; K. Olzscha, *Die Sprache der Etrusker. Probleme und neue Wege der Deutung*, in *Neue Jahrbücher für Wissenschaft und Jugendbildung*, XII, 1936, pp. 97 ff.; *Interpretation der Agramer Mumienbinde*, 1939, pp. 3 ff.; M. Pallottino, in *Studi Etruschi*, XIII, 1939, pp. 331 ff.; *Nuovi orientamenti nello studio dell'etrusco*, in *Archiv Orientalný*, XVIII, 4, 1950 (*Symbolae Hrozný*, v), pp. 159 ff.

13. *Acts of the First International Congress of Etruscan Studies*, pp. 187 ff.

14. Cf. *Studi Etruschi*, XI, 1937, pp. 206 ff.

CHAPTER TWELVE

THE RESULTS

The Alphabet

THE problem of Etruscan concerns the interpretation of the language and not that of its writing, for even though inscriptions cannot be clearly understood, they can be read with a fair degree of accuracy since we know the phonetic value of each Etruscan letter. These values were gradually established between the eighteenth and the beginning of the nineteenth century, by comparison with Greek and Latin alphabets to which Etruscan is closely related. Since 1833, when R. Lepsius determined the value of the Etruscan letter ‡ = z, the cycle of research has been considered closed as far as the alphabet is concerned: correct and complete reading of inscriptions was guaranteed in every case. Nevertheless, a very important and recent discovery has again brought the question of the alphabet to the fore by showing that even in the most recent studies, one of the symbols of the archaic Etruscan alphabet had been erroneously interpreted. This is the symbol ×, until lately confused with t, but demonstrated with all certainty by Miss E. Fiesel to be a sibilant which she transcribed ś.[1] As a consequence of this discovery, a whole series of suppositions concerning certain important archaic inscriptions had to be radically modified.

The origin of the Etruscan alphabet has provoked discussions that have not yet been completely settled.[2] On the basis of the equivalence ↓ = χ, it has been classified by some among the Western or 'red' alphabets and thought to have been transmitted to the Etruscans by the Chalcidian colony of Cumae. Others have spoken of an ancient proto-Greek alphabet or put forward even more unlikely hypotheses. The whole question of the origin of the Etruscan alphabet should be considered foreign to that of the origins of the Etruscan people.

What is certain is that during the seventh century, the Etruscans adopted an alphabet of twenty-six letters, whatever its origin, which may be found reproduced in its entirety on the margin of an ivory writing tablet (found at Marsigliana d'Albegna) and upon a number of vases: obviously didactic models. But the practical use of such an alphabet must have been the result of an elaborate process of adaptation. The letters β, δ, Phoenician *samech* and o were discarded and do not appear in inscriptions for they do not correspond to any of the sounds present in the Etruscan phonetic system: the latter, in fact, lacked the series of voiced plosives while the vowel o was confused, at least originally, with u.[3] The letter γ was not used to represent the voiced palatal plosive, but the unvoiced plosive (as with Latin c), together with the letters χ and q, the use of which becomes rarer in later inscriptions.[4] The complementary symbol ×, which in the eastern Greek alphabets carried the value of χ, and in the western, and in Latin, of the consonant cluster *lks*, is only met in a number of archaic Etruscan inscriptions with the value of the simple sibilant s. In the case of the labio-dental fricative f (different from the aspirated bi-labial consonant ϕ), the original alphabet lacked the appropriate symbol; at first, in the oldest texts, it was represented by the group *vh*; later, towards the end of the sixth century, a new sign 8, of uncertain origin, was introduced for it and placed last in the series of letters of the alphabet. The persistence of the two sibilants M and Z (corresponding respectively to the Phoenician letters *sade* and *šin*) is also worthy of note: it was justified by the existence in Etruscan of two allied sounds

Typical Letterings	Archaic Letterings (*vii–v cent.*)	Late Letterings (*iv–i cent.*)	Modern Equivalents	Typical Letterings	Archaic Letterings (*vii–v cent.*)	Late Letterings (*iv–i cent.*)	Modern Equivalents,
A	A	A	a	⊞			(s)
B			(b)	O			(o)
⅂	)	C	c(k)	�q	q	�q	p
◁			(d)	M	M	M	ś
⅀	⅀	⅀	c	Q	Q		q
⅂	⅂	⅂	v	D	D	D	r
I	I	‡	z	⟨	⟨	⟨	s
⊟	⊟	⊟	h	T	T	ⷭ	t
⊗	⊗	⊙	δ (th)	Y	Y	V	u
l	l	l	i	X	X, +		ṡ
K	K	K	k	Φ		Φ	φ (ph)
⅃	⅃	⅃	l	↓		↓	χ (ch)
M	M	m	m		8	8	f
⅄	⅄	n	n				

Figure 6 – THE ETRUSCAN ALPHABET

which were originally quite distinct; they are generally transcribed ś and s. Apart from the adoption and the rejection of certain signs, the evolution of the Etruscan alphabet features a number of variations in the shape of letters which allow the dating, if only approximative, of inscriptions.

In modern transcriptions of Etruscan, the corresponding Latin letters are used, modified at times by diacritical signs, with the exception of the aspirates (*ph*, *th*, and *ch*), for which the Greek letters φ, δ, and χ are used.

Writing proceeds from right to left in the great majority of inscriptions, contrary to the usual direction of Greek and Latin writing. In a few exceptional cases, writing runs from left to right or alternates the direction with each new line. In archaic inscriptions, words are run together, whereas in later texts one or two dots are often interposed. A recent and important discovery in the study of Etruscan is due to Vetter's researches on Venetic punctuation: working back from the latter to archaic Etruscan inscriptions, Vetter established the characteristics of a system where simple open syllables (e.g. *ma*, *lu*, *ke*, etc.) are considered normal and left, therefore, unpunctuated; whereas isolated letters, whether vowels or consonants, appear distinguished by one or more dots. This system is very widespread in archaic inscriptions, especially from southern Etruria, and it is present even in the Capua tile. Is it perhaps a relic of a syllabic system of writing?[5] It is worth noting, in this respect, that an archaic vase found at Caere possesses, besides the alphabet, a complete syllabary.

Phonetics

After the fundamental preparatory work by Lattes in the field of Etruscan phonetics, research on phonetic problems came to a comparative standstill, from which it only recovered as a result of the work by Trombetti, Devoto, and Miss Fiesel. The latter two have concentrated their attention upon Etruscan phonetic tendencies as revealed by the transformations undergone by Greek mythological names in Etruscan inscriptions. Mention should also be made of F. Slotty's contributions on syllabism.

The elementary sounds of Etruscan seem to have been the following:

(a) four vowels: *a*, *e*, *i*, and *u* (*o* is confused with *u*);

(b) one semi-vowel: *v*, which, at times, replaces the vowel *u;*

(c) one aspirate: *h*, found almost exclusively at the beginning of words;

(d) six plosive consonants: *c*, *t*, *p* (unvoiced), and χ, δ, φ (aspirated);

(e) one labio-dental fricative: *f;*

(f) three dental fricatives: *s*, *ś*, and *ᴢ;*

(g) two liquids: *l* and *r;*

(h) two nasals: *m* and *n*.

It should be noted that fricatives, liquids, and nasals may all possess at times syllabic value and become sonants, i.e. behave as if they were vowels, as in words like *cnl*, *clδi*.

The Etruscan vowel system is a good deal more developed in the earlier than in the later phases of the history of the language. There is much instability in the quality of vowels, as in *Ràmaδa*, *Ràmeδa*, *Ràmuδa*, *Ràmδa*, all variants of the same woman's name. There are also many examples of vowel harmony, i.e. of the assimilation of vowels in neighbouring syllables, as in the form *Cluδumusδa* derived from the Greek Κλυταιμήστρα, and in the frequent occurrence of words with a predominant vowel, e.g. *siricima*, *Fuflunsul*, *acnanasa*. Five diphthongs are known: *ai*, *au*, *ei*, *eu*, and *ui*, but *ai* generally tends to change to *ei* or *e*, whereas *au* and *eu* tend to become, in later Etruscan, *av* and *ev*.

The most characteristic phenomenon affecting Etruscan

consonants is the so-called *Lautverschiebung:* the tendency of unvoiced plosives to become aspirates and of aspirates to become fricatives. Thus, *c* tends to change to χ, *t* to δ, and *p* to ϕ or *f:* e.g. a.Etr. *zac* becomes in later Etruscan *zaχ.* In the most recent texts, there is oscillation in the spelling of unvoiced and aspirate consonants; both are used indifferently: e.g. *suti* and *suδi*, *zic* and *ziχ*, *uple* and *uφle.* In the initial position, aspirates and fricatives weaken sometimes to the simple aspirate *h:* e.g. *Fasti* and *Hasti.* The absence of voiced plosives (*b*, *d*, and *g*) in Etruscan may perhaps have been originally due to the same phenomenon, i.e. they may have changed to the corresponding unvoiced consonants in prehistoric times.

In the matter of stress, the most noticeable and striking characteristic of Etruscan is the strong initial stress of the word and the consequent fall of unstressed vowels (syncope). It is most marked in neo-Etruscan and results in the formation of complex consonant clusters and the development of sonants: e.g. a.Etr. *lautun:* n.Etr. *lautn;* Greek *Ἀλέξανδρος*: Etr. *Aleχsantre, Elχsntre.*

Grammar

Considerable progress has also been made during the last few years in the domain of Etruscan morphology. We are indebted to Trombetti for stressing the importance of morphological phenomena in the interpretation of Etruscan, on the ground that the understanding of a text cannot be arrived at merely by knowing the lexical values (i.e. the meaning of word-roots) concerned, but requires in addition an accurate appreciation of syntactical relations and grammatical functions. Trombetti was the first to attempt, upon a sound critical basis, the splitting of the Etruscan word into its formative elements, and it is to him, as also to Rosenberg (within the framework of the combinatory method), that we owe the concept of a grammatical structure for Etruscan independent of that of Indo-European languages. This is especially evident in the singular indifference with which different suffixes are used in word-formation, the vague fluidity of certain grammatical categories, the probable nominal character of the verb, the poverty of development of plural and feminine formations, and especially in the superposition of suffixes. We have defined as 'morphological redetermination' (a term suggested to us by Trombetti) the group of facts pointing to the typical tendency of Etruscan grammar to reinforce or redetermine the syntactical function of a form by the superposition of suffixes. For example, *Larδ*, a masculine personal name, becomes *Larδ-al* in the genitive, which, in its turn, may acquire another genitive ending *-ś* to form *Larδ-al-ś*, used indifferently instead of *Larδ-al*. We may truly speak of an actual inflexion of forms that have already been grammatically inflected, as in the case of *Uni-al-δi* 'in the (sanctuary) of Juno' from *Uni-al*, the genitive of *Uni* 'Juno'. The concept of morphological redetermination, however repugnant it may appear to the structure of classical languages, has to-day been universally accepted by scholars as fundamental to the interpretation of Etruscan grammatical phenomena.

The Etruscan noun does not possess a characteristic ending for the nominative, with the exception of a few masculine proper names that end in *-s*. Adjectives are formed by means of special suffixes: e.g. *śuδi* 'tomb': *śuδi-na* 'funerary'. Feminines only show differentiation in personal names (both proper and common) by means of special thematic suffixes and endings in *-i*, *-ia*, *-a*, and *-δa*: e.g. *pui*, *puia* 'wife'; *śeδra*, the feminine form of *śeδre*, a *praenomen*; *Mutunai*, the feminine form of the gentilitial name *Mutuna*; *lautniδa* 'freewoman', from *lautni* 'freeman'. Also in the case of plural formations, it is difficult to establish a rule: we know of several plural and collective nouns characterized by the suffixes -r, -l, and -a: e.g. *clan* 'son': *clen-ar* 'sons'; *murŝ* 'sarcophagus': *murs-l* 'sarcophagi'.

As regards the declension of the noun, we can distinguish groups of genitive and dative suffixes (-*a*, -*l*, and -*al*; -*s*, -*ŝ*, -*si*, and -*sa*), a locative suffix (-*t(i)* or -δ(*i*)), and other endings belonging to oblique cases with advantage, instrumental and locative values, etc. (-*i*, -*e*, -*eri*). It is not easy to draw up actual paradigms of inflexions, though it is possible to consider cases such as the following:

nominative	*meδlum*
genitive	*meδlum-eŝ*
dative of advantage?	*meδlum-eri*
locative	*meδlum-δ*.

Broadly speaking, we are able at present to distinguish two separate groups or 'declensions', characterized principally by their genitive endings: one in -*s*, the other in -*l* (a.Etr. -*a*). To the first group belong all nouns ending in a vowel, with the exception of feminines in -*i*, and the majority of nouns ending in a consonant; to the second, feminines in -*i* and certain nouns, mostly personal, in -*s*, -δ, or -*n*. E.g. for the first group, *hamφe*: gen. *hamφe-ŝ*; *ramδa*: gen. *ramδa-ŝ*; *fler*: gen. *fler-ŝ*; for the second group, *ati* 'mother': gen. *ati-al*. Morphological redetermination, particularly in the declension of proper nouns, was much developed: we have already mentioned genitive forms obtained by adding the suffix -*s* to a genitive in -*l*; when, on the other hand, it is the suffix -*la* that is added to a genitive in -*s*, the result obtained is a 'genitive of the genitive', i.e. a genitive in the genitive case. E.g. *Vel Avleŝ* 'Vel, (son) of Aule': gen. *Vel-uŝ Avles-la* 'of Vel, (son) of Aule'. Complex forms are thus obtained in which no less than three genitive endings may be found superimposed: e.g. *Arnδ-al-iśa-la*.

The identification of the particles *mi*, *mini* with the personal pronoun of the first person (they were at first believed to be demonstratives), was first made by Sittig and confirmed by the author by the application of the method of comparison of parallel texts, and is now generally accepted.[6] The following demonstrative adjectives and pronouns are also known: *ca*, *eca*, *ta* and, perhaps, *ei*, together with some of their declensional forms (e.g.: *ca*, *cś*, *cla*, *cn*, *cei*, *clδi*, etc., where forms in -*n* appear to be accusatives). It is probable that the demonstratives, used as noun determinants, came to be reduced to mere articles and ended by being employed enclitically as particles incorporated in the noun itself: e.g. *esvi-tn*, *huslneś-tś*, *śacni-cla*, *śacni-cleri*, etc.; the phenomenon was first noticed by Torp and has to-day been accepted by the majority of scholars. Other particles of a pronominal type, such as δ*i*, χ*i*, *in*, *an*, *ipa*, etc., may have been demonstratives, relatives, or indefinites, but their employment and interpretation are still far from clear. The composition of pronominal roots in forms such as *ancn*, *cnticn*δ, *ipeipa*, etc., is, on the other hand, fairly obvious.

The classic problem of the Etruscan numerals resides in the correct identification of the six words written on the facets of the well-known Tuscania dice (now kept in the Louvre in Paris) with the first six digits. It is as yet unsolved. If the thesis upholding that the majority of the numerical formulas in the text of the Zagreb mummy are dates becomes, as we believe, generally accepted, the series proposed by Torp (δ*u* = 1, *zal* = 2, *ci* = 3, *śa* = 4, *ma*χ = 5, and *hu*δ = 6) will doubtless become recognized as the most probable. At most there may be some discussion as to whether *hu*δ may not represent 4 (owing to the classic comparison of the pre-Hellenic place-name Ὑττηνία = Τετράπολις) and *śa*, 6.[7] Other numerals are represented by *cezp*-, *sem*φ-, and *nur*φ-. The word *za*δ*rum* was probably equivalent to 20. Multiples of 10 are formed by the addition of the suffix -*alc* or -*al*χ: e.g. *cial*χ, *śeal*χ, *hu*δ*al*χ-, *muval*χ-, etc. Counting appears to have proceeded additively as far as 6 (e.g., *huδiś zaδrumiś* 'on the twenty-sixth (day)?' and subtractively from 7 to 9 (e.g. *esl-em-zaδrumiś* 'on the eighteenth (day)?'; cf., also, Greek δυῶν δέοντα εἴκοσι, Latin *duo-de-viginti*). Mention should also be made of the numeral adverbs, formed by the addition of the suffix -*z* or -*zi*: e.g. *ci-z* 'thrice'.

Many and important problems arise out of the study of the Etruscan verb. Pauli's opinion, that it had a nominal origin, appears to be back in favour: many forms derived from verbal roots and with verbal meaning do, in fact, possess both structure and inflexions identical with those of nouns. The only really certain verbal forms, from the point of view of morphological structure, are the third person singular 'perfects' in -*ce*, such as *mulveneke* 'has dedicated', *turce* 'has given', *svalce* 'has lived', etc. Other suffixes frequently encountered with verbal roots are: -*a*, -*e* (e.g. *ama*, *ame*), -*u* (e.g. *lupu* 'has died'), -*ri* (with a value probably identical with that of the Latin gerundive: e.g. δezeri *'faciundum est*, *fieri oportet'*), -*aś*, -δ*as* (with participial or relative meaning: e.g. *svalδas* 'having lived, who has lived'). There are also hypotheses, built on fairly sound foundations and tested by the combinatory method, concerning the possible passive nature of the Etruscan verb as in the case of the Basque verb.[8]

Very little is known for certain on the subject of adverbial expressions and copulative particles. It is generally difficult to distinguish between pronouns and pre- or post-positions. The old fundamental discovery of the enclitic conjunction -*c*, corresponding to Latin -*que*, has been joined by that of enclitic -*um*, generally used to co-ordinate sentences and possessing a slight antithetical value. Some still doubt, though wrongly, the conjunctive value of the particle *etnam*, also found, as it seems, in an enclitic form -*tnam*: it probably corresponded to Umbrian *inumek* and to Latin *item, etiam.* A few more adverbial or conjunctive particles are known, such as δui 'here'; *matam* 'above'?; *iχ, iχnac* 'as'; etc. Very little attention has been given as yet to questions affecting the syntax, word-order, and style of Etruscan texts.[9]

Interpretation of the Texts

In the present condition of our knowledge of Etruscan, it may be affirmed that the very great majority of inscriptions can be understood and translated perfectly. This statement may surprise the general public and all those who continue to retain Etruscan as a sphinx enveloped in impenetrable mystery. It is necessary, however, to add that by far the greater part of epigraphic material in our possession consists of very brief explicative texts (accompanying the painted or carved figures of mythical personages), of a number of legends on coins and sundry objects (giving, in the latter case, the name of the owner), but especially of funerary inscriptions with the name, and, occasionally, the age, of the dead person; all documents, in fact, that contain little but proper names. On the basis of certain inflexions found in funerary inscriptions (such as the genitive of the patronymic or matronymic) and by the comparison of the epitaphs of related persons buried in the same tomb, it has been possible to establish from the very beginning of etruscological research the meaning of certain very common words, such as *clan* =son, *seχ* =daughter, etc. At the same time, the meanings of the words for 'to live', 'to die', 'years', and 'age' were also fixed. Here is an example of the complete formula of a funerary inscription, with a literal translation:

Partunus	*Vel*	*Velδurus*	*Satlnal-c*	*Ramδas*
Partunu	Vel	of Velthur	and of Satlnei	Ramtha

clan	*avils*	*lupu*	*XXIIX*	
son	of years	dead	28	(*C.I.E.* 5424)

i.e. 'Vel Partunu, son of Velthur and of Ramtha Satlnei, who died when 28 years of age.'

Difficulties begin to arise when we pass to funerary inscriptions containing information on the life and career of the dead person, or inscriptions recording the dedication of monuments and furnishings. Words of obscure and uncertain meaning begin to make their appearance, and their meanings become all the more arduous to determine as the etymological problems which they present are further complicated by archaeological and historical difficulties. The combinatory method, even when assisted by the new bilingual processes, has not yet allowed us to pin down the value of, say, political, administrative or priestly titles that accompany the names of the dead, or the exact significance of sacral and funerary terms such as *śacni* (whence the verb *śacnisa*), *acazr*, *atrś*, etc. The value carried by the words for 'tomb', 'sarcophagus', 'to do', 'to give', etc., is, on the other hand, much clearer. Biographical funerary inscriptions are quite frequent, and may assume the character of the Latin *elogia*, such as the well-known inscriptions in the tombs of the Scipios. Here is a brief and simple example of such an inscription:

Aleδnas	*Arnδ*	*Larisal*	*zilaδ*	*Tarχnalδi*	*amce*
Alethna	Arnth	of Laris	*zilath*	in Tarquinii	was

(*C.I.I.*, Suppl., III, 322),

i.e. 'Arnth Alethna (son) of Laris: he was *zilath* (probably= *praetor*) in Tarquinii'. Here is a longer and more complex inscription:

Arnδ	*Xurcles*	*Larδal*	*clan*	*Pevδial*
Arnth	Churcle	of Larth	son (and)	of Pevthi

zilc	*parχis*	*amce*		*marunu*
zilc	*parchis*	did belong to the		*maru* (college of the

spurana	*cepen*	*tenu*
marones?) civic	priest (who)	held office?

avils	*maχs semφalχls*	*lupu*
of years	seventy-five?	dead

(Fabretti, *C.I.I.* 2070),

i.e. 'Arnth Churcle, son of Larth and of Pevthi: he was *zilc parchis*, with the functions of priest of the town "marones"?, died when seventy-five? years of age'. In this inscription, we meet titles of office the precise meaning of which it is naturally impossible to determine (see, however, pp. 146 ff.). The longest biographical funerary inscription in our possession is, as we have already mentioned, the one carved on the sarcophagus of Laris Pulena (*C.I.E.* 5430). Beginning with a very full genealogical account of the dead man (going back to his great-grandfather), it lists the offices and religious honours of this important personage; but the text is unfortunately still very obscure, except for the introductory formula and a number of isolated words. It appears that Pulena was the author of books on divination (*ziχ neδśrac acasce*), had filled an important civic office in his native city of Tarquinii (*creals Tarχnalδ spureni lucairce*) and was connected with the worship of the gods Hermes, Catha, Pacha (Bacchus), and Culsu. Among the inscriptions that do not refer to individuals but to a tomb in general (a record of its foundation and ornamentation), the most notable is that belonging to the hypogeum of San Manno, near Perugia (*C.I.E.* 4116), commemorating the opening of the sepulchral chamber and its decoration with urns and other furnishings by members of the Precu family.

The inscription of the great cippus of Perugia (*C.I.E.* 4538) is particularly noteworthy. From the time it was first discovered, it has provoked the greatest interest among etruscologists, with especially keen attempts to interpret it correctly on the part of Torp, Trombetti, Ribezzo, Goldmann, and Devoto. Two distinct families are recorded in

the inscription, the Velthina and the Afuna, and explicit
reference is made to the tomb of the Velthina; the text also
deals with borders (*tularu*), measurements (*naper*), property
and cessions (*turune*, *ścune* =he gave, or similar phrase) and
the writing of documents (*ziχuχe* =he wrote). It is now
almost impossible to doubt the juridical character of the
text: it probably records a purchase-and-sale transaction or
a donation of funerary properties, analogous perhaps to the
iura sepulcrorum of certain Latin inscriptions. It is possible to
explain not only single words, but even whole phrases, and
the general meaning of the document is understood. Many
obscurities, uncertainties, and unsolved problems are still
scattered widely in the text, however, and there are still
insufficient data to fix an accurate and precise translation of
many words (e.g. *vaχr*, *tezan*, *fuśle*, *falaś*, *spelδi*, etc)

Votive inscriptions are the most common texts pertaining
to the religious sphere. They are numerous on archaic
vases and follow the classic formula:

mini	mulvanice	Mamarce	Velχanas
me	has dedicated	Mamarce	Velchana

(Caere: *Notizie degli Scavi*, 1937, 388),

i.e. 'Mamarce Velchana dedicated me'.

In these formulas, many are the known forms and variants of the 'perfect' of the verb *mul-* =Greek ἀνατίδημι,
and, with it, other verbs with analogous meaning (e.g. *tur-*,
al- 'to give, to offer'). The longer archaic votive inscriptions are usually extremely obscure, partly owing to the
difficulty of separating the words from each other. Neo-
Etruscan dedications found on statuettes and other objects
are generally easier to decipher, though not always fully
intelligible; next to the name of the dedicator, they often
bear the name of the divinity to whom the offering is made.
A sacral document of considerable importance is contained
in a leaden lens-shaped plaque found at Magliano and

spirally inscribed on either side (*C.I.E.* 5237): it contains the names of a number of gods (*Cauδa*, *aiseras*, *Marisl*, *Calus*, *Tins*) and records of funerary offerings. Despite the valiant attempts made by Torp and Trombetti to decipher it, it is still impossible to offer even a partial translation of the text. Other inscribed lead tablets in our possession consist most certainly of '*tabellae defixionum*', i.e. the consecration to infernal deities of persons whose death was ardently desired. The most notable, found at Monte Pitti, near Populonia (*C.I.E.* 5211), contains the curse of a freewoman upon a number of partly related persons, a type of document well-known to the Greek and Roman worlds. Unique, on the other hand, is the bronze model of a liver found at Piacenza, to which we have already had occasion to refer in our chapter on religion, with the names of gods, mostly abbreviated, inscribed in the appropriate spaces, presumably for the use of divinatory priests.

Finally, there remain to be considered the two longest Etruscan texts in our possession: the text of the Capua tile and that of the wrappings of the Zagreb mummy. They are the only two that appear to contain transcripts of complex ritual documents, if we except occasional brief prescriptions found inscribed upon objects. They have in common the prescriptive formulas proper to a liturgical manual for the guidance of sacrificing priests, a characteristic shared by the Umbrian texts of the Iguvine tablets and by Roman rituals as handed down in literary sources (e.g. those contained in Cato's *de agricultura*). The difference rests in the nature of the ceremonies described. The Capua tile is closely connected with funerary rites performed in the honour of infernal deities (*Šuri*, *Leδam*, *Aφe-*, *Calu*, *Larun*, *Fulinuśna*, *Natinusna(i)*, *Tinun-*, *Seδum-*, etc.; but there is also mention of Tinia, Uni and, perhaps, Bacchus). Within the text, it is possible to distinguish brief sentences, rather uniform in structure, with the verb in the imperative, the indication of the offering preceded at times by a numeral and the name of the divinity in the genitive case. Of a more difficult nature, on the other hand, is the determination of the exact technical meaning (i.e. the correct translation) both of verbs expressing sacred acts (*acas-*, *picas-*, *sac-*, *tul*, *ilucu*, *apir-*, *utu*, *scuv-*, *fani-*, *nunδ*, etc.), as of the nouns describing the offerings or the things offered (*vacil*, *tartiria*, *cleva*, *riδna*, *zusleva*, *turza*, etc.). Here, for example, is how the meaning of one of the prescriptive phrases may dimly be seen:

Leδamsul   ci   tartiria   ci-m
To (the god) Letham   three   *tartiria*   and also three

cleva   acasri
cleva   ought to be offered (or similar phrase).

Mention is probably made in the text of officiating priests (*cipen*), and perhaps also of the family (*lavtun*) of the dead man. We have already noted the possibility that the Capua ritual may be connected to the 'salvation' sacrifices contained in the *Libri Acherontici* and remembered by some late classical authors.[10]

It is only natural that the greatest effort in the deciphering of Etruscan became concentrated on the longest text available, the *liber linteus* of Zagreb, which owing to good editing, the evenness of the script and regular word-division, the recentness of the language and the frequent recurrence of words and formulas, offers the most favourable conditions for decipherment. The text was first studied with only partial success by Lattes, Torp, Rosenberg, and Trombetti; more recently, it has become the object of repeated and more thorough probings on the part of Runes, Cortsen, Olzscha, Vetter, and the author of the present book.[11]

The hypothesis that the text contains a funerary ritual in some way connected with Egypt and the mummy on which the wrappings were found has now been definitely discarded in favour of the view that it comprises a series of prescriptions connected with partly public ceremonies regulated by a religious calendar. The most remarkable section of the text consists of a liturgical sequence, repeated, with small variants, at least four times, in honour of the 'gods' (*eiser śi-c śeu-c*), of a god *in crapśti*, and of Neptune. As in the case of the Iguvine tablets, the sacrifices were made on behalf of institutions of a religious nature (a sanctuary) or a political nature (a city or nation?), indicated by the words *śacnicleri cilδl śpureri meδlumeri-c enaś*. Less important paragraphs prescribe, more or less summarily, ceremonies in honour of other divinities (Veltha, Tin, Culsu, and Uni). Each paragraph appears to be preceded by a date (day and month): e.g. *eslem zaδrumiś acale* 'on the eighteenth of the month of Acale (June)'. Of the words found repeated in the text, some are understood with sufficient clarity and precision (e.g. *vinum* =wine; *ais*, *eis* = god; *fler* = sacrifice, offering; *tur* =gives; etc.). Others are understood only in a general sense and no precise translation can be given with any certainty (e.g. *zeri*, *vacl*, *faśe*, *eśvi*, *zusleva* =sacred ceremonies, offerings; *fardan*, *nunδen*, *δezin*, *tul*, all verbs connected with religious worship, etc.). Finally, there are a number of words on whose meaning there is much doubt and disagreement among scholars.

In this case too, the step most likely to lead to a complete decipherment of the text consists in the isolation of the syntactical units corresponding to complete phrases and the identification, as far as it is possible, of the essential elements of such phrases: subject, verb or nominal predicate and complements. To achieve this, much help is obtained from the isolation of conjunctive elements (like the enclitic particles -*c* and -*um*, and, perhaps, also the word *etnam*) and, especially, from the distinction of nominal and verbal forms and the definition of the syntactical functions of certain morphemes. In many cases, no satisfactory result can be

attained or seems attainable, but in the most favourable
instances, the structure of the Etruscan text is revealed as a
complex net of syntactical relations where only the semantic
content of the lexical elements is missing. Thus, in the phrase
cis-um pute tul δansur haδrδi repinδi-c, it is possible to recognize in *tul* a verb in the imperative, *δansur* as the object and
haδrδi repinδi-c as the complement in the locative. Occasionally, however, even the semantic values of the component
words may be arrived at with a greater or lesser degree of
accuracy, so that the general meaning of the phrase can be
made out, as if through a gradually lifting fog. Here are
some examples:

(1) Column VI, lines 9 ff.:

zaδrumsne	*lusaś*	*fler*
on the twentieth (day?)	of *lus-*	the offering

hamφisca	*δezeri*
that concerns the *hamphe-?*	should be made,

laivisca	*lustreś*	*fler*
that concerns the *lae-?*	of the *lus-?*	offering

vacl-tnam	*δezeri*
and moreover the *vacl* (libation?)	should be made.

(2) Column VIII, lines 3 ff.:

Celi	*huδiś zaδrumiś*
(on the month) of Celi (September),	the twenty-sixth

flerχva	*Neδunsl*
(day)? the offerings to the god	Neptune

sucri
should be consecrated (or established or similar verb)

δezeri-c . . .
and should be made . . .

(3) Column IX, lines 6 ff.:

raδχ	*tur*	*heχśδ*	*vinum*	*trin flere*
to the left?	give	place	the wine,	invoke (or propitiate)

Neδunśl un   *mlaχ*   *nunδen*
the god Neptune,?   the vow,   beseech (him)
zuśleve . . .
(with the offer) of one *zuśleva . . .*

(4) Column XI, lines 14 ff.:

cntnam   *δesan*   *fler*   *Veiveś*
and on the same   morning   an offering   to Vejove
δezeri   *etnam*   *ais(na) . . .*
should be made   and moreover   the divine service . . .
huδiś zaδrumiś.
as on the twenty-sixth (day)?

The strenuous efforts made to interpret the Zagreb text with the help of the combinatory and the bilingual methods are now well on the way to success. The journey is long and difficult and the goal can only be reached in slow successive stages. But we may confidently state that, once the major hermeneutic problems of the Zagreb text have been solved, the obstacles that still bar our way to the comprehension of the other texts will become much easier, even if new Etruscan texts of some length were to be added to our stock, as we most ardently hope.

Lexical Values

So as to provide a more complete picture of the state of our knowledge of Etruscan, we now give a list of those words whose meaning is known with certainty or near-certainty, classified according to their semantic content:[12]

I – DEITIES AND RELIGIOUS WORSHIP:

ais, eis 'god'; *aiser, aisar, eiser* 'gods'; *aisuna, aisna* 'divine, divine service';

fler 'offering, sacrifice'; *flerχva* 'offerings'; *flere* 'god, deity'; *śacni, śacni-cn, śacni-tn, sacniu* sacred place or action; *śacnisa* 'consecrate';

zeri sacred act;

vacl sacred act, perhaps 'libation';

δ*ez*, δ*ezi*, δ*ezin*, δ*ezine*, δ*ezince*, δ*ezeri* 'to make (an offering)';

mula, muli, mulu, mulune, muluni, mulunice, mulvanice, mulvenice, mulvunce, muluvanice, etc. 'to dedicate'; *mulaχ, mlaχ* 'vow, anathema';

tur, tura, ture, turi, turu, turune, turce, turuce, turunce 'to give'; *turza* 'gift'?

al, ale, alce, alice, aliqu 'to give'; *alpan, alpnu* 'gift'?

acas, acasa, acasce, acasri 'to do, to give';

nunδ, nunδen, nunδene, nundend 'to beseech (with an offering)';

cver 'gift';

trutnut, trutnvt 'divinatory priest, soothsayer'?

netśvis 'haruspex'; *ziχ neδśrac* 'liber haruspicinus'?

frontac 'fulguriator';

cletram 'trolley for offerings' (cf. Umbrian *kletra*).

2 – THE FUNERARY WORLD:

δ*aur*, δ*aura* 'tomb'; δ*aurχ* 'funerary';

suδi, śuδi 'tomb' (prop. = Lat. *sedes*): *śuδi neśl, śuδi zivas, śuδi hinδiu* 'abode of the dead = tomb'; *śuδina* 'funerary';

cela 'cell';

munisule-, munsle, munδ, 'repository, *loculus*';

murś 'sarcophagus, urn';

mutna, mutana 'sarcophagus';

cesu, ceseδce 'to lie';

lupu, lupuce 'to die';

leine 'to die'?;

hinδial 'soul'; *hinδiu* 'of the souls';

φ*ersu* 'mask'.

3 – MAN, FAMILY RELATIONSHIPS:

clan 'son';

śec, seχ, daughter';

pui, puia 'wife';
ati, atiu 'mother';
tuśurδir 'married couple';
ati nacna 'grandmother'?;
papa 'grandfather'?;
papacs, papals 'grandson'?;
nefiś, nefts 'nephew';
prumaδs, prumts 'great-nephew'.

4 – MAN, LIFE AND ACTIONS:

ama, ame, amce 'to be';
svalce, svalas, svalδas 'to live';
ar, arδ, ara, araś, arce 'to do';
caru, carsi, caresri, cerine, ceriχu, cerχunce 'to make, to build';
  cerur 'pottery'?;
śaδe, śaδena, śaδene, śaδas, setirune 'to establish';
suδ, sutanaś, suδce 'to place, to stand'?;
heci, heχśδ, heczri, hecce, hecśce 'to put, to do';
teśamsa 'to heal'; *tesinδ* 'healer';
ziχuχ, ziχne, ziχuχe, ziχunce 'to write'; *ziχ* 'written, book'.

5 – POLITICAL AND SOCIAL ORGANIZATION:

lautn, lavtn 'family, gens'; *lautni* 'gentilitial';
lautni 'freeman'; *lautniδa* 'freewoman';
etera 'servant' or member of the lower classes; *eterau*
  'relating to the *etera*';
śuplu (Lat. *subulo*) 'piper';
δanasa 'actor';
*δruna (Hesychiuᶜ δροῦνα) 'power, sovereignty';
*lauχume (Lat. *lucumo*) 'king, prince'; *lucairce* 'to fill the
  office of *lucumo*'?;
zilc, zilχ, zilaδ magistrature, probably = 'praetor'; *zilaδ
  meχl rasnal* 'praetor Etruriae'?; *zil(a)χnu, zilaχnδaś,
  zilaχn(u)ce* 'to be a *zilath*';
maru, marunu, marniu, marunuχ magistrature = Umbrian

maro; marunuχva 'belonging to the *maru*'; marunu, marvaś 'to be a *maru*';

camδi magistrature; canδe, canδce 'to be a *camδi*';

cepen, eisnevc, ceχase, celu priestly titles;

macstrevc 'magister';

tenve, tenine, tenu, tenδas, tence 'to have the functions of . . .';

spur, śpur 'city, *populus*'; spureni, spurana 'civic';

tuδδi, tuδiu 'state'?;

meχl, meδlum 'nation, league'?; meχl rasnal 'Etruria'?;

raśna (Dionysius Ρασέννα) 'Etruscan, Etruria';

rumaχ 'Roman'.

6 – NATURE, HOUSEHOLD OBJECTS AND BUILDINGS:

*anδa- (Hesychius ἄνδας, ἄντας) 'north-wind, eagle';

*arac (Hesychius ἄρακος) 'sparrow-hawk';

*arim- (Strabo ἄριμος) 'monkey';

*capu 'falcon';

hiuls 'screech-owl'?;

*δamna (Hesychius δάμνος) 'horse';

δevru 'bull';

leu 'lion';

vinum 'wine';

verse 'fire'?; versie 'concerning fire'?;

zamaδi 'golden'?; zana 'precious'?;

cape, capi names of vases;

culiχna (Greek χυλίχνη) 'cup';

cupe, χupe 'cup';

δapna 'cup';

leχtumuza (Greek λέχυδος) 'small pitcher';

pruχum, pruχś, prucuna (Greek πρόχους) 'pitcher';

putere, putiza (Greek ποτήρ) name of vase;

qutun, qutum (Greek κώδων) name of vase;

aδre part of building, 'atrium', 'aedes'?;

δamce 'has built';

tular, tularu 'border, limit';

naper measure: 'feet'?;
sren 'figure'; *śrenχve* 'figured'?.

7 – TIME AND ITS DIVISIONS:

tin 'day';
δ*esan* 'morning, day';
tivr 'months';
avil 'year, years';
ril 'at the age of . . . ';
*velχitna? (*Velcitanus*) 'March';
ampiles 'May';
acale (*Aclus*) 'June';
δ*ucte* name of a month?;
**t(u)rane*? (*Traneus*) 'July';
*hermie? (*Ermius*) 'August';
celi (*Coelius*) 'September'.

NOTES

1. In *American Journal of Philology*, 1936, pp. 261 ff.
2. On the whole question of the origin of the Etruscan alphabet, see G. Buonamici, *Epigrafia etrusca*, pp. 133 ff., with bibliography; see also M. Guarducci, in *Studi Etruschi*, XIV, 1940, pp. 281 ff., and R. Carpenter, in *American Journal of Archaeology*, XLIX, 1945, pp. 452 ff.
3. The exceptional presence of *o* in *frontac* (=*fulguriator*) in the bi-lingual inscription of Pesaro (C.I.I. 69) may be explained by the fact that this very late inscription belongs to the border region of Etruria.
4. The Latin use of the letter *c*, derived from Greek γ, is certainly due to Etruscan influence. In archaic times there probably also existed small differences in the pronunciation of the letters *c*, *q*, and *k*, as attested by their use with the different vowels: *c* was normally followed by the front vowels *i* and *e*, *k* by the middle vowel *a*, and *q* by the back vowel *u*.
5. E. Vetter, in *Glotta*, XXIV, pp. 114 ff.; XXVII, pp. 157 ff.; G. Buonamici, *L'interpunzione sillabica*, etc., in *Studi Etruschi*, XVI, 1942, pp. 263 ff.; F. Slotty, *Beiträge zur Etruskologie, I, Silbenpunktierung und Silbenbildung im Altetruskischen*, 1952. The latter author tends to

regard the phenomenon as due to purely phonetic causes, as a mark of syllabic division; objections to this view will be found in K. Olzscha, in *Gnomon*, 1953, pp. 271 ff.; M. Pallottino, in *Studi Etruschi*, XXII, 1952–3, pp. 478 ff.

6. S. P. Cortsen, in *Glotta*, XXVI, 1937, pp. 10 ff.

7. See K. Olzscha, in *Neue Jahrbücher für Wissenschaft und Jugend-bildung*, 1936, p. 105.

8. K. Olzscha, *Interpretation der Agramer Mumienbinde*, 1939, pp. 103 ff.; see also V. Pisani, who, in *Archivio Glottologico*, XXXIV, 1942, pp. 116 ff., prefers to speak of an 'intransitive' nature of the Etruscan verb.

9. On the subjects of Etruscan phonetics and morphology, see also M. Pallottino, *Elementi di lingua etrusca*, 1936, with the modifications required by recent progress in the science. H. L. Stoltenberg's recent synthesis on Etruscan grammatical structure, *Etruskische Sprachlehre mit vollständigem Wörterbuch*, should be consulted with care.

10. See F. Ribezzo, in *La Parola del Passato*, I, 1946, pp. 286 ff.; M. Pallottino, *Sulla lettura e sul contenuto della grande iscrizione di Capua*, in *Studi Etruschi*, XX, 1948–9, pp. 159 ff.

11. Cf. *Studi Etruschi*, vols. VI ff.; E. Vetter, *Etruskische Wort-deutungen*, I, 1937; K. Olzscha, *Interpretation der Agramer Mumienbinde*, 1939, and *Glotta*, XXXI, 1948, pp. 105 ff.; XXXII, 1953, pp. 283 ff.

12. See Müller-Deecke, *Die Etrusker*, 1871, II, pp. 508 ff.; S. P. Cortsen, *Vocabulorum etruscorum interpretatio*, in *Nord. Tidsskrift f. filol. fjerderække*, VI, 1917, pp. 165 ff.; A. Trombetti, *La lingua etrusca*, 1928, pp. 211 ff.; M. Pallottino, *Elementi di lingua etrusca*, 1936, pp. 87 ff.; E. Vetter, *Etruskische Wortdeutungen*, I, 1937; H. L. Stoltenberg, *Etruskische Sprachlehre mit vollständigem Wörterbuch*, 1950 (with reservations as to many of the proposed translations).

GENERAL BIBLIOGRAPHY

Works on particular aspects of Etruscan studies will be found
listed in the notes to the relevant chapters of this book.

Acts of the 1st International Congress of Etruscan Studies, Rinascimento
del Libro, Florence 1928.

BUONAMICI, G., *Epigrafia etrusca*, Rinascimento del Libro, Florence
1931.

DENNIS, G., *Cities and Cemeteries of Etruria*, London 1883 (3rd ed.);
also in Everyman's Library.

DUCATI, P., *Etruria antica*, 2 vols., Paravia 1927.

DUCATI, P., *Storia dell'arte etrusca*, 2 vols., Rinascimento del Libro,
Florence 1927.

DUCATI, P., *Le problème étrusque*, Leroux, Paris 1928.

GIGLIOLI, G. Q., *L'arte etrusca*, Treves, Milan 1935.

HÜLSEN, C., *Etruria*; THULIN, C., *Etrusca*; KÖRTE, G., *Etrusker*;
SKUTSCH, F., *Etruskische Sprache*, in *Paulys Real-Encyclopädie* by
WISSOWA, G., VII, 1907, cols. 720 ff.

LOPES PEGNA, M., *Saggio di bibliografia etrusca*, Olschki, Florence
1953 (to be consulted with care).

MÜLLER, K. O. and DEECKE, W., *Die Etrusker*, 2 vols., Heitz, Stütt-
gart 1877.

NEPPI MODONA, A., *A Guide to Etruscan Antiquities*, Florence 1954.

NOGARA, B., *Gli Etruschi e la loro civiltà*, Hoepli, Milan 1934.

PALLOTTINO, M., *Elementi di lingua etrusca*, Rinascimento del Libro,
Florence 1936.

PALLOTTINO, M., *Gli Etruschi*, Colombo, Rome 1940 (2nd ed.).

PALLOTTINO, M., *L'origine degli Etruschi*, Tumminelli, Rome 1947.

PARETI, L., *Le origine etrusche*, Bemporad, Florence 1926.

PARETI, L., *Etruschi: Storia*; DEVOTO, G., *Lingua*; NEPPI MODONA,
A., *Religione*; DUCATI, P., *Archeologia e arte*; CESANO, S.L.,
Numismatica, in *Enciclopedia Italiana*, XIV, 1932, pp. 510 ff.

PONTRANDOLFI, G., *Gli Etruschi e la loro lingua*, Barbèra, Florence
1909.

RENARD, M., *Initiation à l'étruscologie*, Lebègue, Brussels 1941.

RENARD, M., *La question étrusque*, in *L'antiquité classique*, Brussels 1940.

SOLARI, A., *Topografia storica dell' Etruria*, I–IV, Spoerri, Pisa 1915–20.

SOLARI, A., *La vita pubblica e privata degli Etruschi*, Rinascimento del Libro, Florence 1928.

TROMBETTI, A., *La lingua etrusca*, Rinascimento del Libro, Florence 1928.

INDEXES

1. HISTORICAL AND GEOGRAPHICAL INDEX

(The names Etruria, Etruscans, and Tuscany will not be found listed in this index. Numbers in italic refer to plates)

2. INDEX OF ANCIENT AUTHORS

3. Index of Modern Authors